CW01597044

POLITICAL PHILOS

Political Philosophy Now is a series which deals with authors, topics and periods in political philosophy from the perspective of their relevance to current debates. The series presents a spread of subjects and points of view from various traditions which include European and New World debates in political philosophy.

For other titles in this series, please see the University of Wales website: *www.wales.ac.uk/press*

POLITICAL PHILOSOPHY NOW

In Defence of Multinational Citizenship

Siobhán Harty
and
Michael Murphy

UNIVERSITY OF WALES PRESS • CARDIFF • 2005

British Library Cataloguing-in-Publication Data
A catalogue record for this book is available from the British Library.

ISBN 0-7083-1853-3 hardback
0-7083-1852-5 paperback

Siobhán Harty's views as expressed in this book are her own and do not necessarily reflect the views or position of her employer, the Government of Canada.

Flag images on cover by Graham Bartram
Printed in Great Britain by Cromwell Press Ltd, Trowbridge, Wiltshire

Contents

Preface

As the twenty-first century gets under way, no one could have predicted that political thinkers, activists and leaders would be as engaged in theorizing, practising and shaping nationalism as their counterparts were a hundred years ago. On the surface, we seem to be as preoccupied with issues of identity, territory and self-determination as were those who shaped the age of nationalism at the end of the nineteenth and beginning of the twentieth century. However, scratch that surface even a little bit and one realizes that the conditions of our preoccupation have changed dramatically. People today might continue to have a strong preference for a form of belonging – of citizenship – that is based on the history, traditions and identity they share with others, but the nations to which they belong occupy a very different place in relationship to the state and international society. Due to processes of cross-border integration and globalization, not to mention developments in liberal conceptions of rights and equality, substate nations and Aboriginal peoples today have reason to hold out hope that their demands for differentiated citizenship will be recognized by the state.

Consider the case of the Métis in Canada who in September 2003 won a historic ruling from the Supreme Court: they were recognized as 'distinctive peoples who, in addition to their mixed ancestry, developed their own customs, and recognizable group identity separate from their Indian or Inuit and European forebears'. The Court decided that 'A Métis community is a group of Métis with a distinctive collective identity, living together in the same geographical area and sharing a common way of life' (SCC, 2003). The Court's ruling will forever change the relationship between the Métis and the Canadian state by obliging Canadian governments to come to terms with Métis customs and traditions and to negotiate their specific parameters within the Canadian Constitution.

The Métis struggle for recognition, and for just, fair and equal treatment by the state, is a struggle that is played out by substate nations and Aboriginal peoples around the globe. In cases like those of the Métis, legal solutions are often essential because of the state's unwillingness to address these claims in the political realm. In some cases, legal principles may have to serve as a surrogate in the absence of a political framework for substate national self-determination. However, under more ideal circumstances, and many of the Canadian Aboriginal cases are a good illustration of this, legal decisions may form the basis (and incentive) for future political negotiations between states and the nations residing within their borders. For at root, we are not dealing with a legal claim but, more fundamentally, with a struggle for political self-determination. And, indeed, the political will to resolve historic claims to self-government is making its presence felt, even in the most unexpected of locations. A case in point, twenty years ago, no one could have predicted that the United Kingdom would move towards a devolved state or that Australia would declare a policy of self-determination for its Aboriginal peoples. Yet despite these movements towards forms of political recognition and self-determination at the substate level, changes which are often welcomed by the substate nations they are intended to benefit, state responses to nationalist demands frequently are not based on nation-to-nation negotiations. As such, they cannot be construed as agreements struck among equal partners, a fundamental nationalist demand. Moreover, the unilateral tenor of many of these initiatives means that they frequently fail to address key aspects of the claims to which they are directed. Consequently, in numerous cases there continue to be demands from substate nations for more devolution, more autonomy and more self-government. A quick consideration of some of the demands for self-government currently on the table in North America and Europe reveals something of the political expectations of nationalist groups: independence by the Scottish National Party and the Parti Québecois; free-associated state by the Partido Nacionalista Vasco; reunification with the Republic of Ireland by Sinn Féin; and shared sovereignty with Spain by the Catalan Convergència i Unió. Meanwhile, land claims by Aboriginal peoples in Canada, Australia and New Zealand also create high levels of expectations among members of these groups that their quest for increased control of their territories, resources, economies and citizens will be realized.

On one level, it is easy to appreciate the reluctance of states to respond to all of these demands. Established understandings of state stability and domestic order have rested on the assumption that there can only be one legitimate political authority in a given territory, to which should correspond a single nationality and a single citizenship regime. Multiple sites of authority, loyalty and allegiance – which would result from fulfilling nationalist demands for political autonomy –

are believed to be a fundamental source of domestic instability. Moreover, some states are faced with armed conflicts by nationalists, a situation which turns the question of state stability into one of citizen protection.

Nevertheless, there are signs that the conception of internal (domestic) sovereignty on which our definitions of state stability rest is changing. One result of this change is that some nations are seeking out solutions to self-government that do not require independent statehood. Secession is a costly route to self-government and it is not clear that the citizens of 'stateless nations' are willing to bear that cost. It should be possible to find alternative forms of self-government without changing the state's borders. It is certainly true that, for some nationalist groups, alternatives to independence will not satisfy their particular aspirations for self-rule. Moreover, some states will be reluctant to entertain new ideas about shared sovereignty or 'states' residing within states. But in between the inflexibility of some states and that of some nationalists lie ordinary citizens who would welcome recognition of their right to make their own decisions about their collective future.

This book is about those citizens and the alternative political solutions to self-government that they seek. More specifically, this book is about one possible alternative, which we argue can guide the various nations residing within a state towards a resolution of their often competing claims. We call this alternative 'multinational citizenship' in recognition of the fact that in some states, relations between citizens and the state will be mediated by substate nations or Aboriginal peoples having their own institutions for self-government. We focus our attention on Western Europe, Canada, Australia and New Zealand. There is ample evidence that this process is already occurring; yet prevailing models of citizenship have not adapted. As one scholar claims: 'the state needs to adapt to the shape of its nations rather than the other way around' (Resina, 2002: 394). In chapter 1 of the book, we provide a justification and explanation of multinational citizenship that is anchored in a discussion of changing conceptions of citizenship and sovereignty. We do not agree with many scholars that the state is on its way out and that it will be replaced by new transnational or cosmopolitan forms of belonging. On the contrary, we are of the view that states will continue to be the most important actors in domestic and international politics. Nevertheless, we agree that the twenty-first-century state has changed in important ways that provide substate nations and Aboriginal peoples with the opportunity to reconceptualize how they 'belong' to the state.

Of course, this is not the first time such an opportunity has presented itself. In chapter 2, we return to inter-war Europe, where liberal debates about citizenship and belonging in multinational states were theoretically innovative but, unfortunately, institutionally inadequate. An important debate took place in this period about the relationship between the 'nation' and the 'state' that was prompted by the introduction of the term self-determination. We review the debate and draw the conclusion that, in the absence of principles and institutions by which to make new forms of citizenship work, states defaulted to a type of citizenship that was organized around the majority nation. There are many lessons to be learned from this period that can enrich our own approach to multinational citizenship. But we are not the only ones to have caught on to the capacity of liberalism to respond to complicated cases of multiple nations coexisting within the state's border. There is a group of liberal scholars whose interest in national identity and culture has impelled them to develop a liberal approach to understanding and responding to the group-based demands for citizenship rights by substate nations and Aboriginal peoples. The work and arguments of liberal nationalists, as they are known, is the subject of chapter 3. There is some overlap between their approach to citizenship and our own, with one significant exception: we have a democratic understanding of self-determination, whereas they have a cultural one. This difference, which we examine and explain at length, is the starting point for our model of multinational citizenship.

Chapters 4 and 5 are devoted to multinational citizenship. We develop the five dimensions of multinational citizenship in chapter 4, discuss these in relationship to existing scholarship and illustrate them with examples from contemporary cases. In chapter 5, we take a more practical perspective of multinational citizenship by analysing it in relationship to several cases of substate nationalism. It is not our intention to conduct a systematic case-study analysis but rather to describe, and evaluate, how certain dimensions of multinational citizenship are today working in practice, and to address the potential of our model of multinational citizenship as a means of reducing political tensions in other cases. There will be critics of our approach; perhaps the most serious of which will come from those who argue that the relevance and draw of national identities will decline in a globalized world. The postnationalist critique is an influential one and is based on arguments about changing conceptions of sovereignty that are very similar to our own. As such, we review and discuss the postnationalist argument in chapter 6 and cast our response as a defence of our alternative model of multinational citizenship. Finally, we review our main arguments in the conclusion to the book.

1 • Citizenship and Belonging

There has been much debate over the last decade about the decline of the Westphalian model of the nation-state and the implications of such a decline for a series of norms and relationships that govern our understanding of domestic and international society. The crux of the debate has focused, first, on the link between territory, state sovereignty and the effective and legitimate exercise of political authority and, second, on the idea of nationality as the primary principle around which states organize and institutionalize their notions of political and social community. This book focuses on one relationship that has featured prominently in this larger debate: citizenship. If citizenship describes the link between individuals and the state in a bounded national community, then several developments have emerged to challenge it: the transfer (both intentional and unintentional) of sections of the state's sovereignty to supranational and subnational political authorities in the context of intensified regional and global integration; the increasing penetration of the boundaries of the national community by the forces of multiculturalism, mass migration, and the rise of cosmopolitan culture(s); and the creation of alternative communities or spaces of political mobilization – some 'actual', others 'virtual' – above and below the state. Our traditional forms of belonging need to adapt to this changed reality in order to retain both their meaningfulness and their corresponding political efficacy. It is no wonder that we have seen such explosive growth in the literature on citizenship theory as a result (Kymlicka and Norman, 1994; Isin and Turner, 2002).

For a little over a decade now, the literature has extensively debated the meaning and function of citizenship and the relevance of its ongoing association with nationality and territory, advancing theories of multicultural and transnational citizenship in the process (Parekh, 1991; Kymlicka, 1995; Carens, 1995; Heater, 1996; Archibugi et al., 1998). For many observers, the new world of regional and global integration is bringing an end to the sovereign nation-state and ushering in a post-national era characterized by transnational forms of citizenship and self-government that are more in tune with the new geometries of global interdependence. According to their proponents, these new forms of citizenship are capable of expanding the bounds of justice and moral obligation beyond parochial communities anchored in arbitrary divisions such as language, culture, ethnicity or nationality, to emphasize the universal community of humanity. Moreover, it is argued that postnational or cosmopolitan citizenship can help reduce the democratic deficit engendered by regional and global integration through the increased power and policy capacity that is available in transnational political communities or demoi.

In this book, we too argue for new forms of citizenship that challenge the iron link between state, nation, territory and sovereignty, and which are therefore capable of meeting the challenges presented by domestic diversity and transnational interdependence. Nevertheless, our intervention in the citizenship debate differs from many of those available in the current literature, especially those of theorists of cosmopolitanism or postnational citizenship. In our view, changing norms and practical configurations of sovereignty provide the opportunity not to transcend but instead to reaffirm the importance of territory and national identity for citizenship claims, while changes to liberal theory provide the vehicle for doing so. In making this argument, we focus on a particular subset of citizenship claims that have been advanced by substate national and Aboriginal peoples. As we see it, the demands of these groups for meaningful recognition, self-determination and a corresponding measure of state sovereignty, cannot be met by the various forms of global and transnational citizenship on offer in the literature. Postnational forms of citizenship and self-determination do not, in our view, conform to the reality of either subjective or collective identity and patterns of mobilization in most states. We do not deny that global and transnational forms of identity exist but they do not trump territorial ones. Whatever normative argument might be levered in support of them, they do not resonate with the preferences of most individuals, who continue to express strong loyalty to territorial forms of identity. This is as true for members of substate nations as it is for those of so-called 'majority' nations. The political strength of substate national groups in Europe and Canada, and increasingly of Aboriginal peoples in Canada, Australia and New Zealand, provides evidence for our claims. But so does the strength of state nationality in these same countries.

The alternative we develop in this book is an argument for multinational citizenship that is sensitive to the perspectives of and demands for self-determination and differentiated forms of citizenship advanced by substate national and Aboriginal peoples. Our argument has both a political and a normative dimension: not only are people still mobilized around national identities, they feel they are entitled to be organized in this way as a matter of right. Stated differently, their national identities matter for them and they will judge state action and government policy in relation to its respect for national identities and its fair treatment of them. Hence, multinational citizenship, as we define it, gives equal recognition to the citizenship regimes of state and substate nations through a democratic argument for self-determination at the substate level and a revised conception of state sovereignty that is divided and shared. By the end of the book, we hope to have demonstrated that it is more appropriate to place the obligation on states to defend their refusal to recognize the citizenship claims of substate nations and Aboriginal peoples rather than to maintain that these groups must prove something about their cultural distinctiveness in order to stake a claim to differentiated citizenship. In this way we differ from many of the multicultural approaches to differentiated citizenship and self-determination for Aboriginal and substate national groups. Multicultural approaches overemphasize the cultural dimensions of citizenship and consequently underplay the importance of its democratic component – which forms the normative core of our conception of multinational citizenship. Another key shortcoming of multicultural approaches is that, intentionally or not, they continue to privilege state nationality over substate nationality. This fact gives rise to an uncomfortable tension in the work of theorists of multiculturalism who want to support differentiated citizenship claims but who worry that such claims will interfere with the integrative function of citizenship. Although this tension is unresolved in the multicultural approaches on offer, we maintain that it does not need to exist in the first place.

What do we mean by substate nations and Aboriginal peoples? Also known in the literature as 'stateless nations' (Keating, 1996) or 'nations without states' (Guibernau, 1999), substate nations[1] seek a greater degree of self-determination, a share of state sovereignty by way of control over a portion of the state's territory and substantial autonomy to design and implement their own democratic institutions. While some substate nationalists are committed to the project of secession and state breaking, many others are calling for forms of citizenship and self-determination that provide them with a share of sovereignty within the framework of a multinational state; statehood is no longer viewed as a necessary condition of self-rule. Aboriginal peoples differ, often dramatically, from traditional substate nations in terms of their empirical characteristics. Together, their smaller populations, relative lack of resources and economic capacity, and correspondingly higher levels of interdependence with surrounding non-Aboriginal populations, mean that secession is almost never a viable option even if it were desired. Despite these empirical differences, Aboriginal peoples claim an identical normative right to self-determination based on their historic occupation and sovereign control of their traditional territories. This normative claim to self-determination carries no less normative weight than that asserted by conventional substate nations, even though its implementation may look very different. Moreover, like other stateless nations such as the Québécois and the Catalans, Aboriginal peoples demand more than the right of consultation or other subordinate forms of political power – they demand a true share of state sovereignty (Murphy, 2004a).

Neither the groups we have defined above nor their demands are new but the time is right for a reconsideration of how states should best respond to them. We consider the claims of substate nations and Aboriginal peoples in the context of a political and institutional opportunity created by the effects of cross-border integration and international regimes on traditional understandings and practices of state sovereignty. There is an emerging consensus in international law and international relations that globalization and changes in international rule-making have challenged the principle of the legal equality of states (Crawford and Marks, 1998; MacCormick, 1999). The rise of new rule-making institutions at the suprastate level has implications for the state's internal sovereignty regime. The emergence of these regimes of transnational multilevel governance creates interdependencies among regional, state and suprastate authorities that in turn have reconfigured forms of collective action, decision-making, cooperation and monitoring. As a result, suprastate institutions challenge the position that the state holds ultimate political authority over domestic matters, particularly the economy (compare Strange, 1996; Weiss, 1998). While some argue that the nation-state has been rendered increasingly irrelevant as a result (Ohmae, 1995), we take a different view: the emergence of new loci of rule-making at the suprastate level simply reconfigures the distribution of power in the international system such that the state is one among several important actors that exercises influence in processes of decision-making. Indeed, states are and will continue to be the most important actors in both domestic and international politics (Paul et al., 2003; Weiss, 2003).

We are of the view that even if states will continue to be dominant actors, they will face ongoing challenges to their autonomy that are the result of growing interdependencies among levels of government and spheres of collective action. So, even if state power has not necessarily weakened as a result of regional and global integration, it certainly has changed in nature. The most significant way in which this change has played out is in debates about the concept of state sovereignty, which in turn have unleashed new ideas and expectations about how the claims of substate nations and Aboriginal peoples should be managed. Consider, in this context, the fact that territorially concentrated national identities have not receded – as many post-nationalists had predicted – and in many cases have even been invigorated by processes of regional integration. There are many reasons for this reinvigoration, ranging from materialist theories of the emergence of regional economic units in the global economy to post-materialist explanations of identity-based mobilization. Whatever the cause, it seems that territorially based nations – at both the state and substate level – will continue to be the primary units around which citizenship and self-determination claims will be organized for the foreseeable future. But this fact, when considered in combination with shifting sovereignty norms, brings into question the viability of linking democratic self-government and citizenship practices exclusively to nation-states. Indeed, in practical terms, states are already sharing some of their sovereignty with suprastate and substate authorities. So, where substate national and Aboriginal peoples are concerned, it makes sense to give this practice a normative dimension and we do so by arguing for a more *equal* distribution of sovereignty in multination states to meet the citizenship demands of stateless nations. The theoretical transformation of liberalism over the last decade provides the means by which such normative arguments can be constructed. Will Kymlicka's (1989) influential argument that culture is a primary right has opened a path to the liberal recognition of group-based claims. However, we view the claims of substate nations and Aboriginal peoples to be about much more than the protection of their culture (Harty, 1999; Murphy, 2001b). We believe it is crucial to seek the normative grounds for the claims of these groups in fundamental principles of democracy and non-domination rather than in principles tied primarily to issues of culture or cultural distinctiveness.

Our position therefore takes us down a slightly different path than that proposed by other liberal theorists working in the field of nationalism; in our view, the path we chart is more consistent with increased concerns around democratization at both the domestic and international levels. As the literature documents, citizens' expectations around democratization have shifted from formal representative institutions – political parties, legislatures – to more informal and direct ones – public consultations, town hall meetings, referenda, etc. (Smith and Wales, 2000; Saward, 2001). As Inglehart (1997) has argued, this shift is due to a decline in deference and a rise in post-materialist values that are not captured by established class-based parties. Demands for democratization, citizen engagement and government accountability have been used to champion local forms of decision-making through principles such as subsidiarity, devolution or self-government. Such forms of decision-making are more meaningful where there is rule-making capacity provided through political autonomy: for example, municipal or regional bodies having primary legislative responsibility or, at the very least, some legislative capacity so as to give life to collective decision-making and self-rule. For reasons of policy efficacy, other areas of decision-making are best located at the regional or even global level – most citizens recognize and accept this fact. Yet existing regional and global institutions are mostly undemocratic and, as such, render opaque decision-making around important issues of global concern. For example, the democratic deficit in EU institutions is well established in the theoretical literature[2] (Lindseth, 1999; Bellamy and Castiglione, 2000; Lord and Beetham, 2001), to which the European Commission responded with a series of recommendations for reform (CEC, 2001). There is also an ongoing debate about how to democratize and render more effective institutions of global governance (Hirst and Thompson, 1996; Dahl, 1999; Norris, 1999; Nye and Donahue, 2000), for example, by changing their systems of representation, allowing more opportunities for public or NGO consultation, or by rendering their decision-making processes more transparent (Scholte et al., 1999; Woods and Narlikar, 2001). The multinational model of citizenship and self-determination developed in this book is characterized by the domestic redistribution of state sovereignty to satisfy demands for democratic reform at the substate level. This process can in turn be combined with democratized systems of regional or global multilevel governance where sovereignty is shared among substate, state and suprastate actors to help increase their capacity to meet the normative and empirical challenges of cross-border interdependence.[3] We outline this approach in greater detail below, but to set the stage we first need to define and explain the key concepts around which our analysis is developed.

Conceptual anchors: citizenship and sovereignty

In order for our argument to be persuasive, we need to be clear about our use of certain key terms and concepts and the relationship between them. We are writing on themes and issues that have already been examined extensively in the literature, so conceptual confusion is likely. Often, arguments turn on nuances or distinctions that need to be properly captured in order to convince. The two central concepts around which the book is structured are citizenship and sovereignty and the relationships they bear to principles of nationality, democracy and self-determination. Citizenship most fundamentally refers to the rights, entitlements and responsibilities that fall to an individual by virtue of her membership in a particular political community. Although an important body of contemporary theory deals with the subject of the duties of citizenship, our focus, like that of early citizenship theory, is more on the rights as opposed to the duties dimension of citizenship. According to T. H. Marshall's classic liberal formulation (Marshall, 1950), the rights of citizenship include civil rights such as life and liberty, and freedom of expression; key political rights such as the right to vote and stand for political office; and social rights such as access to benefits, income supports and labour standards. In the traditional liberal model of the nation-state, the rights of citizenship are determined on the basis of nationality (Preuss et al., 2003: 7), which on one level is simply an expression of an individual's legal membership in the polity. On a more fundamental level it is also an expression of an individual and collective sense of identity, and a sense of belonging to and solidarity with a larger community of co-nationals. A common sense of national identity can be based on a variety of factors such as a shared history, language or cultural background, but it can also be based on subjective factors such as the perception of a common external threat, an attachment to a particular piece of territory or simply a commitment to a particular set of institutions. More often than not, it is based on some combination of these two factors. Citizenship and nationality are further linked by the principle of national self-determination. Self-determination is simultaneously a crucial dimension (or right) of citizenship and the primary political vehicle that affords different national communities the autonomy to design and implement their own distinctive regimes of citizenship and self-government. Self-determination is most fundamentally an expression of the democratic dimension of citizenship. It entails the freedom of a national community from external interference or domination, the freedom of that community to design and control its own democratic institutions, and that community's freedom to negotiate its governance relationships with the representatives of other communities or governments.

Ascertaining the relationship between citizenship, democracy and national self-determination also brings us up against the concept of sovereignty. In the literature on state theory, the principles of sovereignty and self-determination have been inextricably linked. In the modern period international law located the right to self-determination in peoples (nation), which it assumed to coincide with states. States were recognized as the legitimate sovereign authorities in the domestic and international spheres. No other actors, at either the substate or suprastate level, could lay legitimate claim to this authority, which empowered states to organize their internal forms of citizenship and self-government as they saw fit. For the most part, states have organized citizenship and self-government around the notion of a single, homogeneous national community with a common identity and sense of solidarity or fellow feeling. Sovereignty is understood here as a form of power, with both a *de jure* dimension – the legal recognition and institutionalization of an actor's legitimate right to exercise authority in and over a particular jurisdiction – and a *de facto* dimension – the actual capacity of an actor to exercise that authority and to achieve its desired ends (Litfin, 1998: 6; MacCormick, 1999: 126–9). Given the focus of this book on questions of rights and the creation of institutional structures rather than on the actual exercise of power, we place most of our emphasis on the *de jure* dimension of sovereignty, but the *de facto* dimension of sovereignty does figure prominently in our discussion of the challenges to the state posed by regional and global integration.

Sovereignty is also usefully understood in terms of both its internal and external aspects. Internal sovereignty refers to the principle that the state's full and final internal authority in a particular territory is not subject to limitation by a higher or coordinate domestic power (Litfin, 1998: 5; MacCormick, 1999: 127). This internal aspect of sovereignty is distinguished from its external aspect, which in legal terms refers to the authority granted every state by international law to its territorial integrity, exclusive control of its internal affairs and freedom from external interference by another state (MacCormick, 1999: 129; Krasner, 2001: 20). No matter what the domestic distribution of power might be (unitary, federal, consociational, etc.), the established understanding of sovereignty is based on the position that the power exercised internally is not legally subject to a higher power exercised by some external actor (MacCormick, 1999: 29). To say that state sovereignty has been challenged is not to say that states have lost all control of their territory to a higher external power – far from it. MacCormick has argued that in the case of the member states of the EU, we have instead witnessed a distribution and pooling of their internal sovereignty that has enhanced their external sovereignty with reference to states outside the EU (MacCormick, 1999; see also Millwood, 1992). Member states do not have to worry that the institutions of the EU represent a higher legal or political authority, because the EU is neither a state nor does it exist independently of the will and decisions of its members. Therefore, in MacCormick's view, external state sovereignty has not been weakened, just reconfigured. In this book, we are interested in the potential implications of the reconfiguration of state sovereignty for the equality of nations within the state's borders.

New forms of citizenship: liberal national, postnational and multinational

Citizenship and sovereignty are being re-examined and reconceptualized in rapidly changing domestic and global political environments and these processes of change present new opportunities for drawing their corresponding relationship to nationality, democracy and self-determination. Like other scholars and commentators, we believe that the changes we have outlined above present an opportunity to reconceptualize the very nature of state sovereignty as it relates to the demands for recognition on the part of substate nations and Aboriginal peoples. But there has to be a vehicle by which to do so. Contemporary liberal theory, marked as it is by a significant reappraisal of the importance of differentiated claims to citizenship on the part of such groups, offers a way. In this section, we consider two normative responses by liberal theorists to changes in the international environment: liberal nationalist and postnationalist.[4]

We use the term 'liberal nationalist' to describe a group of political theorists who examine how differentiated claims related to cultural distinctiveness can be accommodated in liberal states (Kymlicka 1989, 1995; Tamir, 1993; Halev, 1994; Miller, 1995, 2000; Moore, 1998, 2001; Patten, 1999, 2002). Liberal nationalists critique the conventional nation-state model of liberal citizenship for its failure to account for either the multinational character of many liberal states or the associated claims to self-determination and group-differentiated forms of citizenship asserted by minority nations within the borders of these states. Liberal nationalists were among the first to draw attention to the fact that, for most of the twentieth century, liberal theory and state practice overwhelmingly tended either to deny minority claims to national self-determination or to pass over these claims in silence. When denying these claims, appeal was most frequently made to core liberal doctrines such as the incompatibility of group rights with the principle of equality of individuals, or the importance of state neutrality with respect to questions of cultural or national differences. Liberal nationalists have raised important objections to each of these liberal responses to minority nationalism. First, they argue that the principle of state neutrality as regards issues of culture and nationality has never played a serious role in liberal state practice, and in fact does not stand up to careful scrutiny as a theoretical response to minority nationalism. Instead, under the mantle of neutrality, citizenship and the state in both liberal theory and practice have always been constructed around the ideal of a homogeneous national community with a single national culture. The liberal nationalist critique helps us see how the neutrality response to substate national or Aboriginal claims in fact evokes a normative double standard, by denying these groups the very right to national self-determination that dominant nations comfortably assume and exercise for themselves via control of the state. Liberal nationalists argue for the elimination of this discriminatory practice by granting substate nations and Aboriginal peoples forms of group-differentiated citizenship that entail substantial powers of autonomous self-government. In their view, these rights, rather than violating liberal equality, are in fact central to upholding it, based on the logic that treating people with equal concern sometimes entails treating them differently. Minority rights in this case provide substate and Aboriginal nations with equal access to the democratic right of self-determination already enjoyed by the dominant nation with whom they share a state. What results is a state with multiple forms of citizenship and, correspondingly, multiple forms of citizen identity.

Liberal nationalists have been followed by a new wave of liberal theorists – we call them postnationalists – who stake out a position in opposition to both state and substate nationalist claims. The complexity of this literature can be daunting, with cosmopolitanism (a strand of postnationalism as we understand it) being a particularly diverse body of theory. For example, one finds distinctions between cultural, political and legal forms of cosmopolitanism (Waldron, 2000: 227–31) and between ethical and institutional cosmopolitanism (Pogge, 1992: 49). Others, meanwhile, speak more specifically of cosmopolitan liberalism (Beitz, 1999), cosmopolitan democracy (Held, 1999) or simply a cosmopolitan point of view on diversity (Waldron, 1995, 2000). A second challenge with this literature is a tendency to conflate the concepts of 'nation' and 'state', which leads to some confusion over whether the goal of postnationalism is to transcend the mononational in favour of the multinational state or to transcend the principle of national self-determination altogether. For example, in one account of postnationalism Kymlicka is deemed a postnationalist because of the challenge he mounts against the dominance of majority nations within multination states (Tambini, 2001: 201–2). However, this account seems oblivious to Kymlicka's fundamental purpose, which is not to transcend nationalism entirely but to defend a liberal version of nationalism, and thereby to seek political accommodation among minority and majority nations in multinational states. Another theorist observes (correctly) that there is no necessary relationship between cosmopolitanism and the fate of *states*, but then draws from this the conclusion that a cosmopolitan politics is not necessarily a post-*national* politics (Cheah and Robbins, 1998: 8), as if the nation and the state were indistinguishable.

There are normative and empirical dimensions to the challenge postnationalists present to nation-states and citizenship regimes grounded in the principle of national self-determination. In normative terms, postnationalism represents a desire to reconnect liberal theory and practice to its core principle, which is the sanctity of the individual as a member of the community of humanity, and thus to divorce contemporary liberal doctrine from its morally arbitrary and ultimately unjustifiable marriage to the principles of nationality and national self-determination. Postnationalists feel that this return to liberalism's normative roots is made both possible and necessary by the impact of regional and global integration on the dominance, if not the very survival, of the sovereign nation-state. There are several different dimensions to this logic. First, it is based on the conclusion that globalization has drastically eroded the governing capacity of the nation-state, thereby casting serious doubt on its continuing viability as the locus of citizenship and democratic self-government in a post-Westphalian world order. Second, as the value and security of citizenship regimes grounded in the principle of national self-determination are inexorably eroded by globalization, postnationalists predict a sharp turn away from territorially grounded national identities to forms of identification and citizenship grounded in transnational polities and transnational communities of fate. These new forms of citizenship and democratic polity are deemed to be both more capable of managing the challenges and opportunities presented by global integration and providing for the needs of populations whose safety, security and basic rights are not being met within the framework of nationality based citizenship and self-determination.

Our own approach to citizenship and self-determination overlaps and diverges from the liberal nationalist and postnationalist positions in important ways. We agree with postnationalists that regional and global integration pose significant challenges to state sovereignty, which create the need for reforms to the domestic and international architecture of power and governance. However, we disagree with those who envision the complete transcendence of the state and its replacement with regional and/or global polities and forms of authority. Instead, we envision a political system wherein states continue to be important actors, but their sovereignty is redistributed, both internally to provide equally for the self-determination of all nations in multinational states, and externally where it can be pooled in suprastate institutions that increase the capacity of their members to cope with the new realities of global interdependence. We also disagree with the postnationalist emphasis on alternative forms of collective identity and political community that explode the boundaries of both nations and states. In this we share some common ground with liberal nationalists, who emphasize, on both practical and normative grounds, the continuing necessity of grounding citizenship and self-determination in national communities from the principle of national self-determination. Similarly, we share the liberal nationalist concern with providing all nations in multinational states with equal access to the right to self-determination and the citizenship status it entails. Nevertheless, we differ from most liberal nationalists in the greater emphasis we place on the democratic and political as opposed to the cultural dimensions of citizenship and self-determination. That is, we view self-determination not as a right that depends on an argument relating to the cultural distinctiveness of a national community (and its corresponding connection to a liberal principle such as individual autonomy), but as a democratic and political right that itself justifies a national community's authority over matters of culture and a wide range of other matters or jurisdictions. In our estimation, even those liberal nationalists who espouse only a thin version of the culturalist argument do not engage in a deep enough discussion of the political aspects of self-determination. We favour an argument about the institutional dimensions of regional political decision-making that does not privilege the state and that does not rely on culture. Compared to liberal nationalists, we are prepared to draw out the fuller implications of a political argument and this forces us to engage with issues of states' exclusive claim to sovereignty. In so doing, we hope to contribute to an emerging literature that seeks a post-sovereign basis for citizenship and self-determination in the twenty-first century (MacCormick, 1999; Keating, 2001; Murphy and Harty, 2003).

Our intention is not to construct an argument for secession nor do we assume that it is possible to overturn international relations norms regarding state sovereignty. Indeed, one of our primary goals is to illustrate the potential benefits of institutional solutions to substate nationalist demands that stop short of secession. Secessionist solutions perpetuate the misleading idea that only states can enjoy sovereign rights, and in this sense they are both unimaginative and out of step with current political trends. Whereas, historically, secession was the only solution for substate nations seeking full control over their territory, we argue that such demands can be accommodated within the existing state structure if we are prepared to accept that there can be multiple sources of legally sanctioned political power that exist in parallel, concurrent or overlapping forms that correspond with different territories within a state's borders. New arrangements for organizing domestic sovereignty, by breaking with the notion of the state's ultimate authority, can promote a just coexistence between national groups through equal political rights and decision-making powers. We refer to these equal political rights as 'multinational citizenship'. Multinational citizenship is capable of providing a substate community of citizens with the exclusive authority to choose their own political representatives, who in turn will exercise decision-making powers that are not subject to unilateral interference or override by an external authority. These powers can be exercised through institutional designs that include some combination of joint, segmented or exclusive jurisdiction over particular issues, territories or peoples, so long as they enshrine the basic principle of equal consideration of the multiple national identities they are intended to serve. This approach would deliver greater autonomy to substate national groups and retain the political and territorial dimension of citizenship on which nationalists are unwilling to compromise, while accommodating traditional state demands relating to stability, social cohesion and multilevel intercommunal interdependence.

Approach

In developing our argument for multinational citizenship, we use an approach that combines normative political theory and empirical case studies. In part, this approach speaks to our distinct strengths as researchers, but our decision to adopt it was driven by much more than convenience. There are two reasons for doing so. First, there is the question of accuracy, by which we mean a correct understanding and interpretation of the nature of ethnic demands or conflict in a given state. We have long been concerned with the fact that, while the excursion of political theorists into the field of nationalism has brought an added dimension to debates about justice, equality and autonomy, their normative contributions have often lacked a full understanding of the political history, circumstances and demands of substate nations and Aboriginal peoples.[5] In particular, some theorists do not fully appreciate the political character of nationalism and national identity. As Moore (2001: 34) argues, 'nationalist identities are *primarily* political identities: they are concerned with the political community with which one identifies, and are normally characterized by the aspiration for some kind of political or institutional recognition of this community'. What this means, in analytical terms, is that theorists need to move beyond essentialist views of nationalism and national identity which characterize it as 'backward', 'pre-modern' or 'tribal'. Obviously, many liberal theorists have already done so, but many others continue to view the expression of nationalism as being on the edge of barbarism and therefore not rationalistic (McKim and McMahan, 1997). It is true that nationalism is an ideology that differs in many respects from modern forms of social organization and political mobilization that originated in market relations (liberalism, conservatism, socialism and communism). To declare oneself a 'nationalist' does not reveal anything about one's market preferences. Because the market has had such a thoroughgoing effect on modern societies, it is difficult to avoid the temptation to view non-market relations as pre-modern; it is for this reason that modernization is often advocated as a solution to the expression of nationalist will. But citizens today choose to be nationalists just as they might choose to be socialists, because to declare themselves nationalist speaks to their preference for self-government through political institutions of their own design.

Second, there is the question of relevance, which is closely tied to the problem of accuracy. Failure to appreciate the nature of nationalist demands can lead to prescriptive advice or practical solutions that, in the end, will not solve anything. As McGarry and O'Leary (1995: 858) have noted for Northern Ireland, 'misinterpreting the conflict has consequences for public policy'. We might also add that the misinterpretation of the nature of a conflict can also produce disastrous consequences for the lives of citizens. So, in our view, even the most theoretically compelling and coherent argument can lack relevance if it claims to address contemporary political realities, but is ultimately unable to cope with the facts and nuances of actual cases of nationalism in practice. As Carens argues in his defence of what he calls a contextual approach, 'the persuasiveness of a theory rests in part upon the sense that it fits reasonably well with current arrangements, so it is important to see whether that is really the case' (Carens, 2000: 3).[6] A test of the relevance of a proposal operates on two levels. First, a proposal will be relevant if it is based on an accurate interpretation of the nationalism in question. Accuracy here requires a balanced approach to understanding a conflict; the theorist must be able to empathize with each side, not advocate for one over another. Second, a proposal will be relevant if it speaks to the claims of the groups for whom a theorist is supposedly developing principled responses. If nationalism and national identity are primarily political, then we need principled responses to the political situations and contexts in which nationalists are operating. Of course, we also need theoretical works that can address the 'what if' situations of the future. This would be one way of categorizing some of the existing literature on secession (Buchanan, 1991, 1995; Moore, 1998, 2001; Patten, 2002). Certainly, the conditions under which secession should be permitted need to be debated, particularly since international law is notoriously silent on the matter. Nevertheless, how many substate nations in the developed West are actually pursuing the secessionist option? Alex Heraclides has produced data on secessionist conflicts between 1945 and 1995 (1997: 302–3), which reveal that most of these have occurred outside Europe. Within Europe, most secessionist conflicts have occurred in East–Central Europe and the former Soviet Union – or, out of the closest approximation to 'empire' that the late twentieth century had to offer. Only two secessionist conflicts have occurred in Western Europe: in Spain (in the Basque Country) and in the UK (in Northern Ireland). As Heraclides's data make clear, these conflicts were waged by a segment of the population acting through a terrorist organization and its legal political wing (IRA/Sinn Féin; ETA/Herri Batasuna and, latterly, Batasuna). This noteworthy feature of Western European secessionist conflicts is confirmed by Keating (2001: 17), who argues that 'the case of the homogenous, territorially concentrated national minority in Western Europe seeking statehood is the limiting exception'. Some nationalist parties have adopted the independence option in their political platform at one time or another while others have occasionally flirted with it – usually as a bargaining chip in relations with the central state. But there are few data to support the claim that the majority of the members of the nation in question favours secession even when there is a nationalist political party that does.[7] Furthermore, how many substate nationalist movements are capable of pursuing secession as a political option? As the Québec case makes clear, even the most ardent nationalists reveal themselves to be risk averse when it comes to state-breaking (Dion, 1996). Taking secession to the people can be a costly political option for nationalist political parties. One could argue, as we do in this book, that, given the remoteness of the secessionist option and the lack of clear evidence that it is the preferred political solution of substate nationalists, other institutional solutions to the claims of substate nations and Aboriginal peoples should also be investigated by political theorists because they would be more immediately relevant. So, we conceive of a reciprocal relationship between theory and practice, wherein theory functions as a guide or as a critical measure of political practice, but is itself also shaped by what is deemed acceptable or possible in particular cases and contexts.

Any examination of the citizenship claims of substate national and Aboriginal peoples needs to be based on an accurate understanding of the problem at hand and needs to be relevant for the groups in question. These two objectives can be met if the demands of substate nations and Aboriginal peoples are presented faithfully and responsibly. So, our strategy for fulfilling these objectives is to consider the demands and claims of substate nationalists and Aboriginal peoples as well as state responses to these demands. Our justification for this approach to case studies is that the demands of substate national and Aboriginal peoples are not made in a vacuum; they are often shaped by the position adopted by a central government or by international events (for example, regional economic integration or the construction of Europe). While the demands of these groups respond to certain universal principles – self-determination, the right to self-government, democratic representation – the form they take is often shaped and influenced by particular political circumstances. So, we keep 'centre–periphery' politics in mind when we examine the demands for differentiated citizenship made by nationalists and Aboriginal peoples. We are not seeking to explain the complicated historical origins of these demands; rather, we want to assess how multinational citizenship can respond to them. We recognize upfront that substate national and Aboriginal peoples are not homogeneous in a political sense: members of these groups can represent many different positions, from the moderate to the radical. So how do we decide which set of demands to respond to in our analysis? Since we are interested in democratic forms of accommodation in multination states, we focus, where possible, on the demands articulated by democratically elected representatives of political parties or associations[8] and leave to one side the demands made by armed organizations. We acknowledge the argument that, in some cases, the recourse to arms might be the only available means of demanding recognition. However, it is difficult to assess the level of support for armed organizations compared to legal political parties. The case of Aboriginal peoples is somewhat more complex, principally because of the larger number of groups within a single country asserting the right to self-determination. The question of representation is also more complex.[9] For example, in Canada there are national-level Aboriginal organizations, such as the Assembly of First Nations, which have a basis in electoral politics and therefore claim to represent the collective concerns of their (more than 600) constituent communities. However, individual Aboriginal First Nations also have their own elected leaders, who alone are mandated to make decisions on local matters and to negotiate, if and when the time comes, on matters of land, resources, and self-government with non-Aboriginal governments. Similarly, in Australia, the Aboriginal and Torres Strait Islander Commission, an elected body whose members are drawn from and represent the interests of indigenous peoples throughout the country, operates alongside a variety of local-level Aboriginal authorities. We will draw on the statements of both of these sorts of representatives in building our analysis.[10]

While we take seriously the demands of substate nationalists and Aboriginal peoples, we acknowledge that the model of multination citizenship we develop might not respond to each and every one of their specific requests. The most obvious instance in which our model will fail to satisfy is in cases where substate nationalists demand secession. We purposefully do not attempt to respond to secessionist demands for several reasons. First, we are interested in differentiated citizenship claims, not claims for independent statehood. Secessionists necessarily reject the possibility that their demands can be met within the existing structure of the state, even if it is reconfigured to allow for shared sovereignty.[11] Second, as we already indicated above, there is an extensive new literature on secession and there is little we could add to it in the context of this book. Third, we believe that there is a gap in the literature on principled institutional responses to differentiated citizenship claims and it is this gap that we are attempting to fill. Like other theorists of citizenship in multination states, we are attempting to develop some basic principles but in doing so we are informed more clearly by the demands of substate nations and Aboriginal peoples: we are, after all, proposing a solution to the problem of justice, equality and recognition in multination states so it seems logical to take seriously the views of those who consider themselves to be facing conditions of injustice.

In developing multinational citizenship, we want to begin by laying the groundwork. The concept of self-determination, which drives contemporary demands for differentiated citizenship, has some complex origins. In the next chapter, we return to inter-war Europe in order to consider the web of political events and ideas that shaped our understanding of citizenship and belonging into the post-war period. This is more than a history lesson; this is a consideration of how liberals have grappled with the problem of minority nations and social integration over time. In chapter 3, we situate the same discussion in the contemporary period by considering how liberals today are responding to the very same set of issues but in a very different world.

2 • Citizenship in Multination States: Historical Precedents

Multinational citizenship is a principled response to some practical political issues that characterize state–society relations in countries inhabited by more than one nation. We do not expect that this is a response that will be readily accepted in all circles. In corners of the academic and political worlds, one will find the view that differentiated citizenship is a threat to the unity of the state. We have already considered how there is very little evidence that demands for political autonomy by nationalist groups will necessarily lead to secession. But there are other threats to domestic stability posed by political autonomy, for instance to social cohesion or solidarity/co-responsibility. Alan Cairns, writing about Aboriginal self-government in Canada, warns that 'proposals that stress what divides us in the service of a comprehensive future separateness simply misperceive where we are' (2000: 212). Many other scholars as well as political leaders have expressed concern that in recognizing difference we are overlooking what unites and unifies us. 'Where Canadians are' for Cairns includes a common citizenship because 'we need bonds of empathy so that our togetherness is moral as well as geographical' (2000: 211). For Cairns, and others worried about the fate of the ties that bind citizens in multination states, there needs to be a common citizenship – presumably a state citizenship – which is compatible with other forms of nationhood residing within the state.[1]

There is a historical precedent for common citizenship in multination states which offers important lessons for present-day attempts to ensure cohesion, solidarity and loyalty in societies that recognize and promote difference. The peace treaties that brought the First World War to an end contained within them important liberal principles related to minority[2] rights and the equality of nations that have echoes in contemporary liberal philosophy (Kymlicka, 1995). Through the Minorities Treaties, the international community imposed upon the new or enlarged states of East–Central Europe a concept of citizenship that was not linked to nationality. But these treaties ultimately failed, suggesting there are 'lessons learned' that we need to bear in mind. In this chapter, we argue that a principal reason for their failure was that the politics of nationalism implicit in the consolidation of the states of East–Central Europe overtook liberal commitments to the protection of minorities and the understanding of citizenship that these commitments implied. In key ways, the conditions which precipitated the failure of the inter-war model have not changed: the politics of nationalism remains the only model on offer for state consolidation and states themselves remain the only constituent unit of international society. While we recognize that the post-cold war international order is not the same as that which existed in the inter-war years, the 'citizenship lesson' of this earlier period will go unheeded unless we acknowledge that 'unnational' forms of belonging – whereby equality between majority and minority(ies) is guaranteed by the 'renunciation by the state of its national character' (Macartney 1934: 421) – will not be possible until we reconsider certain features of the prevailing institutional models of political authority in the nation-state. Two features in particular require attention: the centralized nature of political authority and the view that the state is the only legitimate sovereign authority on the domestic front. As we noted in chapter 1, these two aspects of state rule are being challenged from both a theoretical and political perspective but the possibility of drawing out this challenge to achieve 'unnational' forms of citizenship has not been widely explored.

How can we achieve this? We propose a re-examination of the genesis of the concept of national self-determination as a way of demonstrating that liberal conceptions of membership and belonging were not always closely linked to the idea of a national state. To tell this story, we return to the inter-war period to consider how one particular liberal idea – the equality of national cultures, by which 'majority' and 'minority' cultures would be on the same footing – clashed with that of the national state, which implied a certain way of organizing political authority. Contemporary liberal philosophers have picked up on the liberalism of this period for the way in which it attempted to provide a solution to the problem of ethnic accommodation in multination states (Kymlicka, 1995). Multiple ethnicities were a problem because of the emerging view that state territory 'belonged' to a nation.[3] They were motivated by the need to find a practical solution to a pressing political problem. In the inter-war period, liberals grappled with the possibility of accommodating multiple ethnicities by extending rights to groups in addition to individuals. Nevertheless, they ultimately rejected group rights in the aftermath of the Second World War, primarily in response to negative inter-war experiences with such rights, but also due to internal changes to liberalism itself, which mirrored changing approaches to the study of international relations (Dunne, 1998). The failure of the minority rights regime of inter-war Europe was due to the conflict between two very different principles: that of the nation-state, which privileged one nation's history, traditions and culture, and that of the multination state, which purposefully avoided a hierarchy of nations. Between 1949 and 1989, most liberals opted for the nation-state model. Now, early in the twenty-first century, the multinational state is back on the menu but we have yet to come up with an alternative to a form of nationalism and citizenship that is constructed around one nation. One of the purposes of this book is to develop such an alternative. To do so effectively requires that we imagine forms of community building that do not privilege one nation over another. It is not a straightforward task since our models of political authority and citizen loyalty are predicated on the existence of a common nationality. So this chapter reminds us of the difficulty of the endeavour while underscoring some important lessons for the project we develop.

We begin this chapter with an examination of the emergence of *national* self-determination in the inter-war period through a discussion of the way in which Wilsonian principles reshaped concepts of liberal autonomy. The influence of Wilson's ideas on the international stage forced liberals to respond to new concepts of political legitimacy and self-determination in shaping the constitutional structure of the new states of East–Central Europe. It was not easy: there was much debate about the pairing of 'nation' and 'state' and of the practical need to limit the use of national self-determination. We consider how liberals criticized the former while attempting to institute a new form of citizenship to respond to the latter. As we demonstrate, the results were not very successful because the conception of citizenship they introduced could not keep up with the logic of nationalism, which drove the consolidation of new states in the region. The national minorities of Europe promoted institutional alternatives to the centralized nation-state that might have been able to consolidate unnational citizenship. Unfortunately, liberal theorists and statesmen rejected these. We conclude the chapter by arguing that the failure of the inter-war experiment with a nationally neutral form of citizenship would have implications for how citizenship was shaped in the post-war settlement after 1945.

National self-determination

In British and European circles, the events of the First World War destroyed liberals' faith in progress in that they 'uprooted the political world that Liberals had understood and substituted something which seemed by comparison brash, cheap and contemptible' (Bentley, 1977: 1). The free institutions that were once at the core of liberalism had come crashing down and with them the ideals of tolerance and progress which liberals cherished. In the aftermath of the Great War, the liberal option appeared to be closed in many European countries as well as Russia, but in fact new possibilities for liberal institutions were emerging out of the destruction of the Austro-Hungarian Empire. The possibility of restoring the pathway to progress would depend on the stabilization of domestic society and the states system. Liberal statesmen attempted to do just that through the peace treaties and the creation of the League of Nations. Woodrow Wilson's ideas about liberal autonomy provided them with the opportunity to develop and apply liberalism in a new direction. The Peace Conference acted as the stage upon which they could do so.

Woodrow Wilson's influence in the construction of a new post-war system was set within the context of an emerging school of thought in the field of international relations, which is known as either the idealist or moralist school (Osiander, 1994; Dunne, 1998). The most significant feature of this school, for our purposes, was its liberal commitment to progress, which it believed could be secured through the universal application of certain principles to international society. Wilson's own views on the nature of international society were made clear through a series of speeches he gave in 1918, the most prominent of which were the 'Fourteen Points', the 'Four Principles' and the 'Five Particulars'. In Wilson's estimation, 'the [First World] war had its roots in the disregard of the rights of small nations and of nationalities which lacked the union and the force to make good their claim to determine their own allegiances and their own form of political life' ('The Four Principles').[4] The most important of Wilson's ideas – that which would be of the greatest political significance – was 'national self-determination'. It is difficult to overestimate the impact that his ideas had at the time and how they would transform our understanding of democracy and popular sovereignty. Today, the view that nations are the only unit that can self-determine is uncontroversial – whether or not they should be allowed to do so is a separate question.

However, the twinning of 'nation' and 'self-determination' was a novel development in the period following the First World War and was not without its critics.

'National self-determination' was new in two ways. First, the nation was now regarded as a cultural unit that had the right to decide to which state it wished to belong or, indeed, whether to form its own state. According to Wilson, 'Peoples and provinces are not to be bartered away from sovereign to sovereign as if they were mere chattels and pawns in a game . . . People may now be dominated and governed only by their own consent' ('The Four Principles'). Previously, 'nation' referred to 'the state considered from the point of view of the ruled rather than the ruler' (Cobban, 1969: 30). The French Revolution brought us the idea of popular sovereignty by way of which the right to form a government was transferred from monarchs to the people. The term 'nation' already existed (Hont, 1994), although it did not yet refer to a group of people sharing a history, language, tradition and way of life. The development of the cultural – understood in its broadest sense – meaning of nation took place over the course of the nineteenth century and was encouraged by the wave of Romantic cultural revivals sweeping across Europe. These revivals correspond to Miroslav Hroch's (1985) phase A of nationalist movements, which is marked by cultural, literary and folkloric activities. So, the promotion of minority languages, literature, song and dance is associated with this phase and evidenced by, for example, the restoration of the medieval National Eisteddfod in Wales (1880) or the Jocs Florals in Catalonia (1858). Romantic cultural revivals served to raise awareness among small nations of the characteristics and traditions that marked them off from the majority group. It is fair to say that the success of these movements could be measured by the extent to which they created a foundation for the emergence of a politicized form of substate nationalism by the end of the nineteenth century.[5] The combination of popular sovereignty and broad cultural distinctions that differentiated groups of people occupying separate territories conjured up the idea of distinct political units in the imagination of late nineteenth-century intellectuals and the popular audiences they attempted to influence. It was not long before the group of 'people' to which popular sovereignty referred became equated with the nation. Self-government by the nation was now presented as the quest for autonomy: late nineteenth- and early twentieth-century Europe was replete with regional nationalist movements seeking some form of administrative or governing autonomy from the central state. These nations did not claim self-government as a 'right' – this language did not yet exist – but rather as something that was morally just.

The second way in which national self-determination was novel was that the nation-state, the end result of the act of national self-determination, was now viewed as the democratic expression of the will of the people. Democracy and nationalism were now closely linked in the minds of statesmen and intellectuals. It was for this reason that Wilson could warn that 'self-determination is not a mere phase. It is an imperative principle of action, which statesmen will henceforth ignore at their peril' ('The Four Principles'). This development really dates back to the events of the French Revolution, when popular sovereignty and government by the people became interchangeable in the minds of radical democrats and this continued in their nineteenth-century struggles against autocratic regimes and empires (Cobban, 1969: 43). These campaigns for liberation on the part of culturally homogeneous groups were later categorized as national liberation struggles or, in the cases of Italy and Germany, national unification struggles. But the use of force on the part of some of these nationalists meant that nationalism was not necessarily democratic – for the time being at least. The revolutionary aspect of some nationalist struggles alarmed liberals; nevertheless, they accepted that it was sometimes necessary to use undemocratic means to achieve democratic ends. What mattered to liberals was that the struggle for individual autonomy and emancipation was now pursued by groups mobilized around a concept of themselves as a 'nation'. If individual autonomy was a right – and liberals believed that it was – then the pursuit of democracy (which guaranteed individual autonomy) on the part of national groups must also qualify as a right. Ironically, the unwillingness of liberal statesmen to understand the emerging liberal principles in universal terms – that is, by applying them to their own states – precipitated the breakdown of the very solutions they had put in place. Domestically, there were alternatives to liberalism in Western Europe which, on the face of it, appeared to guarantee stability but which did not include the forms of conflict resolution that the idealists would have wished to extend to the international sphere. For example, while monarchies were no longer considered to be an acceptable form of rule in East–Central Europe after 1918 ('X.7', 1925; Vivian, 1933), they continued to exist in Western Europe, although with constitutional limits. But the power and influence of Wilsonian principles were such that even the Spanish monarch sought guarantees from Presidents Wilson and Clémenceau that the participants in the Peace Conference would not attempt to dethrone him (Nuñez Seixas, 1995: 235).

The existence of a 'right' to national self-determination was not understood as such – Wilson referred to it as a 'principle of action' – but liberals and nationalists were beginning to reason along these lines by the inter-war period. The impact of Wilson's principles, and particularly of the promise of national self-determination, was such that many small nations across Europe expected that the simple declaration of their wish to be self-governing would be sufficient to be granted autonomy, not by the state authority which had acted as their effective oppressor, but by the international community. Cobban has noted that public opinion during the First World War supported

> a right of national independence which the Central Powers had overthrown, and that the primary object of the Allies was the reinstatement of this right. The democratic conception of government being added to it, the combined ideal obtained widespread recognition as the principle of national self-determination. (Cobban, 1969: 18–19)

As one Catalan commentator remarked in the wake of the many defences of the rights of small nations made by Wilson and the then British Prime Minister Lloyd George, if Catalonia did not obtain autonomy once the peace treaties were signed, then its citizens had only themselves to blame for not 'having declared in time before the world who we are, where we come from and what we want' (Roca i Codina, 1918: 40).

This was exactly the kind of thinking that opponents of national self-determination feared. The principle of national self-determination was by no means acceptable to all liberals. For critics such as E. H. Carr and sceptics such as Alfred Cobban, the problem lay with the union of the concepts 'nationality' and 'self-determination'. In Carr's estimation, self-determination was a right belonging to individual men and women, in line with the liberal concept of autonomy. The principle of self-determination 'requires that a group of people of reasonable size desirous of constituting a state should be allowed' to do so (Carr, 1941: 9). It was not entirely problematic that the 'people' were often referred to as a nation until such time as 'nationality' was presented as an objective attribute of a group of people, a label bestowed upon them in response to a shared culture. Carr rejected any notion that nation and state should coincide when a claim to national self-determination was based solely on a common culture: a state required far more than this in order to be viable.[6] Carr was one of the most famous critics of national self-determination, but others echoed his views. Alfred Cobban rejected both the position that 'nation' and 'state' were potentially the same kind of thing (Cobban, 1945: 51) and the claim that the common political loyalty upon which state authority and sovereignty were based should be derived from the cultural unity of the nation. He maintained instead that the attempt to make the culturally united nation-state the sole basis of legitimate political organization had proven untenable in practice, and was never tenable in theory (Cobban, 1945: 63).

Be that as it may, in the aftermath of the First World War liberal statesmen were charged with restoring stability to inter-state Europe through the peace treaties. The outcome of the Peace Conference was to disappoint on many levels (Keynes, 1984; Nicolson, 1937), but fundamentally many participants were uncomfortable with the principles of a 'just' peace, even if they were swayed by the rhetoric that accompanied this idea. In theoretical and practical terms, the statesmen at the Paris Peace Conference were guided by the belief that the international system could be stabilized if it were subjected to the same disciplining procedures for regulating conflicts between parties that were used in domestic society: a form of legal oversight with specifically juridical features (Muir, 1917). As a result, 'the problems of the international sphere would quite literally be domesticated' (Osiander, 1994: 261). For liberal statesmen, at least, stability was dependent on setting limits to the number of nation-states. As far as they were concerned, the carrying capacity of the inter-state system was limited by two important criteria: military and economic power. In the minds of liberals, 'progress' was equated with expansion. This ideal propelled liberals to reject the possibility that small states could be the sites of progress and raised a problem for the fate of Europe's small nations. This position was actually a return to an earlier one that had dominated liberal thinking in 1830–80: the so-called 'threshold principle' by which only nations of a certain size could constitute states. Liberals had argued that the move from small political units – typically conforming to family, clan or tribal patterns of social organization and political authority – to larger ones – in which social and political organizations were regulated by the market and defended by the military – was irreversible. There was no other way to extend human progress but through the merger of smaller nations with larger ones. Liberals never completely abandoned this idea, even if small nations had been the vogue during the Romantic period of nationalism in the late nineteenth century. As Hobsbawm reasoned, paraphrasing these liberal thinkers,

> if the only historically justifiable nationalism was that which fitted in with progress, i.e. which enlarged rather than restricted the scale on which human economies, societies and cultures operated, what could the defence of small peoples, small languages, small traditions be, in the overwhelming majority of cases, but an expression of conservative resistance to the inevitable advance of history? (Hobsbawm, 1992: 41)

In the latter part of the nineteenth century, the capacity for conquest was a criterion for participation in the international society of states; by the inter-war period, conquest had been replaced by economic efficiency and the military capacity for self-defence. In either case, the cards were stacked against small nations. The nation was now regarded as the site of the 'national economy' and small nations were neither capable of producing sufficient resources to sustain the population nor advised to resort to importing the bulk of what they required, since free trade could not be guaranteed. A second problem with the creation of small states after 1914 was similarly related to the need for economies of scale, although this time in military production. One of E. H. Carr's two main conclusions in his study of the future of nations was that the 'right of self-determination must carry with it a recognition of the responsibility to subordinate military and economic policy and resources to the needs of a wider community' (Carr, 1941: 48). For Carr and other critics of national self-determination, the cultural basis of self-determination neither guaranteed recognition of nor the capacity to carry out this responsibility. National self-determination, if it were indeed a universal principle that needed to be carried to its own logical conclusion, would be the cause of inter-state instability. As Hobhouse noted,

> there is no doubt that the general tendency of liberalism is to favour autonomy, but, faced as it is with the problems of subdivision and the complexity of group within group, it has to rely on the concrete teaching of history and the practical insights of statesmanship to determine how the lines of autonomy are to be drawn. (Hobhouse, 1964: 26)

Creating national minorities

From the perspective of statesmen and political commentators, the biggest threat to these dominant ideals of liberal progress in the inter-war period was irredentist nationalism. The driving force behind this form of nationalism was not simply a desire to be united with the nation of which one was culturally a member, although this played an important part. The chief impetus was to pursue union in order to be able to practise one's culture and speak one's language, thereby avoiding the cost of having to learn new ones. As has often been noted, the break-up of the empires of East–Central Europe did not occur along clean ethnic lines. While the international community struggles with its own solutions to the present-day consequences of this reality, inter-war statesmen were most concerned to prevent the creation of new nation-states through irredentist campaigns since it was physically impossible to do so without creating more minority communities. Politically, the principal problem of the region was that no matter where one drew the borderlines, the creation of national minorities was inevitable. The proposed solution, then, was to avoid irredentism by removing the need for it. This was no easy task, given the new discourse on national self-determination and Woodrow Wilson's promise, extended in his 'Four Principles' that 'All well-defined national elements shall be accorded the utmost satisfaction that can be accorded them'.

The challenge facing statesmen at the Peace Conference was to devise a means of curbing the 'natural' inclination of all national groups towards self-determination in order to preserve political stability on the continent. A political assumption accompanied the view that there was something natural about self-determination: ethnic minorities would pursue irredentist nationalism if they were mistreated and discriminated against by the majority population of the state. The recipe for inter-state peace that was devised required some conceptual slippage to make it a reality. Nation-states were believed to be the unit most capable of protecting national cultures and languages; this had been the thinking behind the creation of new nation-states following the First World War. Since the irredentist nations considered themselves to belong to larger nations in an ethnic and cultural sense, they had a persuasive argument – in line with the thinking that had dominated the Peace Conference – for demanding a newly reconfigured nation-state in which they would be the members of a dominant nation. There was no other way for their culture to be protected than by making the nation and state congruent. However, from the perspective of the victors at the Peace Conference, there *was* another possibility: by reclassifying these irredenta as 'national minorities' as opposed to nations, they could continue to maintain that the state offered a protective framework for such groups, even if the nation attached to the state was not their own (Musgrave, 1997: 39). The peace treaties accepted national minorities as a fact – thereby legitimating multination states – and maintained that, if treated with respect and toleration, they would 'forget their own natural determinist nationalism' (Macartney, 1934: 278). It was possible for national minorities to become loyal citizens of the state so long as their status did not become a basis for discrimination. This could be accomplished, first, by recognizing that the members of national minorities enjoyed the right to equality before the law and to the same civil and political rights as members of the majority nation; second, by setting out protective measures to guarantee these rights; and, third, by enforcing the guarantees through collective policing at the inter-state level.

By drawing this subtle distinction between nations and national minorities, statesmen accomplished two things: first, they could approach the problem of minorities using a liberal framework; and, second, they could check the rush on demands for new nation-states. When dealing with the problem of minorities in East–Central Europe, the authors of the peace treaties were strongly influenced by Western liberal ideas about liberty, equality and toleration. The dilemma facing liberals was to establish how national minorities could be placed on an equal footing with members of the dominant culture without being assimilated into the majority nation. They concluded that, so long as national minorities could practise their culture in the private sphere, they would have secured for them an important right that would guard against the threat of assimilation. Liberals had the historical experience of religious toleration to guide them in the development of a solution to the minorities problem, but they were in fact confronted with a more complicated set of issues when dealing with national minorities. The problem of religious minorities was dealt with through the application of the principle of toleration: religious minorities were free to practise their religion in private. It was thought that a similar solution would work with ethnic minorities: the cultural practices of these groups – speaking their language or participating in cultural activities – would be tolerated by the majority group. But whereas religious minorities could be members of the majority nation, the same could not be true of ethnic minorities. Religious minorities might never face discrimination in the public sphere because their ethnicity made them members of the majority.[7] They were not prevented from speaking their language, for example. However, not only did minority nations require the freedom to practise their language and culture, they would not be satisfied with a situation whereby the private practice of their culture was merely tolerated by the majority nation. Toleration of the practice of culture in private, although important, did not provide any guarantee that the members of national minorities would not be discriminated against by public institutions or the social system. National minorities wanted their culture to be equal to that of the majority group. The solution advocated by delegations to the Peace Conference, especially the Committee of Jewish Delegations, was what they referred to as 'cultural autonomy': where numbers warranted it, minorities should have the right to set up their own social and educational institutions and elect their own members to public bodies using a system of proportional representation and their own electoral college. Although forms of administrative autonomy existed in Western Europe, the New States Committee at the Peace Conference rejected the possibility of cultural autonomy regimes in East–Central Europe for two reasons: first, such regimes would undermine the authority of the state and, second, they were not necessary, so long as members of the national minorities enjoyed equality before the law.

Many political commentators of the peace treaties questioned the position that equal rights with members of the majority nation would be sufficient for national minorities. Indeed, before the outbreak of the war, Hobhouse had expressed the view that the smaller nationality 'stands out for a life of its own' (Hobhouse, 1927: 146). Azcárate maintained that national minorities possessed their own 'national consciousness' based on their language and culture (Azcárate, 1945: 24). In other words, in addition to being equal citizens with members of the majority nation, minorities should enjoy rights 'that would enable them to preserve and promote their ethnonational identity in existing states' (Preece, 1998: 12). According to one commentator of the League of Nations, in order for national minorities to be placed on an equal footing with majorities, 'it would be necessary for them to have the juridical, social, economic and cultural institutions which would allow them to preserve their national consciousness and to cultivate and develop their own language and culture under the same conditions as the majority' (Azcárate, 1945: 24). But political commentators and statesmen alike were agreed that national minorities should not be given political rights to self-government or autonomy: 'Any idea of giving the members of minorities such a special organization as would at all emancipate them from the general control of the state was repugnant to them' (Macartney, 1934: 283). Not only would self-government within the state be 'completely impracticable' (Azcárate, 1945: 24), it could also act as the starting point for nationalist mobilization. And, in an age when Wilsonian principles were rewriting the rules of legitimacy for membership in the international arena, such mobilization could pose a real danger.

Citizenship and nationality in inter-war Europe

The main problem with the line of liberal thinking that produced the Minorities Treaties was that it came up against the practical institutional needs of what Brubaker has termed 'nationalizing states' which promote 'nationalizing nationalisms'. These nationalisms

> involve claims made in the name of a 'core nation' or nationality, defined in ethnocultural terms, and sharply distinguished from the citizenry as a whole. The core nation is understood as the legitimate 'owner' of the state, which is conceived as the state *of* and *for* the core nation. (Brubaker, 1996: 5)

From the perspective of liberal statesmen at the Peace Conference, self-determination had not yet entirely reshaped international society such that they could be convinced that its introduction would produce deleterious effects for minorities. There were still other ways of organizing domestic society and inter-state relations. While the empires of East–Central Europe had just collapsed, West European states continued to exercise their imperial powers outside of Europe. The Statute of Westminster, which recognized the autonomy of the member-states of the British Empire and founded the Commonwealth, had not yet come into existence. It is true that the legitimacy of states was to be increasingly founded on the principle of nationality, but it was not yet the case that a homogeneous nation-state, in which citizenship and nationality coincided perfectly, was the only route for ensuring state legitimacy.

Nevertheless, the view that common national identity was a necessary basis for citizenship loyalty was increasingly taking hold in Europe, although the success with which it was pursued varied significantly across the continent. At the Paris Peace Conference, it was clear that there was an attempt to join nationality and citizenship in a potentially irreversible way. Many commentators and statesmen worked to ensure that this would not transpire in cases where this new practice would place minorities at risk (Levene, 2000). The Minorities Treaties were supposed to separate 'citizenship' from 'nationality' by ensuring that the members of the minority nations, like those of the majority, were equal citizens of the state. Citizenship, in other words, was not dependent on being a member of the majority nation nor was it predicated on a *de facto* policy of assimilation into the majority culture. Citizenship was intended as a right bestowed on all peoples – irrespective of their nationality – living within the boundaries of the state.

Even though the Minorities Treaties were integrated into the constitutions of the states which were party to them, the new nation-states tended to privilege the majority nation in their emerging concepts of nationhood and citizenship. For example, the Romanian Constitution stated that 'the Kingdom of Roumania [sic] is a national, unitary and indivisible state', despite the presence of the Hungarian minority within its borders. Similarly, the Czechoslovak Constitution began, 'We the Czecho-Slovak nation [sic], wishing to consolidate the unity of the nation' – a statement which appeared to exclude Germans, Ruthenes, Magyar and Poles residing within the borders of the new state (Macartney, 1934: 209). The status of national minorities' culture or ethnicity was not clearly established by these constitutions, even with the guarantees the treaties supposedly provided. Minority culture had a public face in that the treaties identified certain rights, which members of these groups could claim, and resolved to fight to protect them. On the other hand, these rights tended to operate more like guarantees – perhaps more in the tradition of religious tolerance than in what postwar liberals understand to constitute a right. Equality was interpreted as a 'negative' right; that is, protection against discrimination. Although positive rights were implicit in the concept of equality promoted by liberal statesmen, they were only weakly expressed. But in practice, states managed to avoid implementing the positive measures prescribed by the treaties by insisting on their own interpretation of their obligation to do so (Brubaker, 1996). Moreover, states' constitutions revealed a nationalizing project that was often at odds with the spirit and principle of the treaties. When constitution and treaty clashed, the former invariably won.

The Minorities Treaties were intended to stabilize polities, so why did state leaders undermine them, thereby running the risk of unleashing political conflict within their borders? State leaders behaved in this way because they were responding to their own need to consolidate their authority in the wake of imperial collapse and territorial restructuring. In the old order, before the war, the new majorities had once been dominated minorities. Obviously, they 'could not be expected to keep intact an administration devoted to the national ideals of another state . . . or devote all [their] efforts to the promulgation of a culture which was now that of a minority' (Macartney, 1934: 384). The leaders of the new states faced a particular conundrum: they had no model of state consolidation to fit their particular experience. Certainly, the West European states that housed more than one nation did not have an official 'multination' policy available for export. The 'minorities' question in Canada and the US was of an entirely different nature (Kymlicka, 1995) and thus offered no parallel. The League of Nations did not provide any guidance or expertise on the matter of institutional and democratic development. Thus state officials in East–Central Europe sought to legitimate their political authority in the manner in which the history of state formation taught them: by imposing a national culture across the territory which they were attempting to control. National cultures are important because they can facilitate the business of governing and political legitimacy in two ways: first, a national culture provides some of the key tools – education, language and customs – that allow citizens to access social and economic opportunities. Second, if there is a national culture into which all citizens can be integrated without prejudice, then citizens are more likely to perceive the political system as being fair: opportunities are not withheld because someone has a distinct cultural background (Harty, 2001: 192–3). But the logic behind such nation-building projects clashed with the principle of equality in the Minorities Treaties, which viewed citizenship as being unrelated to nationality. All citizens of these multination states were to enjoy the same social and economic opportunities no matter what their ethnic background. Nevertheless, the leaders and officials of the 'multination' states 'persist[ed] in their theoretically absurd and practically unattainable endeavour to make of these states the exclusive instruments of their national ideals and aspirations', with the result that 'the whole conception of the national state implie[d] a violation of the principle of equality to the detriment of the minorities' (Macartney, 1934: 421).

Of course, a new 'nationalizing' state which had signed the Minorities Treaties did not have the right to 'stamp its own culture on all of its citizens' (Stephens, 1929: 29), but it still had the challenge of gaining the loyalty of all of its citizens, whatever their nationality. This rarely happened. It could be that the scale of the displacement of ethnic nationals in East–Central Europe after the First World War prevented this. It could also be that the new nationalizing states were themselves too unstable domestically to be able to tolerate a rival national group within their borders. Brubaker argues that the new nationalizing states in inter-war Europe were marked by a feeling that their nation was 'not flourishing, that [their] specific interests [were] not adequately "realized" or "expressed" despite [their] rightful "ownership" of the state'. Moreover, the types of policies that were introduced to remedy this situation were viewed as 'remedial' or 'compensatory'; that is, they were 'needed to counterbalance and correct for previous discrimination against the nation before it had "its own" state to safeguard and promote its interests' (Brubaker, 1996: 83–4). The cultural insecurity of the new states is one reason why they frequently evaded their treaty obligations to the minorities within their borders. It was possible to redraw administrative boundaries in order to avoid the concentration of minorities that would have triggered the obligation to provide minority language schools and other services. More drastic measures could be taken if necessary, such as 'disguising' minorities by changing their names or outright repression. If the new states of East–Central Europe, which had benefited directly from the application of the principle of national self-determination, displayed marks of cultural insecurity, then they would hardly be willing to protect and promote the culture of the national minorities within their borders. This is not to deny that the principle of minority rights was itself morally sound. As one observer of the treaties noted: '[A] close examination of the Minority Treaties reveals a body of enlightened legislation far in advance of public opinion in the countries to which they applied' (Stephens, 1929: 28). Rather, it was politically difficult to enforce the principle, given the practical need to build new state institutions and the lack of any alternative to a programme of state consolidation centred around a dominant national culture. Hobhouse drew attention to this apparent conflict of interest facing the treaty states in a comment that is equally applicable today:

> to give scope to national difference without destroying the organization of a life which has somehow to be lived in common, is . . . the problem which the modern state has to solve if it is to maintain itself. It [the modern state] has to . . . make room for diversity and give scope for collective sentiments which in a measure conflict with one another. (Hobhouse, 1927: 147)

Then, as now, the problem was perceived in terms of citizenship and loyalty to the state. Then, as now, it was maintained that the basis for citizenship should be membership in the state's majority nation. There is, as yet, no other mechanism or procedure in place for accessing the full panoply of rights and benefits associated with citizenship. Moreover, aside from the experience of the Minorities Treaties, the rules for becoming a citizen have always been set by states themselves. Not surprisingly, the treaties were criticized by the signatory states for infringing on their domestic sovereignty. Many commentators and scholars writing just prior to the inter-war period maintained that the concept of sovereignty was in decline for much the same reason it is challenged today: developments at the international level meant that the state could not exercise ultimate authority in certain areas of decision-making (Lindsay, 1914; Barker, 1915). But in reality, the scope for outside interference in the affairs of the new or enlarged states after the First World War was quite limited. There was in fact only one condition laid down: 'that the inhabitants of the territories in question shall receive full rights of citizenship and that in the future no distinction shall be made between citizens in consequence of differences of race, religion or language' (Temperley, 1920–4: vol. v, 143). Although the international community judged that the rules for citizenship in the treaties were a hedge against instability, the treaty states maintained something different: the presence of multiple nationalities within their borders made it impossible to devise a principle that would ensure the loyalty of all citizens. The cosmopolitanism of empire was no longer a possibility and between cosmopolitanism and nationalism there were no other options. The idea of creating multicultural nationalism did not square with the prevailing Wilsonian discourse: 'nations' were now recognized as the only political unit that could aspire to self-government. Indeed, only the nation could claim, via the state, sovereignty. By the end of the Second World War, Cobban could observe that the fate of the principle of sovereignty was reversed when 'a strong transfusion of nationalism restored its flagging vigour' (Cobban, 1945: 66). In other words, as the inter-war period progressed, the treaty states opted for a form of sovereignty predicated on the concept of the unified nation-state (Mayall, 1990) and the states of Western Europe were powerless to do anything about it. But Cobban could already recognize what type of problem this would cause for the modern world, problems which we are only beginning to tackle, in theoretical terms, since the end of the cold war: 'If the state maintains its rights of sovereignty over the dissident nation [within its borders], there is no resolving the conflict, except by the destruction of the state or extermination of the nation' (Cobban, 1945: 71).[8] Territory, nationality and citizenship were becoming closely linked and the consequence of this, for minorities, was a form of exclusion.

The response of national minorities

The challenge that faced the new states of inter-war East–Central Europe is much the same as that facing most states in Europe today: how is it possible to create a meaningful overarching identity that responds to the needs of all nations and peoples residing within the state's borders? In the aftermath of the First World War, two solutions were advanced: first, the creation of national states and, second, where this was not possible, the establishment of certain guarantees for the protection of minorities. In effect, no homogeneous nation-state emerged out of the fallen empires of East–Central Europe. Despite this, all of the states of the region would pursue a political development path that converged on the model of the nation-state. They could hardly avoid doing so, given the lack of alternatives on offer. The liberal principles of equality upon which the Minorities Treaties rested provided the seeds for various alternative arrangements for ethnic accommodation in multination states. But these principles had no accompanying blueprint for institutional designs. Liberals took their cue from their historical experience of religious toleration: in states with 'minority' religions, members were given the right to practise their faith (and in some cases, to educate their children through this faith) and to form social and cultural associations around this faith. But while some states in Western Europe, such as the Netherlands, were devising innovative forms of representation to deal with religious plurality (Lijphart, 1968), similar innovations were not considered for the diversity of nationalities in the states of East–Central Europe. In part this was because liberals were set on notions of equality and individualism in the sphere of political representation. The 'politics of accommodation' developed in the Netherlands was not liberal. The absence of institutional innovations meant that there was no way of transforming the ideal of equality in the Minorities Treaties into a concrete and practical reality. Of course, the New States Committee of the Peace Conferences had drawn the line at political autonomy and no doubt viewed the question of political design as irrelevant. Still, there was no mechanism in place for national majorities to consult with minorities over sensitive cultural and political issues. Even some form of consultative structure would have given minorities a stronger sense of their participation in the polity on a group – or 'national' – basis.

During the course of the First World War, most national groups in East–Central Europe – well aware of the political consequences of imperial collapse in the region – considered the need for some level of institutional innovation. During the course of the war, when ideas about the post-war order were already being discussed, minority nations began to pool their resources in the pursuit of common objectives. In fact, the 'most detailed consideration of national minority protection was conducted by private organisations' during this period (Preece, 1998: 70). The Office des Nationalités, based in Lausanne, sponsored two conferences during the middle of the war (1915–16), the outcome of which was the Draft Declaration of the Rights of Nationalities. Both the spirit and the principles of the Declaration were to find their way into the Minorities Treaties: the liberal principle of freedom was applied to racial, linguistic and religious minorities, while the right to self-governing autonomy was also advocated. A second body, the Central Organization for a Durable Peace, located at the Hague, was more concerned with the international system. Nevertheless, it equated international stability with domestic order and towards that end produced the Draft International Treaty on the Rights of National Minorities (1917). The Draft Treaty addressed the issue of the civil and political equality of minority nations by granting them control over their own education and religious institutions and instituting a form of proportional representation in governing institutions.

The work of these two organizations was largely the inspiration for the creation of the Committee on New States and the Protection of Minorities within the League of Nations. The Committee was charged with 'imprinting the new liberal idealism of the inter-war period on the political form of national minority rights' (Preece, 1998: 70). Many small nations of Europe took the work of the Committee very seriously and formed their own Congress of National Minorities in response to the Committee's mandate. The Congress acted as both a lobby group for national minorities and small nations and a watchdog for the enforcement of the Minorities Treaties. But its objective was not only to lobby for the respect of minority rights or their introduction where they did not yet exist: the Congress also sought to champion certain ideals about democracy and autonomy. While some minority nations wanted political independence in the form of their own nation-state, many others only sought a type of local or regional autonomy. The experience of Ireland – first a Free State (1922) and then civil war (1922–3) – scared off many nationalist groups in Western Europe. Of course, any form of autonomy would require a new way of organizing political authority and structuring state–society relations, but it did not necessarily require political independence. Indeed, many substate nationalist groups, whether or not they were liberal, agreed that size mattered when considering the possibility of political independence, not just for economic reasons but for security ones as well. For example, the Parti autonomiste bretonne did not think that 'the absolute liberty of small nations was compatible with the increasing economic interdependence of modern states' (Duhamel, 1929: 168).[9] This position was in line with thinking which had been prominent among advocates of composite states in nineteenth-century European circles. In Catalonia, the journalist and republican organizer Valentí Almirall defined a composite state as an association of several small sovereign states, which ceded a portion of their sovereignty to a designated authority that would be responsible for security issues, while the sovereign states would retain their own institutions of self-government. In Almirall's estimation, a composite state was the only way to balance liberty and equality (Almirall, 1994). By the inter-war period, Catalan political leaders were calling for a federal Iberian Union as a means of responding to the minorities question in Spain (Estelrich, 1929).

The work of the Congress was important for raising alternatives to the institutional design of the centralized nation-state. The most frequently cited solutions to the problem of multination states advocated by members of the Congress were devolution, federalism and cultural autonomy. In the inter-war period, these alternatives were still on the table, politically speaking, and substate national groups worked to keep them there. Ironically, Wilsonian discourse, which substate national groups assumed to legitimize their claims, was in fact making this difficult. For example, the principle of cultural autonomy was viewed by the drafters of the peace treaties as 'dangerous' because it created 'an external rival to the one legal authority of the state' (Macartney, 1934: 282). To the dismay of substate nationalist groups across Europe, the principle of self-determination became neither universal nor overarching; it was in fact in competition with other principles, especially state sovereignty. Statesmen, working collectively, would make decisions about which principle would take precedence in a given context. Because sovereignty was based on mutual recognition, it won out time and again. As Cobban lamented, '[P]ractically every one, including Wilson himself, recognised that self-determination could only be applied with due regard to circumstances. But they are to be criticised for not having made this plainer in their public utterances' (1969: 104). Indeed, in prioritizing sovereignty over self-determination, state leaders closed off political options that had existed in some West European countries before the First World War. For example, prior to 1918, regional or local autonomy was possible in West European states without the threat of secession, but after this date, this threat was ever-present in the minds of some because of the principle of self-determination. State leaders imported the prevalent thinking around stability from East–Central Europe – that the recognition of 'nations' could precipitate demands for self-determination – without also importing the solution: minority rights. Substate nations, for their part, continued to pursue their claims for a political solution to autonomy, believing that the spirit of the peace treaties and the creation of the League of Nations heralded a willingness to work towards practical solutions to the twin imperatives of the rights of small nations and political stability. Of course, this willingness did not really exist. As Mayall notes,

> [I]n human affairs there can be no such thing as a *tabula rasa*: however the political map is re-drawn, there are going to be dissatisfied groups. It is the recognition of this stubborn fact, which has produced, at the international level, the pragmatic reconciliation between the prescriptive principle of state sovereignty and the popular principle of national self-determination. (Mayall, 1990: 44–5)

Although the inter-war period did provide some scope for innovative responses to the problem of political stability, the failure of many of these – as witnessed by regime collapse – forced a turn to conservatism. Authoritarianism was accepted in some corners as a preferable alternative to unstable experiments with democratization. As the Second World War approached, the continent's twenty-year experiment with innovation would come to a close and the type of liberalism that emerged in 1945 was a far cry from Wilson: liberal idealism was to be replaced by liberal realism.

Citizenship in post-war Europe

Out of the period of inter-war instability and the devastation of the Second World War emerged a new set of ideas about how to organize domestic and international order (Latham, 1998). Post-war Europe was not faced with the problem of dissolved empires, as it was in the aftermath of the First World War. This time, the issue was the very survival of the 'old democracies' of Western Europe, which were suffering the severe economic consequences of the war's destruction. The events of Europe's recovery are well-known: the Marshall Plan, the GATT, OECD and NATO became the building-blocks of a post-war international society whose architectural design was based on multilateralism. Domestically, the creation of the welfare state was key for redistributing resources and providing citizens with 'equal' opportunities. Free trade abroad and state intervention at home became known as the 'compromise of embedded liberalism' in Ruggie's analysis of the transition from nineteenth-century liberal *laissez-faire* to late twentieth-century multilateralism (Ruggie, 1982). The embedded nature of liberalism in the post-war period refers to the social control that is exerted over the market: welfare states remain *liberal*, but domestic stability requires that this liberalism be embedded in the domestic social order. As part of the compromise, citizens accept that they have collective responsibility to share the social adjustment costs that markets inevitably produce. This is the notion of distributive justice made famous by John Rawls (1971): all social primary goods (liberty and opportunity, income and wealth, and the bases of self-respect) are to be distributed equally unless an unequal distribution of these goods would be to the advantage of the least favoured. But under what conditions would citizens be motivated to accept an unequal distribution of wealth? According to David Miller (1995), individuals would be prepared to redistribute wealth in a social context in which they recognize, accept and support their mutual obligations to their compatriots. Put differently, when an individual shares a national identity with other individuals, she will experience a particular loyalty towards her compatriots that will make her obligations towards them of an ethical nature. For Miller, nationality implies ethical commitments that are not based on strict reciprocity: I fulfil obligations towards my compatriots without necessarily expecting anything in return because 'I see my own welfare as bound up with the community to which I belong' (Miller, 1995: 67). Thus individuals will support redistributive models of justice 'if they regard themselves as bound to the beneficiaries by strong ties of community' (Miller, 1989: 59, in Abizadeh, 2002: 497). Nationality is what binds us together.[10]

The effect of this new discourse was to dramatically change the concept of liberal equality that had existed in inter-war Europe in relationship to the new states of East–Central Europe and to cause debates about citizenship to veer off in a completely new direction. This was the dawn of 'social citizenship': a set of entitlements designed initially to provide the working classes with the means to access equal opportunities but ultimately becoming the very pillars of the 'Golden Age' of the welfare state in the developed West. Inherent in these programmes was a concept of equality that was directed at the socio-economic status of individuals, not their national status, as had been the case in the inter-war period. In the period between the two world wars, equality and opportunity were believed to be related to the extent to which different nations were tolerated by the state. In the post-war period, equality and opportunity were understood primarily in relationship to the prospects for social mobility, which were believed to be impeded by structural factors, such as class. Liberal equality came to be associated with one's life chances, which should be based on merit since all individuals were equal regardless of race, religion, ethnicity, gender or class. The state's role was now to redistribute resources and to open up channels of access and mobility so as to improve the life chances of lower socio-economic groups. In inter-war Europe, the fear had been that national minorities who did not encounter tolerance would mobilize for self-determination. In post-war Europe, state leaders were concerned that lower socio-economic groups that were denied access to opportunities for advancement would also organize against the state but via revolution not self-determination. The presence of a structure for organizing and funding such a revolution – the Soviet Union – called for an immediate solution.

The solution came, in part, in the form of social programmes that were promoted as *national* programmes with, in many cases, universal access: national health care, national curricula, labour insurance schemes, children's benefits, etc. These programmes became closely associated with citizenship models because they are the outcome of decisions taken around the obligations we owe our compatriots: co-responsibility, the pooling of risk and social solidarity. Canadians often claim that their universal health care system defines who they are and, just as importantly, distinguishes them from Americans who clearly made different choices about the extent of mutual obligation in the area of health care (Maioni, 1998). The association of welfare programmes with citizenship is more than symbolic; it is reinforced over time by public policy recommendations and decisions. In Canada, a recent commission of inquiry into the future of the country's health care drew strong links between health care and the values of Canadians. As the Commissioner, Roy Romanow, reported:

> In their discussions with me, Canadians have been clear that they still strongly support the core values on which our health care system is premised – equity, fairness and solidarity. These values are tied to their understanding of citizenship. Canadians consider equal and timely access to medically necessary health care services on the basis of need as a right of citizenship, not a privilege of status or wealth. (Canada, 2002: p. xv)

So these programmes serve a strong integrative function that is founded on a sense of solidarity and reciprocity that allows for redistribution. Social programmes can also integrate on a territorial basis since they redistribute from 'have' to 'have not' regions, although redistribution can be a politically charged issue in states marked by regional disparities.[11] But where a region of the state is also a substate nation, a complicated politics can emerge around redistribution that affects understandings of citizenship, although it is important to note that this politics has evolved; it was not present at the founding of the welfare state. The Québec government recently concluded a Commission on Fiscal Imbalance, whose mandate was 'to identify and analyze the basic causes of the fiscal imbalance between the federal government and Québec' (Québec, 2002: 1).[12] While there are arguments about economic efficiency and citizen need that can be brought to bear in debates about fiscal federalism, there are also some notable arguments about budgetary autonomy that are related to the need of nations to have the resources to make decisions about their collective public projects. At its most basic level, citizenship is about belonging to a community of people who share something in common. For some individuals, belonging takes place primarily at the regional level: these individuals have more in common with fellow citizens in a delimited territory than with those living elsewhere in the 'imagined community' that is the nation-state. Consequently, it is possible to develop a strong sense of solidarity and reciprocity with fellow citizens at the regional level and to conceive of one's citizenship rights and obligations in relationship to this community. In multination states marked by forms of devolution, autonomy or federalism, political authority will be divided across levels of government. Depending on the constitutional separation of powers among levels of government, it is possible for social citizenship to develop at the regional level. Indeed, Béland and Lecours (forthcoming) argue that

> members of a community that considers itself a nation distinct from the one projected by the central state usually give priority to this sub-state national bond. In this context, nationalist movements will often seek to bring social distributive policies within their version of a national framework.

There is evidence that some nationalist movements have been successful in this regard. Rico (1997: 128) argues that one reason why health care was decentralized to some of the Autonomous Communities in Spain beginning in 1983 (and extended through two further reforms) was 'the existence of an intense and distinctive identity and set of preferences in nationalist communities, which were eager to mobilize in defence of their nationalist claims'. We see a complicated politics of solidarity and redistribution played out in Belgium, which threatens to turn a new federal system into a *de facto* confederal one. While many policy spheres have been decentralized to the Communities (Flemish and Walloon), the federal authority continues to administer the most important social security programmes, thereby giving it some limited tools with which to forge a Belgian identity. However, Flemish nationalists have argued that social security should be decentralized by drawing distinctions between the values and priorities of the two regions. It helps that Flanders is the wealthier of the two regions, since it allows Flemish nationalists to argue that their comparative regional wealth is effectively subsidizing the bad lifestyle habits of the poorer Walloon regions. For Flemish nationalists, Belgian identity is not sufficiently strong for them to accept the redistribution of resources from Flanders to Walloon; Flemish solidarity easily trumps Belgian solidarity on the issue of social security and Flemish public opinion supports its decentralization (Béland and Lecours, forthcoming). Many regional governments, such as the provincial government of Québec, not only have jurisdiction over important services and programmes – education and social services are the most obvious – they have also been particularly successful at promoting relations with their citizens by ensuring that the visibility of the provincial government outstrips that of the federal government. So, successive Québec governments (both nationalist and federalist) refer to Québec as 'État' as in the 'État Québécois' – the Québec state. This is particularly annoying for the federal government of Canada since it transfers substantial amounts of money to the provinces for health and social programmes yet the Canadian 'state' is not as visible in the delivery of these programmes. Scotland, which always enjoyed certain separate social and legal institutions, can now (since devolution) develop its own social programmes. Even if the objectives of these are largely consistent with similar programmes in England and Wales, the fact that they are designed for and delivered exclusively to the Scottish people challenges the integrative function normally performed by state social programmes.[13] Moreover, the Scottish National Party (SNP) has promoted the idea that progressive social policy is a feature of Scottish national identity and has linked the fulfilment of this aspect of Scottish identity to political independence: '[the aim of the SNP is] to create a just, caring and enterprising society by releasing Scotland's full potential as an independent nation in the mainstream of modern Europe' (Béland and Lecours, forthcoming). Therefore, as a result of the services they deliver to citizens, regional governments are able to reinforce communities of reciprocity and solidarity that do not extend to the rest of the country.

Generally speaking, even if there have been substate national challenges to the post-war welfare state's integrative social citizenship, there was little or no possibility of negotiating territorial settlements for substate national groups in the immediate post-war period. The overriding preoccupation of the period was to ensure domestic order as a form of protection against the interference of potentially destabilizing outside influences; in this context, a centralized state was viewed as the path to stability. Security concerns dictated that the discourse around citizenship that had existed after the First World War was no longer a political possibility. More important for our purposes, it was no longer possible from a liberal theoretical perspective either. The 'compromise of embedded liberalism' offers a plausible explanation for liberal theory's move away from advocating culturally neutral forms of citizenship in inter-war Europe to the adoption of a decidedly national form of citizenship in the post-war period. Other explanations for the liberal rejection of minority rights, such as racial desegregation and the revival of ethnicity in the United States (Kymlicka, 1995: 58–69), cannot be generalized beyond this one country. By contrast, embedded liberalism extended across all welfare states and was institutionalized through them, creating a powerful form of liberal citizenship based on universal individual rights that has been difficult to change. Moreover, embedded liberalism covers off the issues that are central to other explanations for the change in liberal theory, especially the need for domestic and international stability.

'Lessons learned'

The form of 'unnational' citizenship that was championed by some liberal theorists in inter-war Europe was an attempted solution to the challenge of domestic stability in multination states. Many liberals of that period recognized that forms of citizenship that privileged and promoted one nation would be exclusionary and quite possibly unjust. In their estimation, the only type of citizenship that could integrate all nations within a state was one that was neutral in a nationalist sense. This project ultimately failed because it was not clear how 'unnational' citizenship could integrate diverse nationalities: what would hold them together? Even if liberals assumed that some form of constitutional allegiance would do the trick, nationalist arguments and mobilization gained the upper hand.

As a result of the post-war experience of citizenship, which settled squarely on mononationality, we now recognize that inter-war liberals were right on one point: privileging one nation excludes others, without necessarily making them go away. As van den Berghe complains (2002: 442):

> there is a fundamental incompatibility between nationalist ideology and multinational populations. Unfortunately, the entire tradition of Western liberal democracy . . . has been inextricably linked with an acceptance of the nation-state as the template of political legitimacy. A better prescription for ethnic strife and genocide could scarcely be imagined.

Contemporary liberals have attempted to correct for this by arguing for differentiated citizenship. At the same time, liberals express concern that differentiated citizenship can work against the integrative function of citizenship. State citizenship is still strongly nationalist in a unitary sense and even though liberal nationalists have revealed this fact in their work, they have offered almost no means of changing it. Differentiated citizenship, on paper, will do nothing to alter the fact that our dominant models of citizenship remain state nationalist. So, it is no surprise that there should be this tension in the work of liberal nationalists (between support for and concern over differentiated citizenship): they will be forced to view their own work (differentiated citizenship) as a threat until such time as they tackle the continued link between state citizenship and the nationality of the majority group. Differentiated citizenship will only work where national states have been transformed into plurinational or unnational ones or denationalized entirely (van den Berghe, 2002). In this chapter, we have considered 'unnational' citizenship; in the next chapter, we consider the liberal argument for differentiated citizenship claims and discuss the ongoing challenge of finding an integrative form of citizenship in multination states.

3 • Liberal Nationalism

For most of the post-war period, the arguments in favour of cultural recognition promoted by inter-war liberals were eclipsed by the view that cultural neutrality was the best path towards the advancement of equality. But by the end of the twentieth century, many liberals had returned to the view that cultural factors could influence the degree to which people feel as though they belong to a wider 'national' community. There are two possible reasons for a reassessment of the role of culture. First, many liberals had come to accept something minority groups had long pointed out: the state was never in fact culturally neutral, as liberal theorists and liberal statesmen had proclaimed. In fact, the national community in question was most often that of the majority group and the history, norms and traditions of this group were the basis for state nation-building projects that projected the symbols and content of the majority's culture back onto the whole population (Tilly, 1975; Seton-Watson, 1975; Gellner, 1983; Harty, 2001; Rae, 2002). Even though the principle of liberal equality was predicated on the assumption of cultural neutrality, the liberal state did not treat all cultures equally. It might be that this fact was not entirely appreciated by liberal political theorists, but it was certainly the subject of the rich investigation of nineteenth- and twentieth-century nation-building in the fields of cultural anthropology, political science and political sociology. This literature documents how state nationalists often purposefully repressed the culture of substate nations within their borders in order to impose the political authority and compliance required for state stability.[1]

There is a second reason for the return of culture to liberal arguments about equality, one which situates this change within a broader context of processes of democratization and liberalization beginning in the 1960s. Whatever the pretensions of post-war liberal universalism, social citizenship has not always operated in the way in which its proponents expected: sometimes, access and opportunity are not available to all citizens, some of whom face structural and institutional barriers to full participation. Such barriers, entirely at odds as they were with the notion of social progress assumed by liberal theorists, had a particularly forceful impact on groups characterized by their ethno-national, linguistic or cultural differences. In this sense, one of the primary challenges posed by structural and institutional barriers to equality is to imagine how citizens of liberal societies can be equal despite their differences. Several important political responses to this challenge were made by African-Americans through the civil rights movement, by women through the transnational 'liberation' movement, by sub-state nations and Aboriginal peoples opposed to 'internal colonialism' and by immigrant ethnic groups in European and North American states combating forces of racism and cultural denigration. Together, these movements underscored how liberal conceptions of justice had missed some crucial marks. Through their struggles, social justice came to be understood as more than just redistributing income; it was also about removing barriers to participation, to belonging, to citizenship.

The struggles bore results. For most of the post-war period, it was assumed that liberal justice could be achieved only by working from the principle that all individuals are equal and the same and therefore should be treated as such by the state. Now, the dominant view in liberal theory is that achieving justice for some individuals requires us to recognize that we are equal *and* different. The citizenship claims of some of our compatriots will therefore be based on how they are different from the majority group; the state's response to their claims must contemplate targeted measures to deal with their particular circumstances, all in the name of equality. 'Differentiated' citizenship is a concept introduced into the justice and equality debate by Iris Marion Young (1990) to confront the effects of oppression and discrimination experienced by individuals who, on paper at least, are deemed full citizens. Her solution is group-specific rights, which seek to give recognition to group differences in order to overcome oppression in the political community. Group-specific rights have challenged conventional liberal theory in two ways. First, their focus is not exclusively on the individual but also on groups of individuals sharing certain ascriptive criteria (race, ethnicity, gender, language) or, in some cases, attributes that have been acquired, such as some disabilities.[2] Second, Young challenged the distributive justice paradigm upon which the post-war welfare state was built for the way in which it ignored the institutional context in which decisions about redistribution are made, thus overlooking how it can give rise to constraints on self-determination and self-development, or what she calls respectively oppression and domination (Young, 1990: chaps 1 and 2).

The efforts of Young and others to transform liberal justice and institutionalize a politics of difference did not proceed unopposed. Liberals like Chandran Kukathas, for example, responded with the argument that there is no reason to modify liberalism in the face of the demands of cultural diversity.[3] Instead, the most effective way to do justice to these claims is via a particular defence of individual rights. In his view liberalism has always concerned itself with the power that majorities may wield over minorities. Liberalism assumes a plurality of interests and attempts to construct a neutral or objective standpoint from which to adjudicate them all – a point which is tied to no particular interest, past, current, or prospective. Group claims have no special primacy and are open to ethical evaluation; moreover, groups have no special right to self-preservation or perpetuation, and are valuable only in so far as they are essential to the well-being of individuals. In Kukathas's liberal universe, cultural groups are more like private associations or electoral majorities; that is, the desire of peoples to live according to the practices of their cultural communities is to be respected, not because cultures have a *right* to be preserved, but because individuals should be free to associate, to form communities and to live by the terms of those communities. This accords cultural communities no 'special' rights, but nor does the larger society have any right to interfere with them (Kukathas, 1992a: 111–12, 116–17).

Such challenges aside, the work of Young and other theorists of group-differentiated citizenship helped transform the debate about the meaning of justice and the importance of reciprocal duties among citizens in plural societies. Her work also underscores the need to address head-on the issue of self-development and self-determination in order to reverse conditions of oppression and domination. It is easy to see how her analysis of the institutional context of oppression and domination might serve as a bridge to an examination of the representation of substate nationalist and Aboriginal peoples.[4] In this vein the work of a group of theorists known as liberal nationalists, who we introduced in chapter 1, stands out. Like Young, they assume culturally heterogeneous societies for which they seek to devise an appropriate corresponding form of justice. The theoretical framework of liberal nationalism, which we will examine in more detail below, is a powerful complement to the distributive model of justice and marks a turning point in the way in which liberals conceive of, first, today's plural and multinational societies and, second, membership in these societies.

Like inter-war liberals, contemporary liberal nationalists recognize that it is difficult to find the right balance between cultural recognition, differentiated citizenship claims and domestic stability. In actual fact, inter-war liberals felt the balance was not possible unless political rights were pulled out of the equation. Only then could domestic stability be achieved through an 'unnational' form of citizenship that recognized and respected cultural plurality. Both inter-war and contemporary liberals express concern that political autonomy for substate national groups can lead to a movement for independent statehood. As we saw in the previous chapter, inter-war liberals sought to reduce this risk by avoiding any discussion of the extension of group-specific political rights to minority nations. In contrast, contemporary liberal nationalists are prepared to extend self-governing rights to substate nations and Aboriginal peoples but acknowledge that they can 'pose a . . . serious challenge to the integrative function of citizenship' (Kymlicka, 1995: 181). A frequently expressed concern on the part of scholars and politicians alike is that, with the granting of self-governing rights to substate nations, state citizenship will become fractured to the point where there will be nothing holding the larger political community together: no common values or sentiments, no overarching culture or sense of solidarity. But concerns such as these are predicated on the view that multiple political communities are necessarily mutually exclusive in terms of their membership, are necessarily in competition for the loyalty of citizens, and that citizens can be loyal to only one community. Things are a lot more complicated than this: individuals are increasingly comfortable holding multiple identities, consider themselves to be members of more than one political community, and do not necessarily consider this to be a source of potential conflict. All the more reason, then, to consider options for self-determination other than secession.

This chapter sets out the liberal national response to contemporary demands for differentiated citizenship and then critiques it through a discussion of the basis of self-determination. The chapter is divided into two main parts: in the first part, we identify some of the events that led to the rediscovery of liberal nationalism and identify its sources and theoretical framework. In the second part, we tee up our model of multinational citizenship by engaging liberal nationalists around a discussion of the basis for the argument for self-determination. While many liberal nationalists take the view that self-determination rests on arguments for culture, we maintain that its foundation is democratic.

The rediscovery of liberal nationalism

The re-emergence of liberal nationalism at the end of the twentieth century did not have a venue comparable to the Paris Peace Conference of 1919. Nevertheless, as at the end of the First World War, external events certainly influenced thinking around the most appropriate response to a rise in demands for political autonomy and self-determination. The collapse of the Soviet Empire, like the collapse of earlier empires at the end of the First World War, took place along ethnic lines, thereby bringing nationalist politics back to life in a frequently violent manner. The explosion in nationalist mobilization since the end of the cold war seemed to take not only liberal theorists by surprise but also scholars of international relations, who struggled to make sense of how ethnic conflict was inducing inter-state instability and regional anarchy (Lake and Rothchild, 1998). The rapid, and for the most part unexpected, collapse of communism in Eastern Europe and the former Soviet Union precipitated a fundamental transformation of the mutually reinforcing domestic and international orders that had prevailed since the end of the Second World War. In actual fact, both sets of scholars were confounded for the same reasons. The euphoria that initially greeted the collapse of communism produced a sense of triumphalism in many liberal circles, which found its clearest expression in the writings of Francis Fukuyama. Fukuyama interpreted the collapse of communism as something akin to a natural stage in the progressive project of liberal Enlightenment. What we were witnessing, he believed, was not merely the triumph of capitalist liberal democracy over communist dictatorship but more fundamentally the last of the great ideological struggles that had characterized the march of history. In this sense at least we had been brought face to face with the end of history (Fukuyama 1992).

Yet history proved itself more resilient in the end, for among the many consequences of the post-communist transition was a tremendous resurgence of nationalist sentiment in Eastern Europe and the Soviet Union. Many had assumed that the national identities and rivalries of old Europe had been tamed if not extinguished under nearly four decades of totalitarian rule. In fact, the end of communism left a political and social vacuum, which ethnicity and nationalism quickly filled as new organizing principles for social and political mobilization (Offe, 1991). Many liberals seemed wholly unprepared for the wave of nationalism that swept the post-communist new world order. They had a similar reaction to an earlier surge in substate nationalism in the states of Western Europe, and in Aboriginal consciousness in British settler societies. In North America, the 1960s brought a surge of Aboriginal nationalism on both sides of the border, with Canada also bearing witness to the Quiet Revolution that marked the birth of contemporary Québec nationalism. In Western Europe, many 'stateless nations' were beginning to flex their political muscles in response to, among other things, the general decline of the culture of deference towards political – read 'state' – authority. In most cases, substate nationalist movements were seeking recognition as legitimate communities. In other cases, such as Spain, they were seeking democratic freedom. As one scholar of nationalism has observed, this wave of nationalism 'has . . . confounded a generation of modernization theorists who saw the consolidated nation-state as the end point of political development' (Keating, 2001: 1). Not only did theorists think that nationalism was confined to the early stages (say, the nineteenth century) of modernization – when it would assist people in making the transition from a local to a state culture (Deutsch, 1953; Gellner, 1983) – it was also considered to be linked to the state. The 'new' nationalisms of the developed West (Tiryakian and Rogowski, 1985) were associated with 'substate' groups, or 'nations against states' (Keating, 1996), which was theoretically problematic.[5]

The reactions of liberal theorists to the new challenge of post-cold war nationalism have been mixed. There was an assumption – which has been proven correct – that the former communist states would have to be recreated in liberal forms if they wanted to join the international community. The imminent expansion of the EU to include many of these states demonstrates the ongoing success of the liberal project in the region. And yet there has been a common view that liberalism and nationalism embody hostile if not entirely antithetical ideals (McKim and McMahan, 1997). Among these critics there was a fairly common perception that nationalism comprised a form of irrational tribalism, an inherently divisive and violent political doctrine that fostered distrust, intolerance and animosity between national groups and that was all too willing to sacrifice the interests and well-being of the individual to those of the nation (Barber, 1992; McKim and McMahan, 1997; Barry, 1998). This is the problem of particularism versus universalism, which for decades has been at the crux of debates about our moral duties towards others and about redistributive justice (Goodin, 1988; Miller, 1995). Others, perhaps sensing that nationalist sentiment is unlikely to disappear, sought to reinvent liberal theory and practice so as to accommodate nationalist demands in terms that respected basic principles of justice and the need for peace and stability in the international system. This emerging school of thought, now commonly known as liberal nationalism, sought both a rapprochement between liberalism and nationalism and support for the idea of self-determination for minority nations in liberal states. Until very recently (Kymlicka and Opalski, 2002), liberal nationalists did not tend to focus their attention on Eastern Europe or regions of the developing world, but almost exclusively on the developed West. The true significance of the Eastern European examples instead lay in the influence they exerted on critics of nationalism *per se* (as opposed to its manifestation in particular cases or contexts). Pointing to the more extreme and violent manifestations of nationalism outside of the developed West, such critics arrived at the conclusion that no liberal theory, let alone a liberal government, could possibly justify self-determination in nationalist terms. Liberal nationalists set out to demonstrate that this conclusion was both empirically and normatively mistaken. This scholarship developed very quickly and the range of ideas it has championed has informed political choices in many of the cases we examine in this book.

Sources of liberal nationalism

In an important sense, the work of liberal nationalists was an exercise in theoretically catching up with political and institutional developments on the ground. Many states in the liberal West had already begun to implement policies to accommodate their multicultural and multinational diversity. So in a sense, the new research agenda of some liberal theorists was to determine whether those reforms could be justified in terms of normative liberal theory (Kymlicka, 1995: 127). Nevertheless, although political events have been key for shaping liberal thinking towards nationalism, the primary inspiration for liberal nationalist interventions in this debate is located in both contemporaneous theoretical debates and the history of liberal thought. From the history of ideas, late twentieth-century liberal nationalists took their cue from their nineteenth- and early twentieth-century liberal predecessors, many of whom were at least grudgingly supportive of the principle of national self-determination, particularly in the case of dominant nations but also to a somewhat lesser extent in the case of national minorities

(Russell, 1994: 228; Kymlicka, 1995: 50–1). It is important to recognize from the outset that these historic liberal arguments in support of national self-determination were not necessarily arguments in favour of minority national self-determination, and in fact were often arguments for the assimilation of national minorities. The most oft-cited example in this regard is John Stuart Mill. Mill makes a clear connection between national self-determination and the maintenance of liberal-democratic institutions and the rights and freedoms they make possible, but he also considered multinational liberal democracy to be untenable. Mill was convinced that free institutions and the benefits connected with them simply could not function in a society made up of different nationalities, particularly if they spoke different languages and had very different cultures. Such societies simply lacked the necessary social solidarity or fellow feeling necessary for the exercise of stable and efficient liberal-democratic government (Mill, 1954: chap. 16; Tamir, 1993: 140; Kymlicka, 1995: 52). The solution, according to Mill, was the assimilation, coercive if necessary, of the national minority into the dominant national group. The latter solution was tied to the idea of a hierarchy of national groups (visited briefly in chapter 2), with designated great nations, such as England, France, Germany, Italy, Spain and Russia and inferior ones, such as the Scots, Welsh, Romanians, Serbs, Croats and Bulgarians. The idea here was that the great nations were the bearers of civilization and progress, whereas the inferior nations were understood to be backward, uncivilized and stagnant. Great nations, as a consequence, were to be accorded the right to self-determination and would assimilate the inferior nations, which would be better off as a consequence (Spinner-Halev, 1994: 8–9; Kymlicka 1995: 52–3). This process of assimilation was seen as a necessary stage in the overall progress and improvement of the human race.[6]

In locating their inspiration in the history of liberal nationalist thought, contemporary liberal nationalist thinkers such as Will Kymlicka, Yael Tamir and Neil MacCormick seek a principled liberal defence of national self-determination, as well as the extension of this principle such that it could be enjoyed equally by both majority and minority nations. For this more inclusive view of national self-determination they drew partly on the thought of liberals like Mill (more on this connection below), but also on early twentieth-century thinkers such as Hobhouse, who defended the connection between liberalism and the protection of rights of national minorities. For liberals of this variety, the prevailing view is that minority rights are not only compatible with but also essential to the liberalization of a multinational society (Russell, 1994: 228; Kymlicka, 1995: 51) The reasons for drawing this link between liberalism and nationalism varied. For some, such as Lord Acton, the very conditions of liberty are more secure in a multinational state. The logic perceived by Acton was that minority nations, in seeking to defend a measure of independence in their own internal affairs, would act as a counterweight to the concentrations and abuse of power by a centralized political authority (Kymlicka, 1995: 53). For others, as was made evident in chapter 2, multination states were something of a historical accident that was politically unavoidable. Liberalism and nationalism were brought together by the necessity of guaranteeing domestic stability.

A second and even more influential source of inspiration for contemporary liberal nationalist thinking emerged from the latter stages of the liberal–communitarian debate that had dominated the theoretical landscape since at least the early 1970s. At the centre of this debate are two key issues, one ontological, the other political. The ontological dimension of the debate is centrally concerned with the nature and development of the self or, roughly, what it means to be human. The political dimension of the debate is focused on the implications of these ontological conclusions in terms of the appropriate relationship that should obtain between the individual and the state, and the corresponding role in this relationship of individual freedom and human rights. In the early stages of this debate, the battle lines between liberals and communitarians appeared to be clearly drawn. Liberals were understood to support an 'atomist' ontology wherein the individual is conceived of as epistemologically and ethically prior to and more fundamental than any particular society or community. Because of this ontological stance, liberals were taken to emphasize maximum individual freedom, individual rights and a minimal role for the state in human development. Communitarian theory, in contrast, was supposed to be marked by a more Aristotelian concept of human nature wherein the individual cannot be properly understood, let alone fully developed, outside of a particular society and without the assistance of others (Taylor, 1985; Sandel, 1997). From this ontological stance communitarians were understood to be driven to the conclusion that the community was at least as important as any individual, that the state has a substantial role to play in human development and that the rights of the community could sometimes override those of particular individuals.

In actual fact, the liberal–communitarian debate was characterized by a variety of more nuanced positions than either of these stock descriptions. Moreover, by the mid-1980s authors from both camps were coming to the conclusion that the terms of the liberal–communitarian debate needed to be framed differently, because the two positions were becoming more and more difficult to distinguish. Most importantly, in spite of their contrasting ontological starting points, liberals and communitarians often ended up with remarkably similar conclusions regarding the proper relationship between individuals, political communities and the state (Buchanan, 1989; Taylor 1995). For those theorists who began to recast the terms of this debate it was clear that liberalism was not unconcerned with the value and importance of distinctive cultural communities, and that communitarianism was not unconcerned with the fate of the individual. The more interesting question was how to achieve the proper balance between these two goods. This transformation of the liberal–communitarian debate was accompanied by a renaissance of theoretical work on the concept of citizenship (Kymlicka and Norman, 1994). The confluence of these two theoretical strands in the early 1990s produced a wealth of literature on the relationship between liberal discourses and practices of citizenship on the one hand, and the political demands of distinctive identity groups and communities on the other (Habermas, 1992; Beiner, 1995; Kymlicka, 1995). One feature of this new debate that distinguished it from its liberal–communitarian precursor was the concerted attempt to distinguish among different types of identity communities and the various rights and entitlements of citizenship associated with each. Liberal nationalists focused their efforts on nations and the distinctive rights and entitlements associated with a liberal theory of national self-determination. Taking a page from the earlier liberal–communitarian debate, Yael Tamir explained that a liberal theory of nationalism incorporates a conception of the person as a contextual individual, combining individuality and sociability as two equally valid and important features of the human personality. It allows for an interpretation of liberalism that is aware of the binding, constitutive character of cultural and social memberships, as well as an interpretation of nationalism that conceives of individuals as free and autonomous participants in a communal framework, who view national membership in Renan's terms, as a daily plebiscite (Tamir, 1993: 33). Defending this relationship between individual freedom and development, on the one hand, and national self-determination, on the other, is the core theoretical concern of liberal nationalism.

Theoretical framework of liberal nationalism

One of the most valuable contributions of liberal nationalists to the debate about nationalism was its success in drawing attention to the silence with which so many post-Second World War liberal theorists had greeted the national question. This silence in fact disguised a number of implicit yet essential nationalist assumptions at the heart of liberal theories of state and society. Citing his agreement with Yael Tamir, Kymlicka argues that most liberals are liberal nationalists in the sense that they assume that nations or national cultures are basic units of political theory, which is to say that liberal goals are to be achieved in and through a liberalized societal culture or nation (Kymlicka, 1995: 125, 194). While liberals have tended to focus their theoretical analyses on *internal* issues of justice, consent, distribution and equality, they have always quietly assumed that these issues would find their resolution within the boundaries of nation-states. Indeed, the success of modern liberalism is in large part based on its capacity to graft onto itself the principle of national self-determination such that it performs the function of closing and bounding a liberal political community, making it co-equal with the national political community (Tamir, 1993: 139). Moreover, Kymlicka argues that liberal states play an essential, even unavoidable, role in preserving and promoting not only a bounded and continuous political community, but also a particular national culture. As such, liberal states have been constituted so as to provide for and protect the rights and opportunities of individuals, but these ends themselves are facilitated through the preservation and promotion of the particular national community of which these individuals are a part (Tamir, 1993: 124–30; Kymlicka, 1995: 110–11). This national dimension of liberal states and politics clearly belies the supposed neutrality of liberalism among different cultures or cultural identities. As Kymlicka argues, this self-declared neutrality is not even coherent, for all states unavoidably (or rather deliberately) promote certain cultures and identities to the detriment or disadvantage of others in their most basic policy decisions, for example, official languages, education, immigration and citizenship (Tamir, 1993: 145–9; Kymlicka, 1995: 108–11).

Liberal nationalists take this argument one step further. Modern liberals had failed not only to acknowledge their national assumptions; they had also proceeded as if the states and societies about which they had been theorizing were mononational when in fact a good many of them were multinational (Kymlicka, 1995: 125, 194). John Rawls, for example, constructs his comprehensive system of liberal procedural justice around the assumption of a state comprised of a single nation or people. Deliberations about justice take place against a background assumption of a single and undifferentiated national body politic with its own particular territory, history, traditions and state structures. Ultimately, it is within this larger national political framework that individuals deliberate among themselves and agree to terms which will govern them all (Rawls, 1971, 1993b). There is room in his theory of justice for religious and cultural diversity but no place for national diversity. When Rawls does turn his attention towards the development of a possible framework for just relations among different peoples or nations, the examples he has in mind are exclusively separate, independent and sovereign states and not multinational states (Rawls, 1993b). Other liberals such as Richard Rorty choose a more assimilationist approach. Rorty outlines a deep moral commitment to seeking out and remedying forms of injustice in liberal societies based on the marginalization of racial, cultural or tribal differences, but the end of this exercise is to assimilate these 'others' into the broader national political community and to treat them according to its standard of right. Like Rawls, Rorty assumes that there is only one 'us' or one nation which makes up a liberal society, and thus only one set of political priorities and institutions in terms of which questions of justice and citizenship need to be framed. Rorty acknowledges that this political framework can and should change over time, particularly when it encounters new forms of difference, but there is never any question of there being coexisting or pre-existing national cultures within a liberal state (Rorty, 1988, 1991).

Another liberal response to multinational diversity, already touched on briefly above, is to treat minority claims to national self-determination as private and cultural issues rather than public and political issues, on the assumption that the state should remain neutral among the interests of any particular national group and any particular national culture (Dworkin, 1984). Kymlicka refers to this approach as benign neglect: the state does not seek to protect or promote particular national groups, but nor is it hostile towards them: it simply leaves them free to pursue their own interests in the private sphere (Kymlicka, 1995: 108). Differences of nationality, in this view, are treated as questions that can best be accommodated through a principle of toleration and equal individual rights. Members of minority nations are to be accorded equal rights of participation and entitlement in the state, whereas the expression of their national or cultural differences will be tolerated, but only in so far as they are confined to the private sphere (Taylor, 1994). This view was very much in line with liberal practice in the aftermath of the Second World War. The revised international order envisioned by the United Nations and embodied in the organization's Charter maintained an ongoing commitment to universal human rights, and also to the right of self-determination, but contrary to the inter-war League of Nations approach, it did not recognize claims to self-determination on behalf of substate nations. Self-determination came to be understood in a very restricted sense as freedom from a former colonial power. This meant independent statehood for colonized territories overseas, but the legitimate boundaries of these states were to be those existing at the time of decolonization, and not those based on ethnic, national, linguistic or historical criteria. Hence, the territorial integrity of existing states came to be regarded as an almost inviolable principle. Satisfaction of minority claims was to be realized in the process of decolonization, but almost exclusively via the protection of individual rights to equality and non-discrimination (Hannum, 1989: 9–13; Anaya, 1995).

In practical terms, the strategy of state neutrality and equal individual rights for members of minority nations was proving to be ineffective in the face of more thoroughgoing demands for collective forms of self-determination and self-government. We noted earlier that, beginning in the 1960s, there was an (re)emergence of 'new nationalism' in the developed West: Belgium (Flanders and Walloon); Canada (Québec and Aboriginal nations); France (Bretagne); Spain (Basque Country, Catalonia and, to a lesser extent, Galicia); the United Kingdom (Northern Ireland, Scotland and Wales). Granted, the recognition and implementation of an equal right to self-determination for national minorities is no guarantee of peace, stability and national integration, but historical experience suggests that these ends are rarely achieved when a substate nation is actively denied the recognition it claims as its due (Horowitz, 1985; Gurr, 1993, 2000; Connor, 1999). Moreover, in normative terms, the exposure of liberalism's implicit nationalism reveals an embarrassing double standard in liberal treatments of demands for self-determination voiced by national minorities. It leaves liberals at a loss to explain why national minorities can justifiably be denied access to a right which majority nations already comfortably assume for themselves. The veil of liberal neutrality had been lifted, and underneath it lay not the mutual recognition and accommodation of differing and sometimes competing identities, but instead the domination of one particular identity and its accompanying cultural markers, which had nevertheless managed to pass itself off as neutrality (Tully, 1995: 191). As Kymlicka concludes, liberal states unavoidably promote certain cultural identities and thereby disadvantage others; therefore, the notion of liberal neutrality or benign neglect of cultural difference is not only unfair, it is incoherent (Kymlicka, 1995: 108–13; compare Tamir, 1993: 145–9).

Liberal nationalism responded to these challenges by first of all deriving a general defence of nationalism in liberal terms and, second, by extending this argument to the case of national minorities in multinational liberal states. Probably the most systematically articulated liberal defence of minority nationalism and a form of multinational (or multicultural) citizenship is found in the work of Will Kymlicka, although the broad outlines of his theoretical framework are shared by a number of other thinkers in this school (Tamir, 1993; Kymlicka, 1995; Miller, 1995). Kymlicka's theoretical framework is an extensive reformulation of his own previous intervention in the liberal–communitarian debate (Kymlicka, 1989). At its heart are two major claims around which a liberal defence of minority nationalism is structured: first, that individual freedom is tied in a crucial way to membership in one's national culture; and second, that group-specific rights are capable of promoting equality between majority and minority cultures. His hope is to prove not only that minority rights are consistent with individual freedom, but that the cause of liberty often finds its anchor in the autonomy of a national group (Kymlicka, 1995: 52, 75). Kymlicka derives his key principles from prominent figures in the history of liberal thought. From Kant he derives the principle that above all else liberals value the sanctity of individual autonomy, and from John Stuart Mill he borrows the principle that our beliefs about the good life are fallible and hence we should always be free to revise them in the light of new experiences and circumstances. Given this assumption, liberals deem two conditions to be necessary to facilitate the good life for liberal citizens: first, individuals need to be provided with the necessary liberties and resources to live their lives autonomously in accordance with their own conceptions of what makes a life worth living; and second, individuals are at liberty to question and revise these beliefs in light of new information and alternatives, which in turn requires that individuals have access to a range of viable alternative views of the good life (Kymlicka, 1995: 81–3, 93, 101, 152).

To apply this theoretical framework specifically to the case of nationalism, the range of viable alternative views of the good life is provided by a nation's distinctive national culture (Tamir, 1993: 6–7, 33; Kymlicka, 1995: 85; Miller, 1995: 85–6, 146–7). Using Kymlicka's terminology, distinctive national cultures provide a rich variety of meaningful and viable options from which individual members can choose in the process of pursuing their own individual life plans. National cultures function as cultural contexts of choice in the absence of which individual autonomy would be significantly impoverished, if not altogether meaningless. Given the centrality of autonomy to liberalism, liberal nationalists argue that states have a vested interest in fostering the conditions essential to its exercise. In other words, states have a compelling reason to preserve and promote their distinctive national cultures because of their instrumental centrality in the facilitation of individual freedom and well-being (Tamir, 1993: 74–6, 150; Kymlicka, 1995: 84; Miller, 1995: 87–8). Extending the argument further to minority nations in multinational states, in order for members of the national minority to have a degree of access to the liberal good of individual autonomy roughly equal to that of members of the majority national group, it is necessary to shelter their distinctive cultural context of choice (their distinctive national culture) from the will of the majority by granting them rights to independent forms of self-government and the group-differentiated citizenship that entails (Tamir, 1993: 150; Kymlicka, 1995: 75–113). Liberal nationalists suggest a variety of institutionalized forms of self-government suited to different cases and contexts (Tamir, 1993: 74–5, 150–2; Kymlicka, 1995: 27–30, 32–3), but whatever its specific institutional or policy correlates, the right to national self-determination finds its primary normative locus in its instrumental importance in preserving a nation's distinctive culture.[7]

It is difficult to exaggerate the impact of liberal nationalism and the multiplicity of discourses on multicultural and group-differentiated forms of citizenship it helped inspire. In less than a decade it has managed to transform what had essentially been a non-issue for liberal theory into one of the most compelling challenges in contemporary political thought. In developing our own approach to citizenship and substate nationalism we clearly have some common cause with liberal nationalists. In particular, we support their conclusion that the most appropriate response to claims to self-determination by substate nationalists are various institutionalized forms of group-differentiated citizenship. However, our approaches diverge in terms of the greater emphasis we place on the democratic and political dimensions of citizenship or claims to national self-determination. Liberal nationalists do not ignore the democratic and political dimensions of these claims, but these questions are often underemphasized and at times obscured by their focus on culture and its instrumental importance to individual autonomy. Part of this difference may be termed merely philosophical in the sense that we simply employ different normative premises to justify a similar principle of self-determination and differentiated citizenship. But these philosophical differences also turn out to have some very important implications in terms of the range of institutional and constitutional solutions that can actually be justified and accepted in practical political terms.

Democratic dimensions of national self-determination

Bringing in the democratic dimensions of self-determination in our view helps compensate for several weaknesses in the cultural arguments developed by liberal nationalists. We focus on four such weaknesses here. To start with, demands for self-determination may have little to do with a nation's desire to preserve its distinctive culture, and everything to do with imperatives such as protection from an external threat or escape from historic persecution (Spinner-Halev, 1994: 169–70). Perhaps no better example exists than the state of Israel, whose existence is linked first and foremost to the imperative of providing a safe and secure homeland for Jews hailing from a multiplicity of geographical regions and cultural backgrounds. Self-determination may also be about more mundane matters, for instance the redistribution of goods such as power, money, land and resources (Barry, 1998: 307–8, 318). For example, while in power in the province of Québec, the nationalist Parti Québécois[8] has clearly been interested in the preservation of Québec's distinctive language and culture, but its demands for control over certain federal jurisdictions, such as labour market training, immigration and taxation, have little to do with culture and everything to do with its desire to take control of its provincial economy. The same can be said of its continual objections to the Canadian government's use of the federal spending power in provincial jurisdictions such as health and social welfare. Even if the federal government took it upon itself to use these powers to help promote Québec's cultural distinctiveness there is little doubt that Québec nationalists would object on the grounds that such a role belongs rightly to the government of Québec and not the government of Canada. In other words, arguments that reduce all self-government demands of substate nationalists to cultural preservation are really unconvincing when set against the history of individual autonomy and popular sovereignty.

Second, the connection between cultural identity and national identity is also more tenuous than liberal nationalist arguments allow. For example, just as the existence of a common language has not led to the abandonment of local political loyalties in favour of an overarching pan-Maori national identity in New Zealand, nor has the existence of a common language and religion led to a strong pan-Arab nationalism in the Middle East. Coming at this question from another direction, strong and competing national identities often prevail between groups whose differences in cultural terms are not that great. Canada and the United States or New Zealand and Australia are examples that come immediately to mind, and similar observations have been made of the Unionist and Nationalist communities in Northern Ireland and the warring ethnic communities in the former Yugoslavia (Moore, 1999: 34–6). Alternatively again, a national community may be characterized by tremendous internal linguistic and cultural diversity and yet maintain a powerful and resilient common national identity. Israel, whose internal cultural diversity is rooted in North Africa, North America, Russia, Eastern Europe and other parts of the Middle East, is a good example. This is not to deny that in many cases national identity and cultural identity may overlap, but simply that this is not true in many other cases, hence a cultural defence of national self-determination may often miss the mark in straightforward empirical terms (Moore, 1999: 36–8; Murphy, 2001b: 373–4).

Third, cultural arguments can also be exploited in order to subject substate nations to a normative double standard in the adjudication of their claims to self-determination. The most obvious manifestation of this double standard is the fact that nations that already exercise the right to self-determination through a territorial state have not been required to justify this right by demonstrating the distinctiveness of their national cultures. Were they asked to do so they would no doubt reply that the question of their cultural distinctiveness was a matter of their own internal self-government, and in any case should have no bearing on their continuing enjoyment of the right to self-determination. Substate nations might similarly ask why their democratic right to self-determination is to be tested against the credentials of their distinctive (or perhaps not very distinctive) cultures. Yet they are frequently held up to this standard. For example, as we argue in chapter 6 this empirical observation is often seized upon by cosmopolitan liberals as an argument against minority rights and as a means of demonstrating that nationalism (and particularly minority nationalism) is an anachronism in a world characterized not by the distinctiveness of local cultures but by cultural hybridism and the so-called mongrelization of citizen identities. At the heart of this cosmopolitan argument is the assumption that most individuals already derive their individuality and vision of the good life from a multiplicity of cultures and cultural contexts, a fact which clearly undermines the claim that a particular or distinctive culture is necessary to provide this function (Waldron, 1995: 100, 103–5). Arguments of this sort are not confined to theory but have also been marshalled in practice, perhaps nowhere more frequently than in the case of indigenous nations. In these cases the argument is given an additional twist, in the sense that the recognition of indigenous rights to goods such as land, resources and self-government is predicated on the centrality of these goods to an indigenous nation's distinctive *traditional* culture. In other words, if practices such as commercial fishing or timber harvesting, a particular form of self-government, or any other kind of activity cannot be linked to an indigenous nation's distinctive traditional culture those rights can be denied recognition in settler-state law. In Canada, the Supreme Court has used arguments of this nature to limit Aboriginal rights to practices such as commercial fishing, land development and business ventures such as the operation of high-stakes bingos.[9] Similarly, in Australia, the High Court has rejected large Aboriginal land claims on the basis that the forebears of the Aboriginal people in question had ceased to occupy their territory in accordance with traditional laws and customs.[10]

Finally, we have a procedural concern with cultural arguments for self-determination. It is neither clear who sets the standards and criteria by which cultures are identified as candidates for self-determination nor is it made explicit who will adjudicate the claims. Liberal nationalists are strangely silent on these points, as though the procedural dimension was neither their responsibility nor a particular concern. But it is. There are very few cases where substate nations or Aboriginal peoples have a say in determinations about their culture and fewer still where they have an equal say. This point is clearly illustrated in Canada by the former Prime Minister Jean Chrétien's controversial efforts in 2003 to reform the Indian Act (the piece of legislation that governs the lives of Aboriginal peoples living on designated Indian reserves). The centrepiece of this initiative was the First Nations Governance Act (FNGA), which the government was determined to pass over the objections of First Nations leadership across the country. The purpose of the Act was to increase the accountability, accessibility and transparency of governance on reserves, which in turn was intended to facilitate gains in governing capacity and socio-economic performance (Nault, 2001). Although the federal government made legitimate efforts to consult Aboriginal peoples on the content of the proposed legislation, the consultation process was entirely determined by the government itself.[11] Moreover, a consultation process is quite different from what some Aboriginals are demanding, namely a co-decision-making process (at the very least), where they have equal capacity to set the agenda and to take part in the final decision (AFN, 2001b). The former provides no guarantees that the views and opinions of Aboriginals will be taken into account when drafting the final version of the parliamentary bill. Moreover, if Aboriginal peoples are left dissatisfied with the outcome of the consultation process, they have no means by which to appeal it. There are no clear rules of the game by which both sides play and to which they are held accountable. In contrast, a co-decision-making process brings both sides to the table with the express purpose of reaching a compromise solution on an issue. The more formal the process, the more transparency and guarantees it is likely to offer all parties to the bargain.

Democracy before culture

In emphasizing the democratic dimension of self-determination our intention is not to assert that culture is irrelevant to substate nationalist and Aboriginal claims. Our point is instead that the democratic right to self-determination should not be subordinated to the choices one makes (or does not make) regarding matters of culture. On the contrary, the democratic right to self-determination is what entitles all nations to make choices about culture, as well as a wide range of other jurisdictions they deem to be key to their interests. Whether they use this authority to develop a distinctive culture, a distinctive traditional culture, some other nation's culture, or not to concern themselves at all about culture are choices which should have no normative bearing on their more fundamental democratic right to self-determination. Understood in this sense, minority nations are asserting the same democratic right to self-determination that is already comfortably assumed by the nation(s) who presently dominate the states within which they reside. Unlike cultural minorities, substate nations question the right of the state unilaterally to assert its sovereignty over them. In their view it is not up to the state to declare whether or not it will tolerate substate nations within its borders, or what degree and form of autonomy they can be granted. A more just framing of the issue is to ask how substate nations and the state can *mutually* accommodate their competing claims to self-determination (Murphy, 2001b, 2003).

When we use the term 'democratic self-determination', democracy in this context implies the right of the group in question to make its own decisions about the direction of its collective future. For example, in Spain, the Basque and Catalan regional governments have repeatedly asserted their right to self-determination. As if to drive home the point, the Catalan parliament passed two such resolutions, one in 1989, the other in 1998.[12] After its strong electoral victory in the regional elections of May 2001, the Partido Nactionalista Vasco (PNV – Basque Nationalist Party) led a movement for a popular referendum on Basque independence. The parliamentary leader Juan José Ibarretxe proposed to ask Basque citizens whether they wanted the right to vote on independence. If the majority answered 'yes', then the Basque government would have sought to negotiate a rereading or revision of the existing Spanish constitution (which prevents territorial break-up) in an attempt to guarantee a non-violent transition to independent statehood. Once that was accomplished, a second referendum would have been held to ask Basques whether they wanted an independent state. As the then president of the Basque parliament, Juan María Atutxa, noted, 'There is nothing more democratic than a popular vote'. However, the view of the then Spanish Prime Minister, José María Aznar, was that 'The right to self-determination is not recognised anywhere in the world' – conflicting views of the rights of nations![13] Similar conflicts have also been in evidence in Canada, where the nationalist Parti Québécois has asserted the right of the Québécois (understand to include all people living in Québec) to determine its collective future through referenda whereas various Canadian governments have argued that any decision to break up the country needs to be made by all Canadians.[14] The federal government of Prime Minister Jean Chrétien (1993–2003) responded to the 1995 Québec referendum on independence with a reference to the Supreme Court on the role of states and nations in cases of secession and followed up with the 'Clarity Act'. The federal government essentially asked the Supreme Court whether Québec has the unilateral right to secede from Canada either under domestic (constitutional) or international law.[15] The Court's response was that 'A clear majority vote in Quebec on a clear question in favour of secession would confer democratic legitimacy on the secession initiative which all of the other participants in Confederation would have to recognize', but noted that 'democratic rights cannot be divorced from constitutional obligations'. Because of constitutional obligations held by all levels of government, a unilateral declaration of secession, the Court concluded, would be unconstitutional; governments would have to proceed to negotiations and a constitutional amendment. Therefore, 'The negotiations [between the federal government and Québec] that followed such a vote would address the potential act of secession as well as its possible terms should in fact secession proceed'. The Court would not pronounce on the negotiation process itself since it felt that process belonged to the political, not the judicial, realm.[16] The federal government's response to the Supreme Court Reference was the Clarity[17] Act (2000), which gives the federal House of Commons a role in deciding whether the question put to Québec citizens is fair and whether the results represent a clear will of the people.

In theoretical terms, very few liberals could disagree with this approach, given that it underpins the legitimacy of contemporary liberal-democratic states. However, in practical terms, the democratic solution raises three problems, which we acknowledge and consider here: (1) the risk of illiberal regimes; (2) the problem of deciding who is a member of the 'nation'; and (3) the risk that self-determination will turn to secession. First, there is the risk, raised by Kymlicka, Spinner-Halev and others, that once constituted via liberal-democratic means, self-governing nations will introduce some illiberal practices that will infringe on the individual rights of some of their members or minority nationals in the new polity. This problem has been raised in the context of Aboriginal self-government in Canada. For example, Aboriginal women have expressed the fear that First Nations governments that are immune to external review by the Canadian Charter of Rights and Freedoms will be male-dominated, unaccountable and unresponsive to their concerns. The two most central of these concerns are, first, their exposure to inordinate levels of physical, emotional and sexual abuse at the hands of their own male community members; and second, their under-representation or exclusion from positions of political power and influence in Aboriginal communities. For many of these women, the Charter represents one of the only means of fighting for political, economic and social justice in their own communities.[18] This dilemma is also clearly demonstrated in cases where language laws have been enacted to protect and promote the use of one particular language in a multilingual context. The Québec case is perhaps the most familiar. After 1976, as part of its legislative initiative designed to protect and promote French language and culture in the province, the ruling Parti Québécois government passed a law proscribing the use of any language other than French on public signs. The legislation was challenged by a group of English-speaking shopkeepers, who argued that their right to freedom of expression under the Canadian Charter was being violated. Both the Québec provincial and the Federal Courts ruled in favour of the shopkeepers, a ruling that was upheld by the Supreme Court of Canada in the case of *Ford v. Quebec*.[19] The Québec government responded initially by invoking section 33 of the Canadian constitution to temporarily override the court's decision and continued to enforce the French-only sign law. They argued that the Court's decision threatened the preservation of French culture and was contrary to the democratic will of the Québec majority. The government's response provoked a public outcry, to which the Québec government eventually responded with a public dialogue, whose ultimate result was a relaxing of the law, bringing it more in line with the standard established by the court.[20]

The linguistic issue has also been raised in other cases, such as Catalonia, where liberalism has been debated. The regional government of Catalonia has passed two language laws since the transition to democracy: in 1983 (the Normalization Law) and 1998 (the Linguistic Policy Act). While the former was designed to re-establish the public use of Catalan through a policy of normalization using government institutions and the education system, the second law was, in the words of Josep Costa, intended to secure 'Catalan speakers' right to use their language in the courts, as well as in social and economic fields' by making the Catalan language the 'default' language and placing an onus on public servants to know and use it (Costa, 2003: 420). Much of the opposition to the law has been related to whether it threatens the individual rights of Castilian speakers residing in Catalonia. Although Castilian speakers can request to be served in their language in public services or to receive government documentation in Castilian, they might find themselves discriminated against, say, if their lack of knowledge of Catalan excluded them from being considered for employment in the Catalan public service. The matter is perhaps most accurately understood as one of group versus individual rights. While many Spaniards reject the validity of group rights, the question remains: 'who has responsibility for protecting the survival of minority languages in Spain?' As Costa notes, the Spanish government has certainly not assumed that responsibility, so it is left to the Catalan government to do so. As Costa argues, the Spanish government could have adopted Catalan as an official language of the Spanish state, but it did not. In this sense, the linguistic policies of the Spanish state 'are anything but neutral towards language' and violate the individual rights of Catalans to use their language in the institutions of the Spanish state (Costa, 2003: 427). At root is a refusal, identified by Costa, of a preference for classical state-centric liberalism, which is quite incompatible with cultural pluralism (Requejo, 1999).

A similar situation prevails in Wales, where Welsh is spoken by a minority of the population, which is territorially concentrated in the north and west. Successive UK governments have passed legislation and implemented policies 'which have both raised the status of the Welsh language and contributed in no small way to the stabilisation in its decline between 1971 and 1991' (WAG, 2003: 1). Through institutions such as the Welsh Language Board and the Welsh television channel S4C, not to mention educational initiatives, the Welsh language was already far along a process of 'normalization' compared to the situation in Catalonia in 1978. And yet, taking a historical perspective covering the twentieth century, the trends and patterns of language use have been a cause for concern: there is wide variation across the country and across age groups and there is a general decline in the percentage of the population speaking Welsh. However, the 2001 Census figures gave some reason to be hopeful, as the percentage of people reporting that they can speak the language increased from 18.5 to 20.5 per cent since the 1991 Census, while 28.4 per cent said they can understand Welsh.[21] Moreover, much of the increase has been reported for south Wales, where historically the use of Welsh has been weakest. Without doubt, education policies to promote Welsh in the schools have paid off. Still, while making Welsh a compulsory subject in school goes a long way towards increasing language acquisition, it will not necessarily improve language use unless there are places to use and speak Welsh in the broader society.

With devolution, the Welsh Assembly Government has its own opportunity to make policy on linguistic issues, which it exercised in 2002 through first, a policy statement ('Bilingual Future', WAG, 2002), and then an action plan ('Iaith Pawb', WAG, 2003). The goal of the Welsh Assembly Government is clear: to make Wales a bilingual society. As in Québec, Catalonia and elsewhere, the need for positive measures in support of a language often raises public debate about the rights of individuals. Of course, in the absence of law-making authority, the Welsh Assembly Government cannot legislate language use and it appears to have no intention of seeking a language bill through Parliament. The Welsh Assembly Government's action plan is extensive in that it moves out from education into social services, business, culture and sports. It seeks to raise awareness among Welsh and non-Welsh speakers of the importance of the Welsh language for the way in which people express themselves and interact as members of a nation. Nevertheless, there are some obvious limitations to what can be accomplished in the absence of new legislation. Currently, only public bodies are compelled by law, under the guidance of the Welsh Language Board, to have bilingual policies – and it is not clear that all of these conform. Legislation, as the Québec and Catalan cases make clear, is the only way to extend language use into the private sphere. However, without a constituency of supporters, never mind full self-governing rights, it is even difficult to introduce and enforce a Language Act.

Generally speaking, the cases considered in this book might involve the introduction of some illiberal practices, but almost certainly not the establishment of illiberal regimes. There is a big difference between the two in terms of guarantees for the protection of minorities. Therefore, it is likely that state, European or international law could be invoked to provide some protective guarantees for minorities within self-governing substate political units. Questions pertaining to the nature and justification of such external review mechanisms are extraordinarily complex, and we do not have sufficient space to cover them here.[22] Debates on this set of issues are frequently polarized by two extreme positions. At one extreme is the claim that self-determination is essentially about individual autonomy and self-rule, hence any restrictions on individual autonomy in the service of collective or communal ends must automatically be either forbidden or at least drastically minimized. External review and interference in defence of individual autonomy is, in this sense, a necessary correlate of any rigorous defence of self-determination. At the other extreme is the claim either that there is a necessary connection between communal and individual self-determination, such that the realization of the former automatically assures the realization of the latter, or that the ends of the community or nation are morally superior to those of any particular individual or minority group. External review and interference in internal community practices is therefore not only unnecessary, but also antithetical to the ideal of national sovereignty or self-government. Suffice it to say that we feel that the answer to these questions is to be found somewhere in between these two extremes, and that the important question to be answered is not *whether* a process of reviewing the institutions and practices of autonomous national communities is necessary, but what form it should take and what parties have a legitimate role to play in it, both internal and external to the national community in question. Lastly, one should bear in mind that these questions are as applicable to states and majority nations as they are to national minorities, hence they cannot be legitimately used to dismiss, a priori, claims to self-determination at the substate level.

Second, there is the problem of determining who should exercise the right to self-determination. Nationalists are not even clear on this point: should it be all residents of the territory in question or should it be members of the ethnic group exclusively? The second, restrictive or exclusive option is not easily defensible in situations wherein the territorial jurisdiction seeking to exercise its right to self-determination is ethnically heterogeneous. Nevertheless, exclusivity *is* somewhat easier to defend in cases of Aboriginal self-determination. For in these cases there is a very real possibility that an inclusive policy of political participation could lead to the Aboriginal residents losing control over their self-governing institutions to non-Aboriginals residing in their territory. For example, when the Sechelt Indian Nation in Canada negotiated a self-government agreement in 1984, roughly half of the residents in their traditional territory were non-Aboriginal. Although provisions were made such that the non-Aboriginal residents had an advisory role in a limited number of jurisdictions, participation in Sechelt institutions was restricted to members of the Sechelt band, precisely so that the community itself would remain in control of its territories, citizens and self-government.[23] Other Aboriginal peoples, such as the Inuit of Nunavut, have agreed to public forms of government where participation is open to anyone residing in their traditional territory, regardless of Aboriginal ancestry or identity. However, the Inuit agreed to this option only because they are guaranteed control of the government as a result of their demographic majority in the territory. Moreover, they have indicated their intention to consider ethnic forms of self-government should the demographic advantage begin to shift in favour of the non-Aboriginal population.[24] Even cases of ethnic Aboriginal self-government are not without complications. These agreements are normally ratified by the Aboriginal group through a referendum, and their powers exercised in terms of their own constitution, which in turn must be ratified by a majority of members, and the question of who qualifies to vote in these referenda can be controversial. A combination of different criteria are most often used, and (in addition to age requirements) may include factors such as ancestry, blood quantum, adoption by an existing member, community recognition, and residence within the community's territory (see Catt and Murphy, 2002: 53–9). Many land claims and self-government agreements further provide for membership enrolment procedures and a mechanism that affords individuals who have been excluded from membership the opportunity to appeal their status (Canada, 1998: 243–6).

For obvious reasons, demands for self-determination on the part of substate nations are of a different sort from the Aboriginal cases. In all of the cases considered in this book, the intermingling of different ethnic and immigrant groups is an irreversible political reality.[25] Given the diversity of the population living on the territory of a regional nationality, many nationalists will agree that all residents of the territory in question should be allowed to exercise the right to vote for self-determination. From a political perspective, this line of reasoning is possibly the only rational one to take where it is not possible to win a democratic majority through the vote of members of the substate nation exclusively. Indeed, this is the case for all of the substate national groups considered in this book. It is not just that cultural heterogeneity and inter-group marriage pose problems but also that not all members of the substate national group are committed nationalists. Nationalist parties have to recruit from among their own ethnic group as well as from among others. So, a politically calculated move would be to take a position on who has the right to exercise self-determination that is as inclusive as possible, even if some 'hard-core' nationalists would prefer more restrictive rules of eligibility. The more inclusive view incorporates ethnic members of the majority nation on the territory, other people who consider themselves members of this nation – even if their ethnic origin is different – and members of other nations or ethnic groups. This seems appropriate since we are not talking about secession: we are not considering the erection of a border where previously there was none or the division of a population that previously belonged to the same state. We are largely talking about existing administrative units or regions that already enjoy some measure of political autonomy. So, for example, there was no dispute over what constituted 'Scotland' or 'Wales' during the devolution referenda of 1997 or over who should be allowed to vote in them. Moreover, since devolution would affect the populations of Scotland and Wales to a far greater extent than the population of England, it was not assumed that the 'English' should vote in either the Scottish or Welsh referenda.[26] Other cases have not been so straightforward; we noted above that in Canada there is the view that the entire population, whether directly or indirectly through elected representatives, should have a say in the self-determination of a sub-unit.

However, some critics might counter that we are talking about the establishment of a political authority that is likely to enact policies and practices that might not be acceptable to members of the majority nation. There are really two versions of this argument. The first is that a nationalist government in power at the substate level might be politically distasteful to people residing elsewhere in the state. The second is that members of the majority nation might view the policies and actions of the nationalist government as somehow threatening their way of life or security. The first version of the argument can be dismissed as an unfortunate by-product of a pluralist democracy. Citizens of a democracy have ideological commitments and ideological differences. We might be opposed to the election of a conservative government because we disagree with its market policies. But if a majority of the population voted for this political party, then it is an electoral outcome we have to accept. The same is true when a nationalist party is democratically elected. The second version of the argument addresses the issues of national security and state stability and when the state can interfere to protect its interests. For example, the Spanish Parliament has considered invoking its constitutional right (Article 155) to suspend the Basque Autonomous Community's regional government on the grounds that the current Basque government's plan to hold a referendum on independence is a manifestation of an action that is against the general interest of Spain. The Spanish Parliament reserves the right to decide what does or does not constitute the general interest of Spain. As we argued above, external review and interference in internal community practices is antithetical to the ideal of national sovereignty or self-government.

A third potential problem with democratic self-determination for some liberal theorists and liberal statesmen is that it is just code for secession. It is an alarmist response to the assertion by some groups of their right to self-determination and a rather unimaginative one at that. Some liberal statesmen and theorists equate references to the right to self-determination with the pursuit of independent statehood and therefore interpret these references as a threat to state sovereignty. In one of his last parliamentary speeches, the former Spanish Prime Minister José María Aznar stated that 'so-called initiatives of free association [on the part of substate nations] are extravagant artifices and attempts to usurp national sovereignty by making supposed spheres of decision making that are nothing but veiled synonyms of independence' (*Avui*, 1 July 2003: 14). But this view of sovereignty is outdated: internal sovereignty does not have to exist in a unitary form to guarantee state stability or the integrity of the state's external borders. Substate nations have been arguing this point since the end of the nineteenth century and have proposed various constitutional and institutional solutions to the fact that their demands for self-government will never be completely met within the existing sovereignty regime. Their solutions involve an extension of the liberal principle of individual freedom of association to the level of self-determination nations which, they argue, should be equally free to determine, and consent to, their political relationships (with other nations) in the absence of coercion or domination (Tully, 1995).[27] As liberal theorists writing about democratic secession have noted, these are also arguments used by nationalists to defend independent statehood (Buchanan, 1991). But that does not mean that each and every argument made by substate nationalists in favour of free association is an argument for secession – far from it. The projects advanced by Québec, Basque and Catalan nationalists are attempts to institutionalize and constitutionalize forms of free association of nations within the Canadian and Spanish states and, for the European cases, the emerging Constitution of Europe. So, the nationalist Parti Québécois has proposed sovereignty association with Canada, which calls for political independence and an ongoing economic partnership with Canada. Sovereignty-association was the proposal put to the Québécois people in the referendum of 1980, which they rejected.[28] More recently, several Catalan political parties (socialist, nationalist and republican) have made separate constitutional proposals that would give Catalonia more independence within the Spanish state. Each party is careful to note that the realization of their proposals calls only for a rereading of the constitution as opposed to a constitutional amendment. The Basque Nationalist Party (PNB) has proposed a free association between Basques and the Spanish state that would be decided through negotiations with Madrid.[29]

None of these proposals is secessionist and each is liberal. Increasingly, the term post-sovereignty is being used to signal a new legal and constitutional order that can accommodate 'difference' without threatening either the state or the international order (MacCormick, 1999; Keating 2001; Walker, 2003). However, in order for post-sovereignty to work, we need to embrace the view that nations can coexist within a state based on a principle of equality. The principle of mutual recognition should apply not only to relations between states but also to relations within states, so that there is no hierarchy of nations.

Principles

In general terms, the democratic dimension of self-determination expresses a people's desire to exercise a measure of control over their individual and collective futures. This broader principle is usefully disaggregated into three subprinciples: internal democracy, external democracy and shared-rule democracy. These principles will be discussed in greater detail in chapter 4, but we will foreshadow that discussion by outlining them briefly here. Internal democracy is likely the most familiar of the three subprinciples, and refers to a nation's right to choose how and by whom it will be governed. This includes the right to design and implement its own democratic institutions, to choose its own representatives and hold them accountable, and to decide what they will govern, whether this refers to populations, jurisdictions, territories or resources. Internal democracy is closely intertwined with external democracy, which is a nation's right to govern itself as free as possible from external interference or domination (Philpott, 1995: 352; Murphy, 2001b: 373–7). This is the same right enjoyed by nation-states under contemporary international law. At the extreme this means secession and absolute sovereignty, but this is not always either a possible or desirable outcome, given the intermixing and interdependence of populations and competing claims to territory and resources that characterize so many multinational states. Therefore, in many cases external self-determination will encompass relationships with other nations or governments, but relationships based on free and open negotiations, freely given consent and secure and binding guarantees (Tully, 1995: 117–24). Shared-rule democracy is probably the most overlooked dimension of national self-determination, which is generally understood as a doctrine that emphasizes the autonomy of nations and the idea of self-rule. Nevertheless, precisely because of the conditions of interdependence that characterize multinational states, it is frequently advantageous, even essential, that minority nations have simultaneous access to self-rule and shared-rule institutions (Borrows, 2000; Catt and Murphy, 2002). Such arrangements are standard practice in federal and consociational forms of government, in the co-management regimes that accompany indigenous self-government in Canada and in forms of devolution characteristic of the recent reforms in the United Kingdom. Shared-rule also applies in the context of global interdependence and the need for forms of multilevel governance.

The subprinciples of self-determination rest on a form of autonomy, the full extent of which is seldom enjoyed by substate or Aboriginal nations. For all three forms of democracy – internal, external and shared – the state continues to enjoy the upper hand on decisions in most multinational states. The solution to this situation should be for majority and minority nations to work from the principle of mutual recognition. In Kymlicka's terms (borrowing from Taylor) there needs to be a commitment to deep diversity on the part of all nations coexisting on the state's territory (Kymlicka, 1995: 189–91). Many states claim to have made this commitment. But a commitment to mutual recognition requires that all parties accept further principles, namely, that all partners are equal and that decisions and outcomes are negotiated, not legislated by one nation and applied to another. Taken on these terms, there are very few multination states where mutual recognition is the chief operating principle. In this sense, any professed commitment to deep diversity is at best incomplete and at worst dishonest.

Conclusion

The resurgence of liberal nationalism, beginning at the end of the twentieth century, has once again opened up the debate on citizenship and belonging in multination states. The possibilities for new forms of justice are manifold and have engaged not only political theorists but also political activists and politicians. Our own contribution to the debate, both in this book and elsewhere, has been to argue for a greater emphasis on the democratic dimensions of self-determination. In this chapter, we have outlined some of the weaknesses of existing cultural defences of self-determination and argued that, ironically, they can perpetuate the very forms of state domination that liberal nationalists are attempting to dismantle. When culture is the key determinant for assessing a nation's claim to self-determination, the state – and the majority population it represents – can still play a dominant role in adjudication. We do not assume that the state will always 'rule' against the substate nation or Aboriginal group, but there is ample evidence to support the claim that it is quite likely that it will do so. States have argued that domestic stability, which it is their responsibility to maintain, is the main reason for taking such action. Traditionally, domestic stability has been assumed to rest on undifferentiated citizenship, which is guaranteed by undivided power and sovereignty. But increasingly, notions of shared or divided citizenship are becoming acceptable in part due to changes in the international environment. Therefore, the sources of domestic stability need to be rethought and, if they are no longer undivided sovereignty, then that opens up the possibility for differentiated forms of citizenship. In the next chapter, we introduce our own version of differentiated citizenship, which attempts to compensate for the weaknesses in recent liberal nationalist arguments.

4 • Multinational Citizenship

If the arguments of the preceding chapters are valid, a multinational model of citizenship and self-determination must respond to the continuing resilience of national identities and the normative claims which are made on their behalf. It must also come to terms with the realities of interdependence and the fact that in many cases it is neither viable nor desirable for all nations to become states. Our aim is to harmonize these objectives in such a way that they do not perpetuate the normative or political subordination of substate nations and Aboriginal groups existing within multinational states. The model of multinational citizenship that we propose is organized around five key dimensions of citizenship and self-determination: democracy (and equality), recognition, identity, trust (and security) and territory. This chapter discusses each of these dimensions in turn, raising occasional country examples in order to illustrate certain points.[1] In the next chapter, we consider multinational citizenship in relation to the demands of substate nations and Aboriginal groups in a few selected case studies.

Dimensions of multinational citizenship

Democracy and equality

In chapter 3 we argued that, in normative terms, national self-determination is best understood as a democratic rather than a cultural claim. That is, self-determination finds its firmest normative roots, not in an argument grounded in the imperative of preserving a nation's distinctive culture, but instead in a nation's democratic right to be self-governing and to determine freely its relationships with other nations and orders of government (Philpott, 1995; Harty, 1999; Murphy, 2001b). Of course, with self-determination, nations gain the freedom to make choices about culture, but the content of these choices, and specifically whether or not nations choose to remain culturally distinctive, should have no normative bearing whatsoever on their continued entitlement to the right to self-determination. In chapter 3 we also briefly outlined three aspects of democratic citizenship and self-determination that are essential for meeting the political demands of substate nations: (1) internal democratic principles and governing practices; (2) external democracy and the corresponding democratization of domestic intergovernmental relations in the multinational state; and (3) shared-rule democracy in common institutions with other orders of government in the multinational state. As we will come to see in the paragraphs below, these distinct aspects of democracy overlap and interrelate in important ways.

Internal democracy for substate nations and Aboriginal groups should not be understood merely as the right to participate in or be represented as equal individual citizens in state-controlled institutions (although this is one important right), but in the first instance as a claim to autonomous and collective forms of self-government. Autonomous institutions of self-government provide nations with the capacity to engage in collective decision-making to determine their own laws, priorities and policies. Meaningful internal self-determination encompasses much more than the right to be consulted or to play an advisory role on matters of law and public policy where the agenda is set and the final decision made by another order of government. It means instead that the group's representatives are to be the primary decision-makers in their areas of jurisdiction. It means that they are to be the active authors rather than the passive subjects of public policies conceived of and executed by others. For example, representatives of New Zealand Maori have harshly criticized government initiatives that seek to equip them with little more than a consultative or advisory role, which in their view constitutes a violation of their constitutional position of co-equality under the Treaty of Waitangi and a denial of *tino rangatiratanga* (roughly speaking, 'self-determination') (McLeay, 1991: 33–4). Similarly, the Assembly of First Nations (AFN) in Canada has mounted strong opposition to the federal government's recent attempts to reform the Indian Act (the legislation which structures governance on Indian reserves), not because they view these reforms as unnecessary, but because they are part of a unilateral process designed and driven by the federal government. In the AFN's view, 'any initiative dealing with First Nations governance should be designed, driven and ratified by First Nations' (AFN, 2001b). This is not to say that there is no place at all for consultation among interdependent governments in a multinational state, but it should be viewed as a supplementary governing function rather than an alternative to autonomous internal self-governance.[2]

Autonomous internal self-government means that members of substate nations must have the capacity to choose their own political leadership and to design the institutions in terms of which representatives are to be selected and held accountable. There are many examples where this has been achieved in practice, including the Québec National Assembly, the Scottish, Basque and Catalan Parliaments and the Legislature in Canada's majority-Inuit territory of Nunavut. It also entails the freedom to design the institutional context that will both structure and facilitate the nation's decision-making authority in ways that reflect the political traditions and priorities of the national group in question. Aboriginal peoples in particular frequently complain that governments require them to adopt institutions and styles of decision-making that were conceived without either their input or their consent. This argument has been voiced by the James Bay Cree regarding the municipal-style institutions they were granted in the James Bay and Northern Québec Agreement (GCC, 1998: 121, 127–8) and by Aboriginal peoples in Australia with reference to the Aboriginal and Torres Strait Islander Commission (ATSIC), a government-designed administrative and advisory body on Aboriginal affairs composed of indirectly elected Aboriginal representatives from across the country (Sullivan, 1996: 121–2). Internal democracy further includes the freedom to decide what will be governed by a substate nation, whether this refers to particular populations, territories, resources, policy jurisdictions, or specific programmes and services. Substate nations may, and frequently do, decide to delegate or share jurisdictions with other governments, but generally with the stipulation that this be based on free and open negotiations and consent, and that the distribution of jurisdictions not be unilaterally determined at the outset by the state. For example, representatives of substate nations frequently complain that their jurisdictional authority is deemed from the outset to legitimately extend only to matters relating to language and culture, when in fact the range of jurisdictions to which they are entitled is something they should be permitted to negotiate with the state.

Internal democracy is closely intertwined with external democracy, which refers to a nation's right to determine its own future as free as possible from arbitrary external interference or domination (Philpott, 1995: 352; De-Shalit, 1996: 911; Murphy, 2001b: 373–7). This democratic sentiment is an expression of a people's desire to gain an increased measure of control over their individual and collective futures by reducing the influence or direct interference of an external governing authority. In the case of stateless nations the primary external governing authority in question is the state. External self-determination for stateless nations can be achieved through a variety of institutional means, including access to exclusive legislative authority in particular jurisdictions, or the enjoyment of concurrent jurisdictional authority where they enjoy legislative paramountcy. It may also additionally entail the formal constitutional entrenchment of their self-governing powers with the intention of further insulating their jurisdictional authority from state interference or override. Whatever the institutional method of choice, stateless nations, unlike other substate groups such as ethnic or cultural minorities, challenge the state's right unilaterally to assume and extend its authority over them. As such, their claim to external self-determination should not be misunderstood as merely a demand for toleration or limited forbearance by the state, but is instead a demand for recognition of their equal political status and their rightful share of political power. Understood in this sense, the call for external self-determination does not constitute an appeal for *special* consideration or a *special* right to self-determination (Buchanan, 1998), but is instead an appeal to the same democratic right to freedom from alien rule that is unproblematically assumed by the dominant nations currently in control of the states within which they reside. From the point of view of stateless nations, the most basic political question to be answered in this context is not why or to what degree the state should accede to their demands for autonomy, but how the various nations – both majority and minority – coexisting in a multinational state can mutually accommodate their equal entitlements to the right to self-determination. The principle of equality is of particular importance in this matrix of self-determination, and we will have more to say about it in the paragraphs below.

Too often, self-determination for stateless nations is understood narrowly to entail more extreme forms of political independence, as was discussed in chapter 3. The most extreme form is, of course, secession, but short of that it is also frequently assumed to entail a state of affairs where the constituent nations in a multinational state govern themselves, to borrow a metaphor from classical federalist theory, in watertight compartments and therefore have very little to do with one another. For this reason there is a strong tendency among many theorists of self-determination to focus almost exclusively on the dimensions of autonomous internal self-government and freedom from external interference (Philpott, 1995; De-Shalit, 1996). While there is no denying the importance of these features of self-determination, the reality for most multinational states is a state of affairs wherein the constituent nations are not so easily divided from one another but in fact are caught up in relations of complex geographical, socio-cultural and economic interdependence. Moreover, cases of stateless nations asserting maximalist demands for political autonomy or even secession and statehood are in the minority worldwide, with most instead seeking some kind of relationship and coexistence within an existing state structure (Connor, 1999: 168–9; Keating, 2001: 17). What this means is that any plausible theoretical framework of citizenship and self-determination for stateless nations must come to terms with democratic forms of shared or cooperative rule, and frameworks of intergovernmental relations that are capable of governing this interdependence in an effective and democratic manner. In this conclusion we share some common ground with Iris Marion Young's metaphor of self-determination as 'relational autonomy', which stipulates the need for cooperative action and certain limitations on the self-governing authority of interdependent national groups in order to maintain the equal right of each to assert and exercise the right of self-determination (Young, 2000: 258–60). We take the analysis a step further than Young by disaggregating our account of the interdependence dimension of self-determination into its shared-rule and intergovernmental components.

As we emphasized in chapter 2, shared-rule in common democratic institutions is probably the most underexamined dimension of national self-determination, given the conventional tendency to emphasize the autonomy of nations and the imperative of self-rule. Indeed, shared-rule in common institutions has frequently been viewed as antithetical to the demands of stateless nations. According to its detractors, shared-rule is viewed as a means of co-opting minority nations, bringing them inside state institutions where their concerns will remain marginalized, while simultaneously distracting energy, attention and resources from the imperative of autonomous self-government. These fears are not entirely unfounded. Aboriginal peoples in particular frequently cite a negative historical experience with shared-rule practices, which were used by settler states as a means of short-circuiting movements for Aboriginal self-government and of assimilating Aboriginal populations as equal and undifferentiated citizens of the state (Fleras, 1985: 555–8; Cairns, 2000: 17–18). One possible way of alleviating these sorts of worries is to conceive of participation in shared-rule institutions not as an alternative but instead as a necessary complement to institutions of autonomous self-government (Murphy, 2004a). Indeed such a complementarity of self-rule and shared-rule is essential to many federal systems of government, wherein the constituent units elect their own governing legislatures while simultaneously sending representatives to serve in government at the federal level. These two complementary forms of rule are also central to consociational systems of government, which combine provisions for segmental autonomy and governance by a grand coalition of the main sub-unit representatives.[3] Another possible means of alleviating concerns regarding marginalization is via the principle of equality in the shared-rule decision-making process. In cases of power-sharing or joint decision-making bodies, equality means that substate nations are not to be included as subordinate or minority participants in decision-making but as co-equal or co-sovereign partners. In other words, the representatives of substate nations must have an equal capacity to partake in the final decisions of power-sharing bodies as that of their historically more dominant and powerful partners. This can be arranged using different institutional mechanisms such as weighted majority voting, parallel consent, legislative veto powers or providing the group with the numerical balance of power in terms of the membership of the decision-making body (Catt and Murphy, 2002).

Participation in shared-rule institutions can serve many key functions for substate nations in a multinational state. In the first instance, where such institutions enjoy the authority to modify or even revoke the self-governing authority of substate governments, representation in those institutions may prove an essential means of ensuring that such modifications cannot be made without their consent. Representation in shared-rule institutions may also prove an effective means of introducing a substate nation's interests and concerns into the country-wide debate. A good example of this is the success of the Bloc Québécois, a federal political party formed with the exclusive aim of representing the interests of Québec in the Parliament of Canada. In 1991 the party returned fifty-four of Québec's seventy-five MPs to Ottawa, enough to form the official opposition (no small irony for a party officially committed to Québec's secession from Canada). The party's popularity waned somewhat in subsequent elections, but after the 2000 elections it nevertheless comprised the third largest party in Parliament with thirty-eight seats. Shared-rule institutions may also play a key role where the populations of different national communities are intermixed and engaged in competition for scarce goods such as land and natural resources. Natural resource co-management institutions have been established in Northern Canada with precisely the aim of governing this sort of competition and interdependence of the Aboriginal and non-Aboriginal inhabitants. These bodies, which generally provide for equal representation of the Aboriginal and non-Aboriginal parties, have been described as a new species of governing institution in Canada. As Graham White explains, co-management bodies exist at the intersection of three orders of government in Canada (federal, provincial and Aboriginal). They are not strictly a form of Aboriginal self-government, but nor are they exclusively federal or provincial institutions. Instead, they are an expression of the unique political relationship between Aboriginal and non-Aboriginal governments that is embodied in historic treaties and the principles of treaty federalism (White, 2002: 92–4). Additional benefits of participation in shared-rule institutions include their symbolic expression of a substate nation's unique constitutional position, and of their right to have a voice in deliberations at the national level. It may also contribute to the development of trust, solidarity and common enterprise with the other national community or communities with whom they share a state, thereby helping to combat the forces of fragmentation or ghettoization that may attend the division or distribution of sovereignty in a multinational context (Borrows, 2000; Cairns, 2000).

Rounding out our discussion of the democratic dimensions of citizenship in a post-sovereign context is the issue of democratizing intergovernmentalism or intergovernmental relations. In the course of institutionalizing their right to self-determination, most substate nations will need to coordinate their governing authority with other orders of government in the state or possibly even delegate some of their sovereign authority to external governing authorities. Such forms of intergovernmental cooperation and coordination are particularly useful, in some cases even essential, given the realities of complex interdependence and corresponding jurisdictional overlaps relating to policy issues, populations and territories in multinational states. What is essential from our point of view is that intergovernmental processes of cooperation and coordination are governed in terms of *equality*. Equality in this context refers to the co-equality of peoples or nations rather than simply to equality of individuals. Equality is linked to the principle of democracy in the sense that it refers to an equal democratic right of national groups to self-rule. Theorists and practitioners often ask why existing states should accept claims to substate national self-determination, but nationalists feel this question should be turned around, such that the state should explain why it has the exclusive right to decide their fate in the first place. In this sense, substate nationalists can be seen as demanding the same democratic right to self-determination which dominant national groups already assume and exercise for themselves via control of a state (MacCormick, 1996: 565–6).

In an intergovernmental context equality means that substate nations should enjoy equal status and authority in the negotiation of arrangements to govern their interdependence with the other political communities with whom they coexist in a state. In other words, both the initial negotiation and the ongoing coordination of its intergovernmental relations remains contingent on the consent of the substate national group, who claim the right to judge whether or not it continues to serve their interest as a nation (Tully, 1995: 26–7; Kymlicka, 1999: 122; Young, 2000b: 258–60). It is important to recognize that interdependence will place constraints on the autonomy of substate nations, as it does on that of existing nation-states, but just as states claim the democratic right to grapple with these constraints on behalf of their members, so too do substate nations. Equal status as a negotiating partner does not, however, mean that equal decision-making powers will be negotiated in all areas where the rights and interests of different national groups overlap. For example, relatively small and less powerful substate nations may judge that their interests in domains such as military security and the administration of criminal justice will best be served by delegating this authority entirely to a larger and more capable central order of government. Alternatively, they may agree to concurrent authority over a jurisdiction such as the environment, thereby allowing an external order of government a fairly extensive amount of legislative authority over their territories and citizens, but with the stipulation that, in cases of conflict, the legislation of the substate government will prevail. Clearly, this view of equality in an intergovernmental context does not call for the end of all hierarchies of authority in a multinational state. As the examples above illustrate, hierarchies of decision-making authority are frequently unavoidable, and often desirable, in managing relations of interdependence in multinational states – as in cases of concurrency when conflicting legislation must be adjudicated or as in cases where a substate nation voluntarily delegates jurisdictional authority to another order of government. Wherever final decision-making authority is assigned to one order of government or another in a multinational state, a hierarchy of authority is preserved. The alternative view of equality we have articulated here refers, therefore, not to the comprehensive absence of hierarchies of authority in a multinational state, but rather to the absence of comprehensive hierarchies of authority where the state is always at the top.

Recognition

The foregoing discussion of equality is closely related to the second dimension of multinational citizenship: *recognition*. What is required here is that each party recognize the other as a distinct people and polity, equal in status and in stature, and each with the right to determine freely their own futures and to be governed by their own traditions, priorities and institutions. Furthermore, recognition refers to mutual recognition of the legitimate claims of each nation to their own distinct histories, cultures, institutions and interests, and to a share of the territory and resources of the state. In Keating's terms, recognition speaks directly to the normative dimension of nationalism – the claim to self-determination – which in a multinational state means the acceptance of a picture of the political order as a pact among entities who bring their own original rights into the bargain (Keating, 2001: 104–5). At the normative centre of the principle of mutual recognition, then, lies the moral imperative of the equality of peoples. For example, Canada's Aboriginal peoples view their historic treaty relationship with the Crown in right of Canada as a consensual pact of mutual recognition among free and equal nations (Canada, 1995d; Tully, 2000b; White, 2002: 90), a view which contemporary Canadian governments continue to resist. Similarly, in the case of Québec, the view among nationalists in the province is that confederation was a pact of mutual recognition and accommodation between the English and French nations in Canada, a view which also meets resistance across Canada from those who hold to the view that Canada is a federation among ten equal provinces, which rules out any 'special' recognition of Québec.

In contrast to the principles embodied by such a framework of mutual recognition, a common assumption when confronting the claims to self-determination of substate nations is that there is only one legitimate or sovereign political entity in the equation – an existing state – which alone has the authority to decide whether or not it will tolerate or grant 'special' rights to 'its' minorities. This understanding of the political relationship simply bypasses the fundamental normative insight that substate nations are not claiming a special right to self-determination, but instead are claiming a right to which all nations should be entitled, not just those dominant nations that presently control the state within which they are housed. The claim to self-determination by substate nations only appears to be a claim to special status or treatment because the claims of dominant nations to exclusive and indivisible domestic sovereignty have not themselves been subjected to rigorous normative critique. Indeed, many substate nations argue that the only reason they are compelled to justify their right to self-determination within an existing state derives from the fact that another nation unilaterally asserted its sovereignty over them at some point in the past and is now strategically ignoring that fact. A more legitimate question, as they might see it, is what justification can the dominant nation offer for the unilateral assertion of its authority over them? Why does their claim to being a distinct national group with a democratic right to choose its own destiny enjoy any less normative force than that of the national group which controls the state (Murphy, 2001b)?

Non-recognition can also have decidedly negative consequences in terms of the sense of dignity and self-respect of the members of the substate national group (Taylor, 1994), which in turn can produce resentment and hostility towards the state and a climate ripe for conflict and instability. Granted, according recognition to substate nations is no guarantee of peace, stability and national integration, but a wealth of evidence suggests that these ends are rarely achieved when a substate nation is actively denied the recognition it claims as its due (Connor, 1999; Freeman, 1999; Kymlicka, 2001a: 63). A failure to recognise national entities as anything more than subordinate minorities has further repercussions on the symbolic level, a dimension of recognition with much more significance than many studies of nationalism have been willing to allow (Keating, 2001: 104–5). Shortfalls in symbolic recognition in turn have their own sets of political correlates. For instance, it is inconceivable that representatives of the Kurds or the Palestinians would even sit down at a negotiating table, let alone engage in earnest discussion, if they were accorded only the symbolic status of politically subordinate minorities.[4] On the flip side of the equation, recognition can play a central role in processes of reconciliation in multinational societies whose histories have been marked by oppressive and unjust relations among their majority and minority nations. The Canadian Royal Commission on Aboriginal Peoples made this principle one of the central pillars of their long-term framework for a renewed relationship between Canada and its Aboriginal First Nations (Canada, 1995b), and similarly mutual recognition of the two competing national communities – Nationalist and Unionist – comprises an essential dimension of the Belfast Agreement designed to bring about reconciliation, peace and power-sharing in Northern Ireland (O'Leary, 1999; O'Neill, 2001).

Identity

It should be clear from the foregoing discussion that, in the absence of secessionist outcomes and the formation of completely independent polities, efforts to accommodate the demands for self-determination within the context of a multinational state necessarily entail the institutionalization of forms of dual citizenship, at least on the level of rights and entitlements. Members of substate nations will possess the rights and entitlements of citizens both in their autonomous substate institutions as well as in various shared-rule and central state institutions. Given the interdependence of nations in a multinational state, such regimes of dual citizenship in terms of rights and entitlements are frequently necessary, if not also desirable, from the point of view of substate nations. For example, we stressed the value of rights of political participation in central institutions in order both to defend the autonomy of substate nations and to share decision-making in areas of common concern with the other national groups with whom they coexist. Economic and social rights of citizenship are also essential in the form of labour mobility, state pension plans and employment insurance schemes, transfer payments to subsidize essential programmes and services, and access to public health care services. Basic human rights and freedoms may also be secured in various forms, ranging from the defence of external borders and protection from foreign threats, charters of basic rights and freedoms, and the administration of criminal justice.

How, then, does the dimension of citizenship as rights and entitlements relate to the dimension of citizenship as identity? The issue of identity raises the question of how it is possible to recognize varying degrees of self-determination that will satisfy the demands of the component national entities, while simultaneously maintaining among them a sense of loyalty or attachment to the larger association of which they are a part. This is a crucial question for students of nationalism, many of whom feel that without this sense of attachment or solidarity it may be very difficult, if not impossible, to sustain the levels of mutual understanding, self-sacrifice, accommodation and cooperation necessary for a healthy, stable and governable multinational polity. For substate nations calling for the recognition of their right to self-determination it is self-evident that their own sense of national identity is not in question. What remains in question is whether or to what degree they also share some form of citizen identity as members of a larger, and multinational, political community.

In previous chapters we have already noted how early liberals such as J. S. Mill expressed worries regarding the very presence, let alone the recognition, of more than one nationality within the bounds of a single state. In Mill's view, where there is more than one nationality, particularly when none either speaks or understands the languages of the others, there is likely to be suspicion, mistrust and jealousy which gravely threatens the possibility of stable government, the maintenance of free institutions and possibly even the very survival of the state (Mill, 1954: chap. 16). Interest also increased dramatically among contemporary political theorists from the 1990s onwards regarding the question of unity and stability in multicultural and multinational democratic states. These theorists have come to the conclusion that, along with its more traditional preoccupation with issues of justice, a liberal theory of nationalism must also address those issues pertaining to the stability and governability of political associations which choose to recognize and institutionalize national diversity (Tamir, 1993; Taylor, 1991; Tully, 1994b; Miller, 1995). These concerns frequently have been cast in the language of citizenship (Parekh, 1991; Habermas, 1992; Cairns, 1993; Beiner, 1995; Kymlicka, 1995; Kymlicka and Norman, 2000), but whatever the language used, each of these theorists professes a similar concern with the relationship between the recognition of multiple national identities within a single state and the maintenance of national unity. For example, liberals such as David Miller express a somewhat different version of Mill's concern, arguing that the recognition of special rights for identity communities at the substate level serves only to focus their attention and their allegiances inward rather than outward towards the larger association of which they are a part (Miller, 1995: 153–4). Miller's sentiment has also been expressed in the writing of many critics of both liberalism and liberal theories of nationalism. Ronald Beiner, for example, cautions against pluralist visions of societies made up of multiple communities of identity. He sees such a pluralist vision as a potential threat to the idea of citizenship because it encourages a form of ghettoization, wherein each community retreats behind the boundaries of its own group-based identity, in the absence of any need or incentive to acknowledge a larger common culture. Citizenship in such circumstances is reduced to what Beiner calls an aggregate of ghettoized subnational identities (Beiner, 1995: 192–3; compare Cairns, 1993: 200).

In spite of their different convictions about liberalism, for Miller and Beiner both, the recognition of multinational or even multicultural rights is the very antithesis of the idea of citizenship for, as Kymlicka neatly summarizes, in their eyes, 'Citizenship should be a forum where people transcend their differences, and think about the common good of all citizens' (Kymlicka, 1995: 175). In other words, the obligations of citizenship should trump the obligations of substate identities in cases of conflict. As Melissa Williams explains, for many theorists this is one of the primary functions of universal and undifferentiated citizenship in diverse or plural societies, for example, as a means of fostering societal unity and civic loyalty, breaking down more localist or subnational bonds (Williams, 2003). To avoid the disintegrative tendencies produced by the phenomenon of multinationalism, theorists who hold to this view of a homogeneous and undifferentiated citizenship often maintain that, where a unified national character or national culture is not present in a liberal state, it must be created, if need be by partition or by movement of populations, but more often by means of assimilation to a single dominant national culture.

Other liberal theorists have expressed a more ambivalent position on the existence of multiple national identities in a single state. In his earlier work on these issues, Kymlicka distinguished between the types of group-differentiated rights one chooses to recognize and their implications for questions of identity and the long-term stability of multinational liberal democratic states. On the one hand, he believes that special rights for ethno-cultural minorities, including special representation in the mainstream political process, exemptions from certain laws that disadvantage or offend them, and limited support for certain of their own institutions, can work to support a sense of overall unity or solidarity. As the argument goes, efforts to acquire special rights of representation characterize a desire among group members for inclusion and more meaningful and active participation in the political life and institutions of the larger society, and thus by their very nature or logic are geared towards integration rather than disintegration. Along with theorists like Bhikhu Parekh, Kymlicka suggests that the creation and maintenance of a strong bond between new immigrants and their new country is often dependent on that country's willingness not merely to tolerate but to welcome cultural difference. 'Cultural rights', according to Parekh, 'express the wider society's respect for its minority cultures, give them the confidence to express their identity and help sustain a climate conducive to cultural diversity' (1999: 463). In summary, the granting of special rights to ethno-cultural minorities tends to promote integration and national unity and as such are consistent with participation in and commitment to those societal institutions essential to national unity (Parekh, 1991; Kymlicka, 1995: 176–8).

On the other hand, when the choice is made to recognize and politically institutionalize national identities at the substate level (through forms of autonomous self-government), Kymlicka suggests that social integration and political unity are far from assured. In this latter case both options – accepting or rejecting such rights – can potentially lead to instability and disintegration (Kymlicka, 1995: 174). Demands for such rights, he argues, frequently indicate a desire on the part of their proponents to weaken the bonds with the wider political community, to question its authority and even its continued existence. In contradistinction to special representation rights, demands for self-government to protect and promote a distinctive national identity are not necessarily predicated on the assumption of the unquestioned authority and legitimacy of the larger political association. Peoples striving for recognition of their right to self-government may assign this larger association a much more conditional role and lifespan, such as the specific and limited terms of a federal or confederal arrangement (Tully, 1995: 27). In this sense, self-government rights can be understood as the most thoroughgoing example of differentiated citizenship, wherein separate peoples each identify with their own political community, institutions, forms of government, territory, etc. These distinct peoples may also reserve their primary allegiance for their own political community, while relegating the value and authority of the larger association to a secondary and inferior status. Given these observations, Kymlicka argues that at first blush it may seem unlikely that the recognition of the right to self-government can serve the cause of national unity, first of all because it promotes a sort of dual citizen identity which could lead to conflicts regarding which community commands greater citizen loyalty; and secondly because there is no natural stopping point to demands for increased powers of self-government – granting an initial set of demands may simply fuel greater demands in the future (Kymlicka, 1995: 181–2; compare Cairns, 1993: 192, 200). As he summarizes:

> Democratic multination states which recognize self-government rights are, it appears, inherently unstable for this reason. At best they seem to be a *modus vivendi* between separate communities, with no intrinsic bond that would lead the members of one national group to make sacrifices for the other. (Kymlicka, 1995: 182)

However, this is not his final conclusion. Kymlicka in fact cautions that a policy of *denying* rights of self-government and pursuing assimilation in its place could itself lead to increasing alienation and resentment, the intensification and possible radicalization of substate national identities, and increased political disintegration. Eventually, such a strategy could provoke calls for more radical forms of self-determination such as secession, which obviously undermine the unity outcome which originally had been sought (Kymlicka, 1995: 183).[5] In considering this point we should also bear in mind the tremendous resiliency of national identity, even in the face of decades, if not centuries, of concerted efforts to destroy it in the case of a wide variety of national minorities (Connor, 1999; Cairns, 2000). In the end, Kymlicka concludes that the goal of stability and governability in a multinational context is to be accomplished by some form of accommodation of different national identities rather than their subordination or attempted assimilation. Parekh (1999) argues that stability and unity in multinational society depends on four conditions: constitutional accommodation of diversity, justice, a multiculturally constituted common culture and a shared sense of loyalty to the political community. Granted, one of the lessons to be drawn from the theoretical literature on the subject is that it is notoriously difficult to identify with any degree of certainty the sources of unity in multinational states (Connor, 1972; Lustick, 1979; Horowitz, 1985; Newman, 1991). Hence, it would be illusory to conclude that we can arrive, a priori, at a definitive list of criteria which would serve to create and/or maintain unity in every multinational democracy which chose to recognize and institutionalize rather than deny its national differences. There are simply too many contingencies, too many vagaries of human will, and too many differences of history, culture and political context to identify any such set of principles or conditions which would provide a blueprint for national unity in all cases. Nevertheless, Parekh (1999:

449) claims that, at a minimum, 'belonging involves mutuality and reciprocity and one cannot belong to a community unless it also accepts one as a valued member'. Therefore, although he proposes four institutional pillars for belonging, he does not claim that they are the only possible pillars. However, in cases where there is no will to reach even the minimum criteria set by Parekh, one may simply have to accept that such a larger association is simply unattainable, and instead set to work on arranging just and workable terms of separation (Buchanan, 1991: 31–2).

The flip side of this argument is that concerns regarding social cohesion provide no grounds for rejecting minority nationalism in general. Specific cases must be judged on the basis of detailed empirical investigation (Kymlicka, 2001a: 63; compare Carens, 2000). And in fact, an abundance of case-study evidence suggests that the recognition and institutionalization of national identities at the substate level tends to contribute to rather than detract from the social cohesion and political stability of a multinational state. Providing rights and recognition to substate national identities may, in fact, serve to diminish the potential for violent conflict, while the denial of these rights could easily escalate tensions to the point of violent clashes (Horowitz, 1985; Hannum, 1990; Gurr, 1993, 2000; Connor, 1999; Kymlicka, 2001a: 63). What is essential is that national communities at the substate level see the larger association as the means by which their distinctive identities and interests can be protected and promoted, rather than as the vehicle through which they will be lost or overridden. Sometimes, small gestures of support can go a long way towards making this the case. There is a constituency in Wales, for example, that views the influx of 'migrants' as a threat to Welsh communities, particularly Welsh-speaking communities. So, when developers and county councils work together on plans for building new houses, many Welsh citizens resort to various forms of protest to make their point: facilitating the settlement of non-Welsh speakers in Wales does nothing to secure the Welsh identity.[6] Others, such as the Welsh language pressure group, Cymuned, have developed a 'Code of ethical practice to clients' for estate agents, which will give house sellers the choice of marketing their property to the local area or for the company to advertise it wider.[7] The public sphere needs to be an open space where diversity is respected. In theoretical terms, there are many reasons to be confident about a strategy of recognition of substate national identities. To begin with, it may well be the case that particular substate national groups do not take the authority of the larger association for granted. Furthermore, they may view its continued existence as conditional in the sense that it must continue to meet their legitimate needs, ends and demands. However, neither always nor in all cases does this automatically indicate a desire on their part either to weaken or to break the bonds with the larger association. Indeed, it may just as easily indicate a desire or an attempt on their part to renew and revise, and thereby to strengthen the bonds which hold the larger association together.

Another argument which can be cited in favour of the unifying potential of recognizing multinational rights and identities is that they can perform the same unifying function as that performed by the recognition of special representation or multicultural rights. This can work on a number of different levels. First of all, such a larger association may provide its constituent national cultures with a sense of physical and cultural security they may not otherwise enjoy outside of the association. Recognizing, institutionalizing and respecting the rights of national minorities also shows a generosity of spirit which is a fertile breeding ground for mutual trust, cooperation and accommodation. In particular, the element of respect for the institutions, values and traditions of other peoples or cultures can contribute immensely to that people's own sense of dignity and self-worth. This sense of dignity, self-worth and cultural self-confidence in turn provides a much healthier base for a stable and lasting relationship than its mirror image of alienation, self-doubt and degradation, and the resentment, suspicion and mistrust to which these conditions generally give rise. Respect also has the potential for breeding a reciprocal respect, and at least the possibility of a bond of solidarity or fellow feeling among different national groups (Borrows, 2002: 156–7).

This message is sometimes lost on those who support the idea of multiple and overlapping political identities in a modern state, but who fear and deplore the insistence of substate nationalists on the primacy of their own national identity. These critics instead insist that the primary citizen identity of substate national groups be directed towards the larger political association and that their substate national identity be accorded a clearly secondary status – perhaps not even as a national identity at all but as a particular kind of cultural identity (Cairns, 2000). We find this argument unconvincing. Even if one accepts that the loyalty or allegiance to the larger association is secondary or subordinate to that directed towards the particular national group in question, this does not automatically mean that this attachment to the larger association is fragile or inherently unstable. Indeed, there is no compelling reason why there cannot be a difference in the relative strengths of these commitments, while each of them remains strong and durable. Keating's empirical research into what he calls 'plurinational identity' in Europe and North America tends to confirm this point of view. Contrary to expectations, public opinion in the countries he studied does not insist on mononationality, but appears to be open to options involving plurinationality; moreover, individuals within stateless nations appear to be able to operate with more than one nationality, and do not seem to make ironclad distinctions between sovereign statehood and advanced forms of decentralization as a means by which this identity can be preserved and promoted (Keating, 2001: ix). He concludes that cases of national minorities asserting an exclusively substate national identity and seeking independent statehood and no relationship or identification with a larger national identity and polity are in fact the exception – multiple identities are more common, wherein people feel varying degrees of attachment to more than one national identity, for example, Scottish and British, Catalan and Spanish, Québécois and Canadian (Keating, 2001: 17, 57–98, 100).

Keating's observations resonate strongly with Charles Taylor's conclusion that in multinational states we require a policy of deep diversity, which means not only accommodating a variety of cultural (and national) groups, but also accommodating them in a variety of ways (Taylor, 1991; compare Tully, 1995; Young, 1995). What Taylor describes is a country where a plurality of ways of belonging would be acknowledged and accepted – and for many substate nations this means being a member of (or feeling a sense of solidarity with) the larger association through being members of their national communities. In these terms, the world needs to explore other models of citizenship and diversity, instead of pushing ourselves to the brink of disintegration or break-up in the name of the 'uniformity of belonging' model (Taylor, 1991: 76). So long as the terms of the association meet the needs, ends and circumstances of the component nations, and if not then they are periodically renegotiated and revised so that they do, this commitment differential is by no means a problem. Critics may argue that any such process of renegotiation and revision is itself an indication of an inherently unstable multinational association, but equally persuasive arguments have been made to the effect that such a process is instead the sign of a healthy, flexible and democratic process in a multinational state (Tully, 1994a, 1994b).

There is one final set of points on this question of identity. Some have argued that the mere formal recognition and institutionalization of a form of deep diversity is likely insufficient on its own to keep a multinational association intact if the various peoples which are a party to that association neither value diversity itself nor manifest a desire to live in a country characterized by a multiplicity of different forms of cultural and political membership. Moreover, simple toleration or a grudging acceptance of diversity also will not suffice – there must be a genuine valuation and respect for the particular forms of diversity or the particular nations or cultures which make up the larger association (Kymlicka, 1995: 191). While this may be true in some cases, we are not convinced of its validity in others. For example, in multinational contexts with a history of enmity, mistrust or even violent conflict there is often a conspicuous absence of a sense of mutual respect or a genuine desire to live together in a multinational political association. In many such situations, coexistence will likely fail, but in others it can be successfully based on what Williams describes as a sense of citizenship as shared fate. What drives this idea of citizenship as shared fate are the straightforward empirical facts of interdependence. In communities of shared fate, the futures of the component national entities are bound to those of the others whether they like it or not, since 'there is no plausible alternative to living together' (Williams, 2003: 9).[8] These relations of interdependence may or may not be valued by the communities in question, but the fact remains that their circumstances require the negotiation of terms of political coexistence that both communities can live with. In this sense, their agreement to terms of political coexistence and their commitment to a form of common political community need not be based on mutual affection or respect but on something much more pragmatic, such as the instinct for self-preservation or a desire to escape from a cycle of deadly inter-communal violence. Northern Ireland and Israel–Palestine are two examples that fit the profile of a shared-fate model of political community.

Ultimately, a stable and governable multinational democratic state will not be possible if the constituent national units have no sense of identification with or commitment to that larger political community. However, two final points can be taken from the foregoing discussion. First, this sense of identification or commitment has a number of different possible sources (Taylor, 1991: 74–6; Kymlicka, 2001a: 64; Abizadeh, 2002: 507–8). We noted earlier a model proposed by Parekh (1999) in which he cited loyalty and attachment to the political community. He notes (Parekh, 1999: 459) that it can have many different sources, depending on citizens' 'political biographies'. These biographies tell the story of their relations with the state. But his view might be over-simplistic since it does not take account of some possible bad chapters or endings in the stories of certain groups of citizens. Second, if a national group feels that it cannot realize its goals within a liberal state or even if it simply wants to liberate itself from the control of that state, then it should, prima facie, have the right to do so. We should not automatically assume that dominant cultures in multinational states have the moral right to deny the right of secession to the less dominant national groups with whom they currently cohabitate and/or associate. In such cases, instead of categorically denying the right of distinct peoples to self-determination, which may include a right to secession, we should instead focus our energies on balancing this moral right with questions of (1) its practicality and viability in social, political and economic terms; and (2) the competing rights and interests of the individuals and the national groups involved, both those seeking greater self-determination and those from whom it is sought (compare Buchanan, 1991: 32). Such a course of action holds greater promise than any approach which refuses from the outset to recognize self-determination and/or secession as options on either a normative or a practical political level.

Trust

Trust and its relationship to political security is the next dimension of multinational citizenship. Trust, or its absence, which in extreme cases is accompanied by overt hostility, violence and bloodshed, is an issue that confronts many multinational states (Catt and Murphy, 2002). In some cases, a lack of trust may stem from the belief among representatives of substate national groups that their interests have been neglected or underemphasized by those who control the state, and by the conviction that non-members will never be as motivated as the group's own members to defend those interests in the future. In other cases, lack of trust stems from a group's historic experience of discrimination, domination or assimilatory pressures at the hands of another national group (Williams, 1998: 13–14, 174–5). For example, historic repression and discrimination by the Spanish state explains why Basques, Catalans and Galicians are vigilant monitors of their hard-won regional autonomy and supporters of continued dialogue with Madrid over centre–periphery relations. In the United Kingdom, suspicion and mistrust abounds on all sides in Northern Ireland. It takes the form of Republican mistrust of the Unionist majority, who they blame for a history of discrimination, or Republican resentment and mistrust of the British, the perceived backers of the Unionist cause, and an impediment to Irish self-determination. Unionists, for their part, have long feared submergence in a Catholic-dominated United Ireland, and have long cited a reluctance to share power with the Nationalists, whom they continue to link with the violence and terror of the IRA. The Scottish and Welsh have enjoyed comparatively more positive experiences under Westminster's rule; hence the degree of trust in these cases can be expected to be much higher than in the case of Northern Ireland. On the other hand, some observers argue that a degree of breakdown in this trust was instrumental in increasing support for a Scottish Parliament (Brown et al., 1998: 230). The relative sizes of competing national groups, and the power differential by which they are often accompanied, are obvious contributing factors to inter-communal fear and mistrust. This is particularly relevant in the examples of Aboriginal peoples who often make up only a small fraction of the total population of the state and are frequently surrounded by the non-Aboriginal population, as in countries such as Australia and the United States. Québécois express a similar fear of being overwhelmed, not just by the rest of Canada, but by a North American continent dominated by some 300 million English speakers. Similarly, some have plausibly argued that Unionists may have been willing to sign on to the Belfast Agreement in Northern Ireland in order to secure themselves against a demographic future fuelled by a higher Northern Catholic birth-rate (O'Leary, 1999: 92).

Depending on the level of inter-communal trust in a given multinational state, different forms and degrees of legal and political guarantees will need to be put in place such that substate nations will feel secure that their rights of citizenship and self-determination are not subject to arbitrary interference or override by the larger and more powerful national communities with whom they coexist. Where there is a deficiency of trust, fairly stringent legal and institutional guarantees will be necessary to provide the requisite level of political security in order for peaceful and cooperative coexistence to be possible. The importance of security under conditions of mistrust is not always sufficiently appreciated, even by those with a measure of sympathy for the claims to self-determination of substate nations. For example, Alan Cairns criticizes what he sees as an excessive emphasis in the Canadian discourse on Aboriginal governance on the creation of powerful legal rights and protections for Aboriginal autonomy, and a corresponding distaste for majoritarian politics and a neglect of the importance of Aboriginal participation in shared-rule institutions of the Canadian federation (Cairns, 2000: 143–4). Although Cairns's comments on the neglected importance of shared-rule institutions is well taken, his criticism of the 'battery' of legal and institutional protections of Aboriginal autonomy is overstated. In particular, he neglects to emphasize the essential role that legal-constitutional guarantees and legal decisions in favour of Aboriginal rights have played in pushing Canadian governments to respect the rights, entitlements and autonomy of Canada's Aboriginal peoples (Macklem, 1995). The Canadian Supreme Court in particular has been instrumental in prodding reluctant or simply uninterested Canadian governments to the negotiating table (Murphy, 2001a).

In states where inter-communal trust is at a minimum, stringent safeguards to ensure an effective voice for substate nations in shared-rule institutions may also be essential. It will be difficult enough for a nation that has faced historic domination by another to join that dominant nation in cooperative decision-making bodies, let alone trust them to look after their interests in a 'one person one vote' majority-rule situation. Those who crafted the quasi-consociational institutions in the Belfast Agreement in Northern Ireland surely appreciated this fact – that shared-rule would be a non-starter for either community without ironclad guarantees that their voices could not be subordinated or overridden with impunity. What is required in states where there is a relatively low degree of inter-communal trust is not shared-rule institutions that will fail to function in the absence of trust, but institutions which can function where trust is not in abundance. Where there are low levels of inter-communal trust, the proper temporal ordering of self-rule and shared-rule institutions must also be considered. In many cases, it may be that the only viable option is first to establish autonomous institutions of self-government for substate nations, and thereby a form of parallel substate citizenship. The idea here is that the self-governing institutions will provide the community in question with a sense of security which might provide a platform upon which sufficient inter-group trust can be established that might in turn support cooperation in a second layer of shared-rule institutions.

Territory

The final dimension of multinational citizenship is territory or territoriality. There are normative and practical issues at stake here. The normative issue was touched on obliquely in our discussion of the continuing salience of national identities in the modern world. Contrary to the expectations of many postnational and cosmopolitan theorists, national identities continue to be strongly linked to a particular territory and, more specifically, to a desire for ownership and governance of that territory. This might even be called the defining feature of nationalist claims. For example, Québec nationalists make continual reference to the territorial integrity of the province in the event of an act of secession from Canada. Meanwhile, the Cree and Inuit of Northern Québec contest this claim by asserting the right to maintain control of their own territories and to keep those territories in Canada, should Québec choose to secede (GCC, 1998; Ramos, 2000). Treaty negotiations with Aboriginal nations regarding land title and governance remain a fundamental part of state reconciliation in Canada and New Zealand, and land rights are a key dimension of Aboriginal–state relations in Australia (Canada, 1995d; Durie, 1998). To leave the territorial dimension of citizenship and self-determination out of the substate nationalist equation is simply to refuse to face the issue squarely. Some might argue that the appeal to international legal norms and universal human rights on the part of Aboriginal nations belies this territorial claim, but this is based on a conflation of individual and collective universal human rights. Aboriginal groups appeal primarily to their universal collective human rights – to land and self-determination – as a means of securing and protecting their universal individual human rights. The appeal, as we mentioned already, is to the universal norm of equality, but equality of peoples not just individuals (Macklem, 1995; Anaya, 1996). This is precisely what Aboriginal groups have been seeking but so far have failed to achieve fully via the UN Draft Declaration on the Rights of Indigenous Peoples, and related instruments of international law (Barsh, 1994; Mayall 1999: 496–500).

The territorial dimension of multinational citizenship will, on the other hand, have to be squared with certain practical limitations on sovereignty and self-determination. First, this means facing up to the fact that secession and independent statehood is not a viable option for a great number of substate nations. Secondly, we must face the fact that competing national groups in multinational states are frequently highly intermixed, interdependent and mount conflicting claims relating both to justice and to jurisdiction over territories and their resident populations. Hence, even for those substate nations that could make it as states, the most just and stable solution may still be shared or co-ordinated sovereignty over particular territories and populations. For example, while the political objectives of the nationalist Parti Québécois (PQ) include sovereignty it is not clear that this can only be fulfilled through secession. The PQ prefers a 'partnership' with Canada that would borrow some of the features of the common market in the EU, not least a shared currency. Within Québec, the PQ recognizes the need to build similar partnerships with Aboriginal and Anglophone groups: for the former, this would include giving Aboriginal First Nations control over their own territories through the establishment of institutions of self-government negotiated together.

Conclusion

In this chapter, we have introduced and discussed five dimensions of multinational citizenship that, we maintain, should define how nations coexist within the borders of the state. We give equal weight to the five dimensions, but we recognize that some will matter more than others, depending on the case in question. To underscore the importance of all five dimensions for multinational citizenship, we apply our model to a range of cases in the next chapter. What we discover is that justice can only be achieved when all five dimensions are working together. A second finding that comes to light is that the process of introducing and using the five dimensions of multinational citizenship is a highly political one.

5 • Multinational Citizenship and Demands for Self-Determination

At the beginning of this book, we noted that our approach to multinational citizenship combines normative political theory and empirical case studies. In chapter 4, we set out the normative framework for our model of citizenship in multinational states. Throughout the book, we have cited specific empirical examples to illustrate and explain our arguments. In this chapter, we engage in a more detailed case study of three states that are confronted with demands from substate nations and Aboriginal peoples. Our intention here is to consider the nature of the demands of these groups and to assess them in relationship to our five dimensions of multinational citizenship. In laying out our approach to multinational citizenship in chapter 1, we underscored the importance of accuracy and relevance; in this chapter, we drive this point home through a discussion and analysis that takes into account the political context of the demands of substate nations and Aboriginal peoples. Understanding the political context within which these claims operate also forces us to deal with the state.

We select three different types of states: Belgium, which is made up of two distinct substate nations; Canada, which faces demands from both a substate nation and Aboriginal peoples; and Spain, where there are three substate nations but also a strong sense of Spanish (Castilian) national identity. How do these states respond to demands for differentiated citizenship? One way of answering this question is to consider the state's interest in preserving a strong 'nation-state' tradition relative to its willingness to develop a form of multinational citizenship: state interest ranges from weak (Belgium) through to strong (Spain) via a 'moderate' position represented by Canada. We invoke state interest here because we argued in chapter 1 for the political character of nationalism and national identity, a character that applies as much to state nationalism as it does to substate nationalism and the nationalism of Aboriginal peoples. There will always be some tension between the political nature of different nationalisms and national identity. While we argue that the five dimensions of multinational citizenship are a means of managing this tension, we do not suppose that it is a straightforward exercise. We recognize that politics can act as a constraint:

political circumstances will sometimes render it impossible to adopt the dimensions of multinational citizenship that we are proposing. In some cases the five dimensions will act as guidelines, but in other cases, they might be objectives that need to be met before nations can negotiate multinational citizenship. Meeting these objectives would signal the presence, in all parties, of the political will requisite for a more formal settlement.

For each of the case studies which follow, we begin with a discussion of the nature and origin of recent demands for self-determination, highlighting the position of different political parties and the state's general response to these demands. We necessarily provide a shortened version of the demands of the relevant case details; in particular, due to space constraints, we cannot address the historical origins and the full range of demands advanced by each of the substate nations or Aboriginal peoples examined. We focus, for the most part, on the constitutional and institutional relationship between the substate or Aboriginal nation and the state.

Belgium

Language, as many scholars have noted, is at the root of inter-group conflicts in Belgium, dating back to the kingdom's creation in the nineteenth century (Keating, 2001; Lecours, 2001, 2002; Hooghe, 2003, 2004). Although the constitution of 1831 guaranteed linguistic liberty, the dominance of French in a highly centralized state, where the majority of the population was Dutch-speaking, prompted the creation of the Flemish nationalist movement, which campaigned for language parity. Asymmetrical bilingualism (bilingualism in Flanders but unilingualism in Wallonia) was followed by the Equalization Act of 1898, which made Dutch an official language alongside French. In the 1930s, a second set of language laws created two unilingual territories (with some provisions for minority enclaves) and a bilingual capital. The borders of these territories were adjusted according to a language census which was conducted at regular intervals. Predictably, this further politicized the language issue, leading to a freezing of the territorial borders in a series of language laws passed in 1962–3. This created four linguistic regions: monolingual Flanders, monolingual Wallonia, bilingual Brussels and a small German-speaking region. There has been much dissatisfaction with the borders as they were drawn in the 1960s, but several attempts to re-examine them have failed. Language has not been the only catalyst for nationalist mobilization in Belgium: economic development issues also fuelled specific nationalist demands over the twentieth century. While Flanders was the economically poorer region in the early twentieth century, fortunes were reversed following 1945, when the place of Wallonia's coal and steel industries declined as a proportion of overall economic activity. Moreover, demographics came into play as the Dutch population grew faster than that of Wallonia, which had implications for political representation in the state parliament.

Belgium is an interesting case in that it was the central state government which recognized, in 1970, that 'the unitary state, its structure and functioning as laid down by law, had become obsolete' (quoted in Hooghe, 2003). Of course, there had been pressures from the regional nationalist parties, such as Volksunie (Flemish nationalists), Rassemblement Wallon (Walloon regionalist) and the Brussels-based Front Démocratique des Francophones. In fact, the pressure exerted by these parties on the traditional 'state parties' (Christian Democratic, Socialist and Liberal) to deal with the linguistic borders issue eventually forced the latter to divide along linguistic lines. The result is that there are no longer any state parties in Belgium; all political parties are divided along linguistic lines, and correspond to a territorial unit: Flanders or Wallonia. The Belgian government took the unusual step, from 1970, of initiating a series of constitutional revisions that, between 1970 and 1993, would move Belgium from regionalism to federalism. As Lecours notes (2002: 61), 'the main reason for the incremental nature of the process was that Flemish and Francophone parties favoured different federal models'. It is no wonder, given the number of permutations and combinations that are possible: there is a complex combination of 'regions' and 'communities' in the Belgian constitution, which can be explained, in part, by the particular mix of linguistic and economic grievances that have shaped Belgian politics (Lecours, 2002: 61–2). The regions are territorial units while communities consist of individuals speaking a particular language, irrespective of where they live. Competencies correspond as follows: regions enjoy responsibilities on matters related to territory while community responsibilities are related to the individual. The state is left with some exclusive federal competencies related to security, justice, social security and fiscal policy (which is, of course, constrained by Economic and Monetary Union at the EU level). While Belgium is certainly the most decentralized state in the EU in that most competencies are exclusive, the federal government does retain control over the general legislative and fiscal framework. As such, there is some potential for conflict between the two linguistic groups, which is managed in two ways: first, through certain institutional legacies of the previous consociational model of the state, which necessarily seek to limit majoritarian tendencies; and, second, through institutions designed specifically to manage territorial conflicts.[1] Of course, another way to manage conflict, as Hooghe observes (2003a), is to devolve further competencies to the regions or communities. This is what happened in 2001, with the federalization of agriculture and free trade.

All of this begs the question, 'what is holding Belgium together?' The fact that there is almost no 'state interest' at play means that there has been a 'hollowing out of the centre' in Belgium, to use Hooghe's phrase. Federal institutions are consociational and are therefore primarily an arena for the representation of regional interests since the linguistic cleavage is the principal one shaping Belgian politics. Under most circumstances, this would create an unusual challenge for state unity and stability, but the fact that Brussels also acts as the unofficial capital of the EU has meant, in practice, that there is strong willingness to keep Belgium together. But beyond this instrumental reason, there is some additional evidence that there is a strong sense of dual identity at work in Belgium[2] (equally Flemish/Walloon and Belgian) (Keating, 2001: 87). Nevertheless, others fear that 'there is no apparent ground of homogeneity that binds its citizens into a strong sense of communal identity based on national belonging' (Van den Abbeele, 2001: 511). It should be noted, however, that there has *never* been a strong sense of Belgian national identity, when compared to say, neighbouring France. State-building in nineteenth-century Belgium never succeeded in creating a unified cultural and national identity. So, it is not the case that the recent federalization of Belgium is responsible for breaking up Belgian nationhood. The historical perspective makes the question about Belgium's future all the more relevant: what is holding the country together? There is strong support for European integration among Belgian political elites and Belgian political parties (nationalist and non-nationalist) more generally. Whether a party thinks that Belgium will one day be split into two independent states really depends on its position on European integration: if it is believed that the EU is moving towards a 'Europe of the Regions' in which states will become unnecessary, then Belgium will disappear. But if integration is viewed in 'multilevel' governance terms, then a party is more likely to support further federalization of competencies but stop short of independence. As Keating (2001: 85) argues, 'there is broad acceptance of the limitations of independence in the modern world and a consensus on the need for European integration'.

One thing that can be said quite clearly is that the Belgian party system is in evolution, partly as a result of the federalization of the country. Thus far, the twenty-first century has been characterized by party splits, coalitions and reorientations across the whole political spectrum. Given this state of affairs, it is difficult to say with certainty what position a given party will settle on as regards sovereignty and state structure. Nevertheless, there is some evidence that Flemish nationalist parties are pursuing the independence option. For example, the Nieuw-Vlaamse Alliantie (New-Flemish Alliance, N-VA), formerly the Volksunie (VU), seeks a republican solution for Flanders as a member state within a 'confederal Europe'. It anticipates that, as European integration deepens, the Belgian state will dissolve, mostly due to its administrative inefficiency. In a refrain that is repeated across the nationalist parties considered in this section, the N-VA maintains that it has a right to self-determination, in accordance with international law. The VU, by contrast, was not a separatist party, although it did support confederation in Belgium.[3] The Vlaams Blok (VB), well known for its ethnic nationalism in Flanders, similarly seeks independence for the region within a confederal Europe, although its vision of Europe is more intergovernmental than a 'Europe of the Regions'. VB's goal is to preserve Flemish nationality, culture and traditions through a tight immigration policy and a form of citizenship that is a reward for effective assimilation into Flemish culture. The current naturalization laws 'give Belgian citizenship away', in VB's estimation. There is a much weaker nationalist current in Wallonia compared to Flanders and where it does exist as a discourse, it is usually directed at Flemish nationalists, who are characterized as separatists. Generally, Francophone Belgians are not seeking further decentralization and would prefer to democratize existing federal institutions and citizen engagement.

Multinational citizenship in Belgium

At first glance, the inclusion of the Belgium case seems unnecessary in this chapter: its two substate nations currently enjoy substantive democratic rights to self-government (the first dimension of multinational citizenship) at both the regional level as well as through shared institutions at the federal level. Unlike other cases considered here, there is no strong state opposition to the demands of substate nations in Belgium, so equality (the second part of the first dimension of multinational citizenship) is not an obvious problem. Moreover, not only do Belgium's two nations enjoy self-government, they also have the capacity to self-determine through institutions for shared-rule that are heavily consociational. So, it is fair to say that the principles of democracy and equality are presently at work, even if they were not always there historically. In part, this is because Belgium's two nations cannot be viewed in 'majority' and 'minority' terms. Even if Dutch-speaking Belgians were disadvantaged historically, this was not because they had minority status. However, it is worth noting that there are some antagonisms around the implications of equality and recognition in a state marked by regional economic differences: Do the more resource-rich Flemish have obligations to the less well-off Walloons? Is it necessary to redistribute resources across the two regions in order to ensure the substantive material nature of equality? Obviously, there is no doubt that recognition (the second dimension of multinational citizenship) is at work here. But how far does the freedom to decide one's future – which is explicit in recognition – extend? Needless to say, there are different responses to this question and, in our estimation, these differences are in part due to the absence of a shared identity at the state level. This point deserves some discussion.

Belgium is an odd twist on our model of multinational citizenship: while it meets the requirements of 'recognition' and 'identity' (the third dimension of multinational citizenship), it suggests that state stability can appear to be at risk where substate nations do not display a strong basis for a shared sense of belonging to the state. As we noted above, Belgian national identity has always been weak and the consociational nature of Belgium political institutions perpetuated this weakness over time. The Belgian case reveals that sometimes the 'problem' of stability antedates the introduction of the differentiated citizenship policies themselves. Indeed, this makes sense when we consider that the cases under examination in the chapter have never been consolidated mononational states: an undercurrent of instability has always been present, due to multinationalism. We might keep this in mind when considering the concerns expressed by liberal nationalists over the potential effects of differentiated citizenship on state stability. The effects of it are clear today: a federal state that appears to be moving towards confederation and, according to some sceptics, dissolution. As we noted above, federalism is not to blame, but rather weak nineteenth-century nation-building. Belgium serves as a reminder that multinational citizenship really does require more than a mere association of different nations. We are not saying that the Belgian state is unsustainable but Belgian politics reveal an uncomfortable cohabitation of Belgian territory by two nations who do not appear to be equally committed to the future of their country. However, the situation is not obviously critical. Moreover, the existence of federal institutions where cooperation and shared-rule are practised means that, in theory, it is possible to build trust across the two substate nations and, potentially, a project for a true multinational citizenship that would make Belgium more than a mere shell. There are some compelling reasons to think that this is possible, since institutions of shared-rule can help foster trust, the fourth dimension of multinational citizenship. Nevertheless, there are signs that, in the absence of a strong overarching Belgian identity, Flemish and Walloons are using these institutions for instrumental reasons: instead of using them to develop inter-communal trust, they are using them to further decentralize Belgium, thereby reducing the frequency of federal issues on which the two nations will be forced to cooperate. Finally, while the status of Brussels does appear to be something that binds Belgium together, in fact Brussels is contested territory for many Belgians. Historically, it is part of Flanders but increasingly its status is international and it is multilingual although more French than Flemish. It is not beyond the realm of possibility to hypothesize that Belgium could break up into two separate nations with Brussels becoming a European city-state and capital of the EU.

Canada

The Canadian case stands out among those considered in this chapter in that it is faced with substate national and Aboriginal demands. Increasingly, the Canadian government is faced with the almost impossible task of responding to these different demands, which are not always compatible from an institutional perspective. The level of government, especially federal government, activity in Canada around the demands of substate national and Aboriginal peoples is unparalleled in the other cases considered here. There are incredible costs associated with constitutional negotiations, referenda, land claims, royal commissions and court cases. And when one considers that the land claims of Aboriginal peoples have fundamentally altered the domestic structure of the state, the implications of recent politics around self-determination are probably more extensive in Canada than elsewhere. In addition, Canada has a relatively more open approach to difference and diversity than some European countries, because of its status as a country of immigrants, but also due to an explicit policy of multiculturalism. Still, multiculturalism has not been accepted by either the nationalists in Québec or most Aboriginal peoples, so other solutions must be sought. In this section, we examine the cases of Québec and Aboriginal peoples separately.

Québec

Contemporary Québec nationalism finds its roots in the 'Quiet Revolution' of the 1960s, in which the institutions of what became know as the Québec 'state' (état) were modernized. Most observers recognize a qualitative shift in Québec nationalism in this period, moving the province from an almost exclusive emphasis on linguistic, religious and cultural differences to a more radical and secular nationalism anchored in the view of Québec as a separate society and the role of the province as the guardian and promoter of that society (Chevrier, 1997; MacIver, 1999: 245). The basic project of the Québec state has been to secure an expansion of its powers in order to preserve and promote French language and culture and the integrity and strength of its society. If the momentum for Québec nationalism was unleashed at this time, so were many complicating factors, the effects of which continue to be felt today. Two stand out. There is, first, the fact that while the modernization of Québec society produced a new political class of Francophones, some of them chose to support Canada over Québec. Former Prime Minister Pierre Trudeau is perhaps the most well-known of these but there are many others, including the current (autumn 2004) Minister of the Environment, Stéphane Dion. While this is not unusual when we consider European cases such as Spain or the United Kingdom, its effect in Canada has been to force several debates, some of them constitutional, over the nature of Québec's relationship with Canada (we also see this outcome in Spain). Many Québec 'federalists' have viewed it as their mission to use federal institutions to challenge one of the founding myths of Canada as a means of weakening Québec nationalism. For example, the 'two founding nations' thesis of Canadian federalism views the federation as a pact between English and French Canada, the terms of which are evident in some consociational arrangements in federal politics. But there are rival interpretations of Canada's origins, particularly when the Aboriginal question is factored into the debate. Another view of the origins of Canada preserves the notion of a pact but extends it to all ten provinces.[4] The problem with this version, from Québec's perspective, is that it treats all ten provinces equally, thereby obscuring, if not rejecting, the distinctiveness of Québec. We see some evidence of this version of Canada's founding in the repatriation of the constitution in 1982, which happened without the consent of Québec's National Assembly. This event was considered as something of a betrayal of Québec by one of its own, Pierre Trudeau, who was prime minister at the time. The fact that it occurred following the defeat of the 'yes' side in Québec's first referendum on independence did not help matters. There was some attempt to redress the post-1982 Canada–Québec divide by the federal government of Brian Mulroney (a bilingual Québécois), first through the Meech Lake Accord (1987) and later through the 1992 Charlottetown Accord, two constitutional initiatives contemplating various changes to Québec's powers and relationship with federal institutions, in addition to the recognition of Québec as a distinct society within Canada. The failure of the two Accords possibly closed the door, for the foreseeable future, on any attempt to constitutionalize Québec's distinctiveness.

A second complicating factor is that the rise of Québec nationalism beginning in the 1960s coincided with the rise of Aboriginal nationalism towards the end of that same decade. In fact, these two nationalisms frequently came into direct conflict with one another in the province of Québec (Ramos, 2000). In the first instance the conflict related to unsettled Aboriginal land claims in areas which the province had slated for the development of natural resources, such as forestry and hydroelectricity. Negotiations to end these conflicts have produced a number of comprehensive land claims and self-government agreements in the province, and significant initiatives to share in the development of and revenues from natural resources in the province's northern reaches

(Feit, 1989; Penn, 1995; Awashish, forthcoming). In the second instance it manifested itself in the form of opposition by the province's Aboriginal peoples to their automatic incorporation into a sovereign Québec in the event of that province's secession from Canada (GCC, 1998). Indeed, in the event of secession, Aboriginal peoples such as the James Bay Cree asserted their own right to secede from an independent Québec and to exercise their right of self-determination in the context of a renewed federal relationship with Canada, a claim which created significant tensions between Aboriginal and Québécois nationalists in the province. Some of this tension has abated in the early part of the new century with the negotiation of a number of groundbreaking partnership agreements relating to the development of natural resources.[5]

Together, these factors have forced Québec nationalism, associated with the Parti Québécois (PQ) since 1976, to adapt its agenda to changing political circumstances and challenges in Canada. Moreover, the PQ leadership has had to balance these exogenous factors with some endogenous ones, namely, the division within the party between 'hardliners' (secessionists) and softliners (who support some form of association with Canada). The PQ has never assumed that a majority of the population would support secession and therefore has always sought some alternative arrangement that might win over more moderate nationalists and risk averse citizens. The party has oscillated between sovereignty-association and outright independence. Sovereignty-association was used in the referenda of 1980 and 1995: in the former, PQ asked for a popular mandate to negotiate sovereignty-association, while in 1995 it asked the Québec people whether they would support a declaration of sovereignty if negotiations with Canada on sovereignty-association failed. The answer in each case was 'no', although the 1995 referendum was lost by a very narrow margin. After the 1980 loss, the PQ pursued what is known as the 'beau risque' and tried to renegotiate its federal relationship with Canada. It failed and, as a result, Québec refused to sign the Constitution Act of 1982.[6] A change in leadership in the party pushed it more towards the independence option by the late 1980s, a move which was rationalized by the Free Trade Agreement with the US and, later, by the North American Free Trade Agreement with the US and Mexico. The PQ's argument is much the same as that made by some substate nations in Europe: free trade lowers the risk of independence (Meadwell and Martin, 1996). But the voters refused to buy this argument in the referendum of

1995.[7] After 1995, the party retreated and opted for a political and economic partnership between a sovereign Québec and Canada. As we saw in chapter 3, Canada's response to the 1995 referendum was a reference to the Supreme Court on Québec's right to declare unilateral secession, a decision followed by the federal government's Clarity Act. Canada, like Spain (see below) is not inclined to support a form of free association, however defined, between so-called equal sovereign partners. One of the clarity 'tests' is whether or not a provincial government asks its population a direct and clear question of the type 'do you wish to secede from Canada?' The Act states explicitly that questions referring to forms of possible association with Canada are not clear. Possibly because of the Act, the PQ is now once again (autumn 2003) pursuing sovereignty (independence). In an obvious reference to the Clarity Act, a recent PQ publication (PQ, 2003: 11) suggests:

> It wouldn't be too much to dream that one day the Québécois could develop a project for a Québec constitution and say 'yes' to themselves in response to a clearly stated question such as: 'Do you support the constitutional Act on the statute of independence of the Québec state?' Québec would then join the concert of the most prosperous and democratic nations on the planet.[8]

Aboriginal peoples

The politicization of Canada's First Nations really took off following the failure of the federal Liberal government's 1969 White Paper on Indian policy. Inspired by ideas of liberal universalism and then Prime Minister Pierre Trudeau's vision of a just society, the federal government sought an end to both its special responsibility for Aboriginal affairs and the differential legal and political status of Aboriginal peoples under the Indian Act. The policy's ultimate aim was to assimilate Aboriginal people as equal individual members of Canadian society. However well-intentioned was the Trudeau government's attempt to improve the social and economic conditions of Aboriginals (Cairns, 2000), it did not resonate with the goals and aspirations of Canada's Aboriginal communities. Indeed, one of the great ironies of this policy of assimilation was its contribution to the flowering of a vigorous period of Aboriginal nationalism and political mobilization.[9] From this point onwards, the idea of Aboriginal peoples being passively acted upon or consulted by Canadian governments as policy clients would be deemed unacceptable. Instead, Aboriginal representatives began more aggressively to assert their right to be the designers and initiators of public policy relating to their rights, and to negotiate their mutual interests and jurisdictional limits on an equal basis with the federal government (Murphy, 2004b).

The roots of Aboriginal nationalism in Canada in fact stretch far back into pre-confederation history. Aboriginal nationalists trace their right to self-government to their status as the original occupants and the original sovereigns in their traditional territories. This is why the right to self-government is referred to as an inherent right: it pre-dates Canadian law and the Canadian constitution. As such, it is viewed as a right that should be recognized by non-Aboriginal legal and political instruments, but a right that finds neither its source nor its ultimate legitimacy in those legal and political structures. Mainstream Aboriginal nationalism has never harboured separatist aspirations. Instead, it conceives of an interdependent relationship with Canada's non-Aboriginals, a relationship whose terms must be negotiated so as to establish cooperation, the distribution of territories, powers and jurisdictions among Canada's self-governing peoples. What is sought is a flexible relationship tailored to the specific needs and circumstances of the group or community in question, and subject to periodic review and renegotiation as these needs and circumstances change. What is essential is that the Aboriginal and non-Aboriginal parties to these negotiations be accorded equal political status, with neither having the power to dictate terms arbitrarily to the other or to interfere indiscriminately in the other's internal affairs. As such, Aboriginal nationalism represents a rejection of intergovernmental relationships based on unilateralism and control in favour of those based on mutual recognition and consent, and the co-equality of Aboriginal and non-Aboriginal governing authorities (Henderson, 1994; Alfred, 1995; Tully, 2000b; Borrows, 2002; Murphy, 2004a).

Canadian governments were slow to acknowledge the existence of inherent Aboriginal rights but a number of factors combined with the rise of Aboriginal nationalism to push them towards increasing levels of recognition. This included breakthroughs in the judicial recognition of Aboriginal rights in the 1970s in cases brought by the Nisga'a of British Columbia and the James Bay Cree of Northern Québec, which in turn led to a new federal policy of negotiating comprehensive land claims and self-government agreements and the subsequent negotiation of Canada's first modern land and self-government treaty in James Bay. Following the entrenchment of Aboriginal rights in the Constitution Act of 1982, Canadian courts began to articulate an increasingly positive Aboriginal rights jurisprudence. This jurisprudence recognizes the *sui generis* constitutional status of Aboriginal peoples based on their occupation of Canada prior to the assertion of Crown sovereignty. Moreover, it describes a Crown fiduciary responsibility towards First Nations, and places strong constitutional limitations on the capacity of Canadian governments to infringe on Aboriginal rights to land, resources and self-government.[10] The court has refrained from explicitly recognizing an inherent Aboriginal right of self-government, although it has entertained, on more than one occasion, the possibility that such a right exists in Canadian law (Morse, 1997; Campbell, 2001). For the most part, the courts have avoided dictating policy on Aboriginal–state relations, and instead have insisted that its decisions constitute a firm basis for political negotiations among Aboriginal peoples and the Crown.

In the 1980s and 1990s, a number of important initiatives were launched, seeking a more explicit recognition and entrenchment of an inherent right of Aboriginal self-government in the Canadian constitution.[11] Although each of these initiatives failed, when the federal Liberals came to power in 1993, they quickly announced their intention to bypass the requirement of formal constitutional entrenchment, and simply to recognize the inherent right of Aboriginal self-government as a departure point for future negotiations with First Nations. Under this policy, the government would consider a variety of different means of realizing this right in practice, including self-government institutions, forms of public government and devolution of programs and services to Aboriginal communities (Canada, 1995a). Even before the announcement of this policy, negotiations had been under way with previous governments since the late 1970s that produced a variety of specific land and self-government agreements across the country. For example, the Sechelt and Nisga'a of British Columbia, the Inuit of Nunavut, Yukon First Nations and the James Bay Cree have negotiated separate deals that supersede the Indian Act in different ways and to varying degrees. For those First Nations who have not negotiated a deal, the Indian Act remains in place.

In practice Aboriginal self-determination will frequently look very different than other cases of stateless nations such as the Québécois,

Catalans in Spain or the Scots and the Welsh in the UK. Factors contributing to this difference include the demographic diversity of the overall Aboriginal population. To give just a small indication of this diversity, Aboriginal peoples are divided into three main legal groups (Indian, Inuit and Métis). The 'Indian' population is itself cross-cut by local cultural, linguistic and identity differences that yield approximately sixty to eighty Aboriginal First Nations. Moreover, this population is distributed across 600 Indian bands and nearly 2,000 separate communities, nearly 50 per cent of which is based in urban centres off a land base. A related issue is the relatively small size and capacity of Aboriginal communities, many of which are still highly dependent on Canadian governments, and which are intermixed with non-Aboriginal portions of the Canadian population. All of these factors must be taken into account in designing governance institutions.

Multinational citizenship in Canada

Canada faces a set of challenges to the federation it has carefully constructed and, in searching for the best possible way to manage them, has to keep in mind several very vocal constituencies: the provinces[12] and territories, regional interests (western and eastern Canada), Québec nationalists, Québec federalists, minority language communities,[13] immigrant populations and Aboriginal Canadians. It is impossible for the government to please all constituencies at once and just as difficult for it to prioritize among them. The Québec question, when it arises, tends to overshadow the others, but Aboriginal self-government has, periodically, moved on and off the top of the federal agenda.

Québec

What does multinational citizenship bring to the table in Canada? Clearly, the principle of democracy (the first dimension of multinational citizenship) has resonance with the goals of the Canadian government, Québec and First Nations, but each actor's interpretation of what democracy requires in practical terms is frequently at odds with those of the others. In the Québec case, the Supreme Court reference did state that a strong majority on a popular referendum on a clearly stated question around independence would place an obligation on the federal government to negotiate. Therefore, national self-determination is now part of any future popular settlement between

Canada and Québec. Equality, the second part of the first dimension of multinational citizenship, is trickier. It has a different meaning for Québec nationalists than it does for the Canadian government. For the former, there should be equality between Canada's two founding nations – English and French Canada – and possibly with First Nations. But Canada treats Québec as equal to every other province in intergovernmental negotiations around major programmes, funding and policies. Québec does not want to deny that, in intergovernmental terms, there should be equality among the provinces and territories. Nevertheless, it views Québec as fundamentally distinctive since none of the other nine provinces is constituted by a nation in the way Québec is. Québec has the choice to 'opt out' of the final agreements on major policy initiatives (while retaining federal dollars) and invariably does. The result is an asymmetrical form of federalism with predictable consequences for a shared Canadian identity. So while the principle of equality is met in the case of Québec, it is actually insufficient for Québec, because the type of equality promoted by Ottawa is between provinces, not between nations.

The tension around equality is, in some sense, repeated for recognition. In public policy terms, the Canadian government tries hard not to recognize Québec as a 'nation' but rather as a province. In political terms, there is a reluctance (at least on the part of the current Liberal government) to recognize Québec as a nation having the right to determine freely its own future and to be governed by its own traditions, priorities and institutions. The Clarity Act is a manifestation of this reluctance: Canada wants to be involved in the final decision. Moving to identity (the third dimension of multinational citizenship), Canada has been moderately successful at trying to respond to this issue. We argue that the issue here is the need to satisfy two aspects of identity simultaneously: first, the differentiated citizenship demands of a substate nation and Aboriginal peoples and second, an overarching Canadian identity. Like many multinational states, Canada has struggled with the very nature of its identity as well as its projection. Nevertheless, it has committed extensive resources to public debates and policy responses on this issue. What the Canadian case shows is that the identity dimension of multinational citizenship is ever evolving and that maybe what matters most is a commitment to having a public dialogue and citizen engagement on this issue. Quick fixes are not possible.

Of course, public dialogue and citizen engagement can only happen where there is a high level of trust (the fourth dimension of multinational citizenship). In Canada, as in many other Western democracies, there has been a decline of trust in government on the part of citizens. There is little indication that trust between citizens – no matter what 'nation' they belong to – is a problem. Rather, citizens do not trust governments to deal with major political and policy issues. That being said, the question of territory (the fifth dimension of multinational citizenship) can reduce levels of trust among citizens. The very real possibility of Québec secession in the mid-1990s raised fears among Canadians of the break-up of their country and about cross-Canada mobility (given Québec's geographical position at the centre of Canada). These not insignificant anxieties raised public debate about who exactly Québec's territory 'belonged' to. As Moore argues (2001: 165), 'territory simply refers to the domain of jurisdicational authority, to the geographical area in which self-government operates'. Nevertheless, the politics of the post-1995 referendum revealed that arguments based on emotional attachment could trump those grounded in questions of ethics.

Aboriginal peoples

Canada has made a moderate amount of progress on the democratic dimension of multinational citizenship for Aboriginal peoples. Groups such as the Nisga'a and Yukon First Nations have negotiated arrangements that provide them with a fair amount of leeway in designing their own constitutions, internal governing structures, citizenship codes and decision-making procedures. Nevertheless, the Canadian government continues to limit the extent to which these internal democratic measures can deviate from mainstream non-Aboriginal democratic practice (Catt and Murphy, 2002: chap. 3), a limitation that continues to be a flashpoint in Aboriginal–state relations (Alfred, 1999; Ladner, 2001). In other negotiated agreements, the resulting institutions of 'self-government' are almost identical in structure to those of standard municipal governments, although groups like the James Bay Cree have partially circumvented this limitation by placing their own chosen representative body, the Grand Council of the Crees, in control of these institutions (GCC, 2000). For those groups that have yet to negotiate their way out from under the authority of the Indian Act, the federal government continues to exercise comprehensive control over the character and structure of their internal democratic institutions and procedures.

The fact that a majority of First Nations in Canada remain under the authority of the Indian Act, a relic of Canada's more openly colonial past, means that their governments enjoy a fairly meagre range of bylaw-making powers, and are still subject to extensive external oversight, and the ever-present possibility of intervention and override by the federal government (Catt and Murphy, 2002: 83–7). Nevertheless, there has also been some progress along the external democratic dimension. For example, the Inuit now effectively control Canada's newest territory of Nunavut, through a form of public government negotiated in tandem with a land claim encompassing some two million square kilometres (approximately 20 per cent of Canada's landmass). The Nunavut government is not ethnically based, and as such is open to participation to Inuit and non-Inuit in the territory, but Inuit are effectively guaranteed control of government since they comprise approximately 85 per cent of the territory's population (2003). The legislature enjoys a broad range of powers, comparable to those exercised by Canadian provinces (Hicks and White, 2000), with the important difference that these powers are not constitutionally entrenched, and thus are subject to override by the federal government. Indeed, for the most part the federal government is reluctant to cede final legislative authority to any Aboriginal group, except in a relatively small number of purely local jurisdictions. In the majority of cases, the legislative authority of Aboriginal governments is held concurrently with the federal government, with legislative paramountcy usually retained by the federal government.[14]

Shared-rule is surely the least developed democratic dimension of multinational citizenship in Canada. This is particularly true of Aboriginal representation in central legislatures. Nunavut has one guaranteed seat in the Canadian senate, and a handful of Aboriginal individuals have been elected to federal and provincial parliaments, but Aboriginal participation in central representative institutions remains an exception to the rule. Some Aboriginal commentators have called for an increase in such forms of participation (Henderson, 1994; Borrows, 2000), but such voices remain a minority. The shortfall in this shared-rule dimension of democracy is partly a result of the federal government's reluctance to implement recommendations for fundamental change to the electoral system that would help facilitate such participation (Canada, 1991; Schouls, 1996). However, it is at least equally a result of Aboriginal opposition to such forms of participation, which is not surprising once one realizes that, historically, such processes of enfranchisement and legislative representation were designed as a means of undermining autonomous self-government and assimilating the indigenous populations. A more promising development in shared-rule democracy are institutions for the cooperative management of land and natural resources that have become a standard part of land claims and self-government agreements in Canada. As we indicated in the previous chapter, some commentators see these institutions, which generally call for equal representation of Aboriginal and non-Aboriginal governments, as a genuine advancement in shared-rule governance (White, 2002). Others, however, are more sceptical, noting that the relevant federal minister still retains final authority to accept or reject the recommendations of many of these boards, a state of affairs that continually threatens to replace the shared-rule dimension with rule by the centre (Rynard, 1999). We will have more to say on these institutions when we talk about the issue of territory below.

In another intriguing recent development (17 June 2003) Jean Charest, the newly elected Liberal Premier of Québec, and Ghislain Picard, Regional Chief of the Assembly of First Nations, announced the establishment of a joint council of elected officials. The accompanying press release notes that this commitment demonstrates the firm desire of the parties to engage in an exchange of ideas among Aboriginal and non-Aboriginal elected officials on various subjects, including the territory and resources, taxation and economic development, as well as the services intended for Aboriginal people living both on and off reserves. The council is to be composed of an equal number of Aboriginal and non-Aboriginal elected officials. Moreover, according to Premier Charest, '[t]he signing of the mutual political commitment and the ensuing exchanges represent a major step forward in the political relations between the Government of Québec and the First Nations, and could eventually lead to a permanent space for political exchanges'.[15]

Equality is also problematic in relations with Aboriginal Canadians, an issue that is also tied to the principle of recognition. Here too there are signs of progress, in particular the constitutional entrenchment of Aboriginal rights, and the Canadian government's decision to proceed on the assumption that this includes the entrenchment of an inherent right of self-government. Yet Canadian governments from confederation onwards have never fully accepted the Aboriginal view of Canada as a partnership among equal Aboriginal and non-Aboriginal governments. They may accept that Aboriginal peoples have rights, but they retain the view that sovereignty ultimately remains exclusively in the hands of the Canadian state. First Nations want to enter negotiations with the federal government as equals, but the federal government continues to view them as junior, and subordinate, partners (Tully, 2000a; Russell, 2001). One of the clearest demonstrations of this was the Chrétien government's efforts to reform the Indian Act. Rather than include representatives of First Nations as equal partners in the proposed process of reform, the government chose instead to treat them as interest groups. This entailed a limited right of consultation on government proposals, but no control over either the legislative agenda or the final legislative outcome (AFN, 2001a; CAP, 2002; Orsini and Ladner, 2004).

On the question of identity, Aboriginal peoples in Canada manifest a strong sense of identification with their local community or First Nation. As we indicated above, this strong sense of identity at the substate level has, for the most part, not been paired with a desire to separate from Canada, but instead with a desire to build a partnership with Canada based on principles of mutual recognition, equality and consent (GCC, 1992: 180; Alfred, 1995; Borrows, 2000).[16] However, the identification of Aboriginal people *as* Canadians is a much more doubtful proposition and, in some cases, such an identification is decidedly absent (Alfred, 1995: 104). This lack of Canadian identity is undoubtedly linked to the Aboriginal experience of more than a century and a half of colonial rule, under which Aboriginal identities were actively discouraged, and denigrated, and the adoption of a Canadian identity became synonymous with the abandonment or assimilation of one's Aboriginal identity.[17] This colonial history and its after-effects has engendered a fundamental lack of trust (the fourth dimension of multinational citizenship) which continues to pervade Aboriginal–state relations in Canada[18] and has clear implications for future Aboriginal identification with a multinational Canada and a sense of Canadian citizenship. If an Aboriginal sense of Canadian citizenship is to develop at all, it is more likely to do so either along the lines of Williams's model of shared fate (a fundamentally pragmatic attachment to Canada), described in chapter 4, or along the lines of an identification *with* Canada (a kind of solidarity not *entirely* without bonds of affection) rather than along the lines of a strong form of identification *as* Canadians. It also remains a possibility that, as Aboriginal peoples become more assured that their own distinctive identity communities are no longer threatened with extinction or assimilation, their desire to identify with

Canada in a more positive way, or perhaps even *as Canadians*, will increase. In the interim, the more attenuated forms of identification described above provide a solid enough basis for a stable and mutually advantageous multinational association.

Territory continues to be an integral part of the self-determination equation for Aboriginal peoples in Canada. Indeed, disputes over control of territory and natural resources continue to be one of the most difficult challenges in contemporary Canadian Aboriginal–state relations. Among the most central grievances of the Aboriginal parties are the relatively small size of the settlement territories compared to their traditional territories, government insistence on the blanket extinguishment of Aboriginal rights in exchange for a defined set of statutory rights, and the failure of land claim settlements to provide for sufficient Aboriginal control over and revenues from the harvesting of natural resources on and around their settlement lands (Canada, 1995d; GCC, 1998: 113, 128–9; Rynard, 1999: 230–2). Governments for their part are anxious to preserve access to natural resources, and to provide the certainty of territorial ownership they feel is essential to attracting business development in disputed lands. Yet it would be inaccurate to say that Canada has made no progress in the territorial dimension of multinational citizenship. Although concerns regarding government domination must be resolved, it is fair to say that co-management bodies hold out significant promise for the cooperative governance of overlapping federal, provincial and Aboriginal interests in natural resources. In fact, there is evidence that many of these institutions function truly independently of government, are able to exercise considerable *de facto* decision-making authority despite government's formal right to veto their decisions and are having a real influence on the policy areas in which they have been assigned decision-making authority (White, 2002: 98–100, 108–10).

New innovations in governance for territorially dispersed Aboriginal populations is another dimension of multinational citizenship that shows signs of genuine progress in Canada. Co-management bodies are one such institutional innovation, in that their decisions can just as easily be applied either to territorially concentrated Aboriginal-specific populations or to geographically dispersed and intermixed Aboriginal and non-Aboriginal populations. As of the time of writing, another interesting innovation was being negotiated among representatives of the federal government, the province of Saskatchewan and the Federation of Saskatchewan Indian Nations. Under discussion is a three-tiered First Nations governance system comprising a single province-wide government, an intermediate layer of regional governments based on tribal or treaty areas, and a third layer comprising local First Nations community governments. The idea is to preserve the independence and autonomy of local First Nations governments, while enabling them to delegate authority upwards to take advantage of increased capacity and economies of scale. The 'Saskatchewan Model' would provide for First Nation jurisdiction both on- and off-reserve. For example, the province-wide First Nations government could design and administer its own system of child and family services, which could then be implemented by local First Nations governments and made available to indigenous (and non-indigenous) children on reserves, and in off-reserve rural and urban settings. Initial negotiations are scheduled to deal with First Nations jurisdiction in education and child and family services, and subsequent negotiations are anticipated in relation to justice, lands and resources, hunting, fishing, trapping and gathering, health and housing.[19]

Spain

The starting point for a consideration of substate national demands in Spain[20] is the ratification of the democratic constitution in 1978. The process of negotiating the constitution was an especially sensitive one, given Spain's history of authoritarianism, during which regional nationalities were repressed in favour of 'España una e indivisible' (Spain one and indivisible). There were two immediate issues that confronted Spain's political leaders in the aftermath of the authoritarian regime of Francisco Franco (1939–75): first, whether to retain an authoritarian ruling structure or make a transition to democracy; and, second, if the democratic option was chosen, whether to retain a centralized state structure or introduce some form of devolution in recognition of the demands for political autonomy on the part of the substate nations of the Basque Country, Catalonia and Galicia. In the end, the terms of the constitutional negotiations put Spain on the path towards a democratic state that, although not a federation in name, shares many of the institutional features of federal states. In particular, the Spanish constitution seeks to reconcile 'unity and diversity' – a common purpose of federal states – through institutional structures that permit self-government at the regional level in the form of an autonomous community. Nevertheless, there is much debate over the precise nature of the constitutional relationship between Madrid and the communities, in particular in those of the three so-called 'historic nationalities' (Basque Country, Catalonia and Galicia). For example, Article 2 of the constitution states that '[t]he Constitution is based on the indissoluble unity of the Spanish Nation, the common and indivisible country of all Spaniards; it recognizes and guarantees the right to autonomy of the nationalities and regions of which it is composed, and solidarity amongst them all'. One might assume from Article 2 that there is only one constituent nation (Spanish) but Article 137 challenges this view: '[t]he State is organized territorially into municipalities, provinces and Autonomous Communities that may be constituted. All these bodies shall enjoy self-government for the management of their respective interests.' But since three autonomous communities correspond to the 'historic nationalities', it is a legitimate question to ask whether these nations are in fact constituent. The debate has never been resolved.

Autonomy is a voluntary right and the constitution specifies three paths for acceding to autonomy. The three historic nationalities were permitted to take a 'rapid' route while most other regions of Spain took the 'slow' route. By the end of this process, there would be seventeen autonomous communities in Spain, including the capital, Madrid. But the varied paths to autonomy conceal what Catalan nationalists have often characterized as a policy of 'café para todos' (coffee for everyone) – or, reluctance on the part of the central government to treat the historic nationalities in a distinctive way. This assessment is not entirely fair or even accurate: in reality, the autonomous communities, especially the Basque and Catalan ones, enjoy a strong measure of regional power. However, it is true that there has been reluctance on the part of Madrid to respond to requests for increased autonomy on the part of the Basque Country, Catalonia and Galicia. One obvious reason for Madrid's position is that, historically, pressures for autonomy from the regions have inevitably resulted in state instability. Given Spain's nineteenth- and twentieth-century experiences with dictatorships, this view just does not seem to want to fade away, even amongst younger generations of Spanish (as opposed to Basque, Catalan or Galician) politicians. The fact that one strand of Basque nationalism continues to be associated with violence does not help matters. Whatever the reason, the conservative and narrow interpretation of the Spanish constitution, which holds sway in Madrid, has resulted in the view that it is 'untouchable'. So, any attempt by Spain's substate nations to seek further autonomy must leave the 'magna carta', as the constitution is popularly known, intact.

Of course, constitutions should not be changed or amended too frequently: they are meant to be the foundation of political legitimacy in a society. But in Spain, the (justified) fear of political instability in the early days of the transition to democracy created a climate where any public debate on the constitutional definition of 'nationality' and 'nation' was interpreted as a threat to the constitution's very authority. Even though this atmosphere has lightened up in response to Spain's obvious success in consolidating its democracy, the dominant view in Madrid continues to be that the constitution must remain 'untouched' because it 'exemplifies and guarantees civic consensus' (Guibernau, 2002: 20): According to the former Prime Minister, José María Aznar, 'No modification of our constitutional trademark is possible without the support of the same representation which was responsible for its birth' (*Avui*, 1 July 2003). This view has strong merit and picks up on Parekh's (1999) argument, discussed in chapter 4, that there needs to be a constitutional accommodation of diversity. Of course, the validity of the prevailing view in Madrid depends on whether the constitution does represent a civic consensus from the perspective of Spain's substate nations.[21]

There are two ways to approach this question: first, were the substate nations at the negotiation table when the constitution was drafted and, second, what was the public response of Spanish citizens to the constitution in the popular referendum of 1978? There might be a third assessment: namely, how is the constitution viewed today in the three autonomous communities that correspond to the substate nations? In August 1977, a democratically elected parliament (Cortes) created a Constitutional Committee made up of thirty-six parliamentarians, who in turn appointed a subcommittee of seven members who were charged with drafting a constitution. While three members of the subcommittee were from substate nations (two Catalans and one Galician), they were not all nationalists: the Galician Manuel Fraga (a former Francoist minister) was a conservative while the Catalan, Jordi Sola Turé, was a communist, although he supported certain elements of Catalan nationalists' demands. Only Miquel Roca was a self-declared Catalan nationalist. So, not all nations were at the table: no Basque representative was there, and only one nationalist perspective – the Catalan one – was presented. Of course, the Spanish constitution was the product of certain compromises around some of the main fault-lines separating Francoist and more liberal thinking, but in the end, there was a strong parliamentary consensus in favour of the constitution: only a handful of deputies or senators either voted against it or abstained. But amongst those who refused to endorse it were the moderate and extremist Basque nationalists. This pattern was repeated in the popular referendum held in December 1978:[22] only 35 per cent of eligible Basque voters supported it, with a large number abstaining; none of the Basque nationalist parties would support it. The constitution received majority support in Catalonia and Galicia. The current constitution continues to be supported by citizens in Catalonia and Galicia and, to a lesser extent, in the Basque Country: according to a poll conducted in 2002 by the Observatorio Político Autonómico.[23] So, in sum, there is some evidence that the constitution represents a civic consensus in Catalonia and Galicia, but it is much less clear that such a consensus exists in the Basque Country.

Civic consensus around the constitution is not necessarily a vote for the status quo. In fact, Spain's three substate nations have repeatedly argued that they would like a 'rereading' of the constitution to recognize the plurinational nature of Spain. Their combined efforts produced the Declaration of Barcelona (16 July 1998), the Gasteiz Agreement (15 September 1998) and the Santiago Agreement (1 November 1998). The first of these called for a public debate on a new political culture that recognizes and supports the plurinational character of the Spanish state, while the second expressed a commitment to work collaboratively in the Spanish Cortes as well as EU institutions to promote their shared objectives and to raise awareness about plurinationalism. Finally, the Santiago Agreement was critical of what they viewed as the centralist and mononationalist tendencies of the institutions of the central state, including the Constitutional Court. The result has been 'the negation of the exclusive competencies of autonomous communities', which must be replaced by a rereading of the 'Constitution that guarantees the juridico-political recognition of the national realities'. The response from Madrid has been either to reject these proposals or to ignore them: the Spanish government is not under any pressure to work with the nationalists in this regard.[24]

In addition to these cross-regional efforts to promote 'plurinationalism', the Basque and Catalan nationalist parties are also pursuing efforts to reform their autonomy statutes. In Catalonia, three political parties introduced proposals for a new autonomy statute in advance of the regional elections of November 2003: the ruling party, Convergència i Unió[25] (CiU), Partit dels Socialistes de Catalunya (PSC) and Esquerra Republicana de Catalunya (ERC). Each of these is based on a set of shared assumptions. First, the Catalan people enjoy the right to self-determination and thus to make collective decisions about their future. Indeed, as noted by CiU, this is the same right that was exercised by all people living in Spain at the time of the popular referendum on the Spanish constitution in December 1978. Second, the Spanish constitution provides the legal means by which to enhance the autonomy of the country's three substate nations. So, none of the parties is proposing to amend the constitution; rather, they are all asking that the constitution be fully implemented so that regional autonomy might be enhanced.

There are, however, some differences over the degree of autonomy being sought. For example, CiU's proposal[26] views Catalonia's relations with Spain as a 'pact' between the Catalan nation and the Spanish state that needs to be renewed in conformity with certain principles: mutual respect, reciprocal loyalty, cooperation and solidarity. CiU is seeking a new self-government agreement founded on the historical rights established in the constitution, which will essentially create a constitution for Catalonia. The new statute will establish a single administration in Catalonia, the Generalitat (which exists already, but alongside some of the institutions of the Spanish administration), which in addition to serving Catalan citizens will represent Catalonia in international organizations, such as the EU, in matters that fall within its jurisdiction. Finally, working relations with the Spanish state would be institutionalized through a bilateral commission. PSC's proposal[27] does not go quite so far in that it settles on a model of interdependence among multiple levels of government extending from the local to the European that is based on reciprocal institutional loyalty, collaboration and mutual assistance. Like CiU, PSC views the existing autonomy statute as a pact with Spain, but one that needs to be renewed to conform to twenty-first-century needs. In particular, the Catalan Generalitat needs to have control over more decision-making in areas affecting Catalan citizens and to be able to represent these citizens in other governing institutions at the Spanish, European and international levels. Overall, the PSC proposal is far less explicit about the nature of Catalan–Spanish relations than is that of CiU. Finally, ERC, picking up on a model the party championed during the Spanish Second Republic, proposes a 'free associated state',[28] which is a step towards independence. Not surprisingly, ERC's proposal has far more to say about Catalonia's relations with European and international institutions than with those of the Spanish state; however, it recognizes that Catalonia must work with the Spanish state to ensure Catalan representation in these institutions. ERC favours increasing Catalonia's decision-making competencies and moving to a form of shared decision-making with Spain on matters that remain within the state's jurisdiction but which might affect Catalonia. Like CiU, ERC proposes a permanent institution for co-decision-making, which would include an equal number of representatives from the two levels of government.

In the Basque Country, the leader (*lehendakari*) of the Basque regional government, Juan José Ibarretxe, presented a plan in September 2003, the 'Plan Ibarretxe', which proposes 'a new political model of relations with the Spanish state based on free association and compatible with the possibilities of developing a composite, plurinational and asymmetric state'. As with the various Catalan proposals, the plan is supported by several principles: the distinctive identity of the Basque people; the right of the Basque people to decide their own future; and the right of the Basque people to be consulted through public channels so that they might decide their own future (PNV, 2003: 23–4). Like the Catalan proposals, one of the central objectives of the Basque plan is to deepen self-government within the Basque Autonomous Community through the acquisition of further competencies. Moreover, the capacity of the Basque institutions needs to be more than 'a mere nominal declaration that is subject to flights of unilateral interpretation on the part of the State, but rather a real objective reality' (PNV, 2003: 34). Ibarretxe is not seeking to move unilaterally, but rather to work first at the level of Basque society and, then, through the Basque Parliament, before, finally, heading to Madrid. The plan is clear on one point, however: throughout the process, the Basque and Spanish authorities are to be considered as equals; relations are to be based on mutual respect, not on hierarchies. Further, the Basque government wants Madrid to recognize the 'political fact of Basque distinctiveness', which is the basis for the proposal (PNV, 2003: 44). Recognition and respect are to be institutionalized through a Basque-State Commission that will act as a forum for dialogue, a process that will build trust and prevent conflicts. Generally, unilateralism is to be replaced by negotiation.

While the Basques view the proposals as statements about their right to self-government, Madrid views things otherwise, and it is not difficult to see why. If put into practice, the plan would provide the Basques with more powers than those presently contained in its autonomy statute, the Statute of Gernika. Under the plan most of the political and legal competencies would be in Basque hands; the only ties between Spain and the Basque government would be the Spanish Crown, the army and foreign policy. Although earlier (summer 2003) discussions on the plan suggested that Ibarretxe would use a popular referendum which might have had a question on independence, the intense opposition he encountered from Madrid is undoubtedly one reason why he changed his mind. It seems that a referendum will only take place as a final form of ratification of a new statute, should one be successfully negotiated with Madrid.[29]

Madrid has always been concerned that Basque nationalist parties will push independence and use a popular referendum as a means of galvanizing support. Although the Partido Nacionalista Vasco (PNV, the party led by Ibarretxe), which enjoys more electoral support than other Basque nationalist parties, is a moderate nationalist party, Madrid thinks it can be pressured by the more radical parties to sell the independence option to its supporters. In summer 2003, Madrid even considered using a constitutional provision to suspend Basque regional autonomy, for fear of a referendum on self-determination. From Madrid's perspective, the historic nationalities of Spain do not enjoy a right to self-determination; only the Spanish nation (of which they are a part) enjoys such a right. While the majority of Basques do not support radical nationalist agendas (especially not the violence of ETA), they are even less supportive of interference by Madrid.

Multinational citizenship in Spain

There is much momentum for multinational citizenship in evidence among the three substate nations in Spain. While all three already enjoy strong democratic rights to self-government, they are seeking to broaden these rights, which has engendered conflict with the Spanish state. As in Canada, there is much disagreement over the limits of self-determination, possibly because of the implications for state stability, social cohesion and Spanish nationalism, however it is defined. The proposals on the table in Spain fall into one of two tracks: a more moderate one, as exemplified by CiU and PSC, which seeks to establish democratic institutions for self-government within Catalonia and to democratize intergovernmental relations through institutions for shared-rule or co-decision-making between Catalonia and Spain. The second track, on which ERC and PNV find themselves, is more 'maximalist' in that it does not discount independence, although ERC is more explicit on this point than PNV. All of the proposals considered here are an attempt to adapt to multilevel governance in the EU by making explicit the need for transparent forms of interdependence, cooperation and solidarity. The principle of the equality of people or nations that underscores these proposals is not readily accepted by the Spanish state, which must uphold a constitution that is notoriously ambiguous on the nature of the Spanish nation – is it or is it not constituted by a single nation or by multiple nations? The divergence of opinions on this question points to problems around 'recognition' and 'identity'. As noted earlier, there is concern among a large segment of the Spanish political class that the recognition of the national identity of the substate nations will result in political instability. It is difficult to overemphasize the weight of history here. And yet a multinational model of citizenship would not create a hierarchy of identities but rather a co-equality of identities: the substate nations of Spain would be bound to respect Castilian identity and to safeguard it on their territory. At the same time, the Spanish state would need to change dramatically the way in which the institutions of the state are presented in each of the substate national territories. But more importantly, there needs to be willingness on the part of the Spanish government to move in this direction and to initiate a public debate on multinational citizenship. Unfortunately, that will is not there at present. Compared to Canada, there is little public discussion or debate on new models of citizenship; what debate there is tends to be presented in black/white terms. The only options are those advanced by the substate nations. This tells us that the rest of Spain is likely very comfortable with Spanish nationalism, as it stands.

Perhaps one of the biggest impediments to moving forward is a lack of trust on each 'side' over the other's true intentions. Although there are historical reasons for the absence of trust in centre–periphery relations in Spain, they should not be perpetuated into the future indefinitely. Madrid is rightly concerned that the true intention of some of the proposals put forward by nationalist parties is political independence. Because of this perception, bilateral negotiations of the type we advocate are not yet possible in Spain, nor does there appear to be an objective mechanism (such as the royal commissions which are favoured in Canada) for examining the issue and consulting with the public. Perhaps it is for this reason that the nationalist political parties plough ahead with their own proposals instead of attempting to draft plans with Madrid. But these proposals seek to change the territorial order in Spain and this is viewed as a first step in the break-up of the country. Even though Spain is a highly regionalized country, there is still a strong discourse around the unity of the country that is based on Spanish nationalism. The fact that some Spanish citizens do not identify with this nationalism is not viewed as a problem to be solved so much as a sentiment to be resisted.

Conclusion

In this chapter, we have attempted to provide an accurate account of the demands of substate nations and Aboriginal peoples and the state's response in three cases: Belgium, Canada and Spain. Further, we have filtered their demands through the lens of multinational citizenship to highlight some of the stumbling blocks in negotiating forms of differentiated citizenship. We paid particular attention to some of the 'politics' of relations between the state and its substate challengers, in order to draw the reader's attention to the fact that the state's perspective needs to be taken into account for multinational citizenship to work. We are advocating a form of citizenship in which all nations are brought to the table as equals, but we are aware that, sometimes, before you can even get to the table, you need to address the competing perspectives of 'state' and 'nation'. While there is a healthy, public debate (some would say too much debate) in Canada, the same is not true in Spain. In our estimation, the debate is almost a necessity for moving the multinational citizenship agenda forward.

We have endeavoured to be balanced in our analysis, highlighting both the progress and the absence of progress surrounding our five dimensions of multinational citizenship. These dimensions are the real fault-lines of the *politics* of multinational citizenship. The politicization of these dimensions varies across cases, but generally speaking it seems as though questions of equality, recognition and identity are paramount: until the state recognizes substate nationals and Aboriginal peoples as equals, in practice as much as in theory, the politics of multination states will continue to be tilted towards division and conflict and away from cooperation and peaceful coexistence. At the same time, substate nations and Aboriginal peoples must be genuinely committed to negotiations and to the possibility of compromise on some of their demands. The idea that the state would fully accede to the demands of these groups is unlikely – even if they are supported by members of substate nations. The state has other interests, which it needs to protect. Recognizing this fact would contribute to building a trusting relationship with the state. After all, political will is needed on both sides to get things going. Once that will is there, the five dimensions of multinational citizenship can serve as a road map to negotiations and then as principles for keeping a new working relationship on track.

6 • Postnational Alternatives

Throughout this book, but especially in the previous two chapters, we have placed the issue of sovereignty on the table. We have maintained that arguments for undifferentiated or mononational forms of citizenship can no longer be buttressed by the view that sovereignty must not be divided. Given both the changes to sovereignty that have accompanied processes of globalization, and the fact that shared domestic sovereignty is already characteristic of many multinational states, demands for self-determination by territorially based nations within states can no longer be dismissed as 'simply unfeasible' or as a certain threat to the integrity of the polity. Shared sovereignty is both a possibility and a reality. On the basis of this observation, we have advanced a democratic model of multinational citizenship that respects an equal right to self-determination for majority and minority nations without threatening either the stability or the integrity of multinational states. In this chapter we confront a serious challenge to this multinational model of citizenship and self-determination. This challenge has been mounted by liberals of a postnationalist orientation and is particularly serious because, like us, they also consider that established sovereignty norms are being slowly replaced by new ideas and practices that call into question the long-term future of the Westphalian order. Like their opponents in the school of liberal nationalism, many postnationalists find their theoretical inspiration in the works of historic liberal figures such as Kant and J. S. Mill, and feel that part of their mission is to bring liberalism back in line with its core commitment to the equal sanctity of all individuals. This core liberal commitment, they argue, is not well served by the principles of national self-determination and national partiality, whether they apply to the state or substate level.

The position we define in this chapter as 'postnationalist' draws together strands from a broader literature that incorporates theorists who identify themselves as either postnationalists or cosmopolitans. Postnationalism, as we understand it, has both normative and empirical dimensions. In empirical terms, the claim is that globalization is calling into question the possibility of effective self-government and even the very survival of the sovereign state. This challenge to the sovereign state is understood to have a corresponding impact on political identities and solidarities by reducing the salience of territorially concentrated national identities and the forms of citizenship which they underpin (Soysal, 1996; Held, 1999; Tambini, 2001). In the place of national identities and forms of citizenship, postnationalists foresee a rise in transnational identities and citizenship practices that transcend the boundaries of national political communities. In normative terms, two issues are important. The first relates to what many theorists have dubbed the global democracy deficit (Crawford and Marks, 1998: 72–85; Held, 1999): democratically elected national governments are increasingly faced with transnational forces and actors whom they can neither control nor hold accountable. As a response to this democratic deficit postnationalists argue in favour of democratic institutions, communities and forms of citizenship which, like these globalizing forces, are not constrained by the boundaries of national states and therefore are more capable of subjecting those forces to the scrutiny and control of those people on whose lives they have a tangible impact (Archibugi et al., 1998; Held, 1999). The second normative claim is that the privilege assigned to nations through the principle of national self-determination is morally tenuous if not entirely indefensible. The postnationalist challenge here is not only to the dominance of the nation-state but more fundamentally to the very idea of organizing citizenship and self-determination on the basis of national identity, whether this be at the state or the substate level. Postnationalists instead feel that our primary allegiance and sense of moral obligation ought to be directed towards individual human beings and the universal community of humanity (Nussbaum, 1994; Preuss, 1998: 148–9; Beitz, 1999; Weinstock, 1999).

Our own multinational approach to citizenship and self-determination bears both similarities and differences to the postnationalist model. In empirical terms, we agree that globalization forces us to rethink the traditional conceptual and institutional dimensions of state sovereignty, but we reject the conclusion that states have been fatally compromised as effective political actors. We argued this position in chapters 3 and 4. We also reject the notion that territorialized national identities are inexorably being replaced by deterritorialized postnational identities, an argument that we first introduced in chapter 1. In normative terms, we agree that there is a need to establish a greater congruence between power and polity in the international system in order to offset the democratic deficits engendered by regional and global integration. Furthermore, we share the postnationalist moral intuition that more needs to be done to safeguard the rights and well-being of individuals whose nations or states are either unable or unwilling to meet their needs. However, we do not accept the conclusion that the complete transcendence either of the state or of territorially centred national identities is either a feasible or desirable means by which these ends can be achieved. Although we are sympathetic to the postnationalist project to extend the benefits and protections of citizenship to 'non-nationals' facing suffering, deprivation or death, we feel that this goal is best viewed as complementary rather than alternative to the goal of a more just distribution of the principle of national self-determination. In this sense, we are more in line with the conclusions of a divergent school of postnationalist thinkers who see nationalism and a proactive concern with the plight of non-nationals as potentially complementary rather than mutually exclusive ethical impulses (Cheah and Robbins, 1998; Linklater, 1998; Nielsen, 1999; Lu, 2000). Similarly, we feel that efforts to reduce democratic deficits via the creation of transnational forms of democratic governance will lack both legitimacy and efficacy if they are incompatible with claims to national self-determination at either the state or substate levels. In this chapter we set out the postnationalist position, and in response to their views and arguments, develop a defence of our alternative model of multinational citizenship.

Postnationalism past and present

Far from being a feature unique to contemporary normative political discourse, postnationalism has a long and established pedigree in the history of political thought. One of the more interesting and frequently overlooked historic postnationalist thinkers is Karl Marx, who argued passionately in favour of the demise of nations and nationalist ideals as part of the necessary and inevitable process of political and human development. Genuine human progress, in Marxian terms, requires more than simply an economic revolution, it also requires a social revolution. Among other things, such a social revolution entails the destruction of what Marx concluded were the many unnatural divisions that existed between human beings based on differences of class, but also of race, ethnicity, religion, tribe and nationality. In his view, such differences served only to foster artificial divisions and conflict among individual human beings and, as such, they are to be deplored and ultimately overcome. Such divisions are, moreover, a distortion of our social nature and of our sense of community with other human beings in a truly universal and cosmopolitan sense. To be liberated from these divisions is to achieve the conscious realization of our authentic humanity and the path to real freedom and human development. Societies which cling to these divisions and distinctions are dismissed as backward and ignorant of the real conditions of their emancipation.[1] In one of the less frequently discussed parts of Marx's work, he held that at a certain stage in history capitalism itself provides the essential means by which such 'backward' or 'stagnant' societies will be liberated from the prison of their traditional religious, ethnic or national identities and set on the historical path towards a more progressive and humanistic communist society. Perhaps the bluntest formulation of this line of thinking in Marx can be found in his short essay 'On Imperialism in India' (Marx, 1978), the logic of which bears an ironic resemblance not only to early liberal ideals of human progress, but also to the liberal capitalist modernization theories which dominated the literature on political and economic development in the early to mid-twentieth century.

Elements of postnationalism are particularly prominent in the history of liberal political theory. Looking back on the conclusions of these early liberals provides a constructive perspective in the formation of our own critical approach to contemporary postnationalism. Immanuel Kant, for many the 'godfather' of liberalism, articulated an eighteenth-century doctrine of postnationalism (Kant himself preferred the term cosmopolitanism) which continues to be influential among contemporary liberal postnationalist thinkers. A postnationalist or cosmopolitan concern for the universal community of humanity was the logical conclusion of Kant's moral universalism and his primary commitment to the autonomy and dignity of individual human beings. Kant, however, mused on this subject with decided ambivalence. Whereas the logic of his ideal philosophical system led him to the conclusion that an international state encompassing all the peoples of the world was the rational and ethical goal towards which humanity ought to strive, pragmatically he reasoned that the vast majority of his contemporaries were not likely to achieve a level of rational or moral awareness sufficient to realize such a goal in the foreseeable future. In the interim, he concluded, the best that could be hoped for was the imperfect substitute of an international federation of sovereign states embracing a more limited set of cosmopolitan principles relating to the proper treatment of non-nationals (Reiss, 1978: 90; Waldron, 2000: 229).

John Stuart Mill also openly expressed his cosmopolitan sympathies, perhaps most clearly in a famous passage dealing with the question of obligations due to members as opposed to outsiders of a particular national community:

> If it be said that so broadly marked a distinction between what is due to a fellow-countryman and what is due merely to a human creature is more worthy of savages than of civilized beings, and ought, with the utmost energy, to be contended against, no one holds that opinion more strongly than myself. (Mill, 1954: 362)

Nevertheless, as distasteful as Mill finds this distinction, he is equally convinced that stable government and the maintenance of free institutions is next to impossible outside the political framework provided by distinctive national communities. His explanation for this conclusion is that a common nationality, based upon factors such as a common language, race and descent, a shared history and territory and perhaps a common religion, is essential to maintaining a common bond among the members of that nation which in turn makes it possible to govern them in a peaceful, stable and prosperous way. Where there is an absence of this national bond, and particularly where members of a polity neither speak nor understand one another's language, there is likely to be suspicion, mistrust, jealousy and a much greater potential for violence and instability (Mill, 1954: 361–2). In Mill's terms this problem is particularly pronounced in cases where one or more of the nations in question is deemed to be uncivilized, in which case he argues in favour of the benefits of their assimilation into one of the designated great nations of his time (Mill, 1954: 363–4). Leaving aside the more subtle differences in their postnationalist inclinations, one crucial point common to the liberalism of Kant and Mill is a yearning for the ideal of a community of humanity, unbounded by the arbitrary constraints of nations and states, a yearning that is ultimately tempered with the recognition of the unattainability of such a community under the circumstances and constraints of the political worlds with which they were confronted. With these constraints firmly in mind, each proceeded to offer both a practical and normative defence of the doctrine of national self-determination.

The second generation of postnationalists, whose arguments we consider below, share the ethical imperatives of their liberal forebears (though, for the most part, minus the hard imperialist edge), but they believe that the logic of globalization is removing the socio-political constraints that have prevented the realization of these core liberal convictions in practice. In other words, by effecting the gradual erosion of state sovereignty and instrumental support base for territorially grounded national identities, globalization is producing a historic opportunity to institutionalize liberal principles in a manner that transcends the narrow and morally arbitrary principle of national self-determination in favour of a postnational world wherein all individual human beings are treated with equal consideration and respect. In our view, this postnationalist position is neither empirically viable nor is it particularly persuasive on a normative level. Globalization has undoubtedly had a profound impact on the international system of states, but the types of constraints that prevented liberals like Kant and Mill from following through on their postnational liberal ideals have not been transcended, and in fact will be with us for some time yet. It is for this reason that these constraints must be incorporated into any viable contemporary theory of citizenship and self-determination. In developing our arguments in this chapter, then, we are guided by the spirit of ethical realism implicit in the works of early liberals such as Kant and Mill. In other words, we are sympathetic to the postnationalist ideal where all human beings are treated with equal consideration regardless of differences of culture, ethnicity or nationality, but we believe that progress towards this ideal is more likely to be achieved by conceiving it as an end that complements rather than conflicts with the principle and practice of national self-determination.

Nations, states and globalization

Emerging postnationalist challenges to the national and multinational citizenship models tend to be driven by the logic of globalization. While globalization is a contested concept, in this book we have defined it as the condition wherein the physical, legal and political borders of states are increasingly and more rapidly permeated by actors, forces and norms that are beyond their exclusive influence or control (Archibugi et al., 1998; Holton, 1998; Coleman and Perl, 1999: 379; Keohane and Nye, 2000). Global integration is not a new phenomenon, but it is differentiated from its historic predecessors by the greater complexity, speed and intensity of cross-border phenomena that challenge the traditional dominance of the state and the principle of national self-determination. Globalization is a complex and multidimensional phenomenon, comprising elements as disparate as international trade and capital flows, internationalization of marketing and purchasing, increases in electronic communication and information transfer across borders, linguistic and cultural interpenetration, global environmental degradation which has no regard for state boundaries, the flow of populations (tourists, immigrants, refugees, labour migrants and various other categories of stateless persons) and the threats posed by international crime and terrorism. Globalization also entails a growth in the number and influence of non-state actors and forms of private authority that at times cooperate with and at other times conflict with state actors (Rosenau, 1995; Cutler, Haufler and Porter, 1999). Examples include large transnational corporations, currency traders, international organizations such as the IMF, World Bank and the United Nations and international non-governmental organizations and social movements (Rosenau, 1995: 13–16; Falk, 1998; Litfin, 1998: 7–8).

Postnationalists argue that globalization fundamentally, some say fatally, compromises state sovereignty. A direct outcome of this sovereignty depletion, in their view, is the reduced political salience of territorially concentrated national identities and forms of citizenship, which are gradually supplanted by new forms of identification and political solidarity that transcend the borders of both nations and states. Although these sorts of arguments tend to be levelled at dominant nations that control states, their implications for the political aspirations of substate nationalists are clear enough: their search for self-determination, whether it be through control of their own state or different forms of institutionalized political power within an existing state, is anachronistic and therefore ill-advised in a world where domestic territorial forms of citizenship and self-determination will soon be, if they are not already, irrelevant. There are a number of distinct but mutually reinforcing strands of this more general argument, each of which poses an important challenge to the idea of national self-determination and its associated practices of citizenship. While each of these arguments raises important concerns, we contend that the case against the persistence of national identities and the corresponding need for national models of citizenship and self-determination is frequently overstated and, more often than not, based on insufficient hard evidence. We will take up our objections to each of these different strands of postnationalism in turn.

Cultural postnationalism

One prominent strand of postnationalism finds its theoretical grounding in questions of culture or cultural distinctiveness. One of its foremost thinkers, Jeremy Waldron, argues that most individuals already have multiple and mixed cultural identities, hence a political project whose end is to preserve a particular distinctive national or ethno-cultural identity is fundamentally out of touch with reality, and almost certainly bound to fail (Waldron, 1995: 96–7, 103–5). The normative equivalent of this argument is that, since claims to national self-determination are justified in terms of the need to preserve a distinctive culture (for example, liberal nationalism), once one demonstrates that distinctive cultures are a pipe dream in the age of globalization, this justification loses its force. In Waldron's view, this leaves the right to culture on roughly the same footing as the right to religion (Waldron, 1995: 100). This argument is particularly popular with reference to claims to self-determination advanced by substate nations. In these contexts, it is intended to undercut arguments that substate nations have a right to assistance or forbearance from the state, such as a 'special' right to self-determination (Waldron, 1995: 96–7, 103–4; Buchanan, 1995: 357).

We have several objections to this argument. On an empirical level, Waldron's position is premised on a conflation of the idea of cultural distinctiveness with that of national identity. Cultural particularity or cultural distinctiveness may be, and frequently is, an element of national identity, but it is wrong to think that it is exhaustive of national identity. As we argued in chapter 3, the persistence of objective cultural differences often has little, if anything, to do with the persistence of distinctive national identities (Moore, 1999). A shared national identity may have little more basis than an attachment to a particular piece of territory, the perception of a common external threat or simply a common commitment to a particular set of social and political institutions (Deflem and Pampel, 1996; Abizadeh, 2002: 507–8). As Charles Taylor has argued in the case of late twentieth-century Québec, it was precisely when Francophone Québécois were becoming more culturally similar to Anglophones in the rest of Canada that a distinct Québécois national identity gained renewed force and vigour (Taylor, 1991). A decline in objective cultural differences, in this case, in fact contributed to an increase in identity-based difference. Kymlicka makes a similar case with regard to national identities in a North American context, arguing that increasing economic and cultural integration has not diminished the desire of Mexicans, Canadians or Americans to retain their own national identities and citizenship practices, and to develop distinctive domestic and international policy agendas (Kymlicka, 1999: 114–15). In the case of Canada, public opinion surveys indicate that, as continental socio-cultural integration has increased, Canadians have actually become both more confident in and attached to their independent national identity; hence they are much less desirous of political union with the United States and less convinced that such a union is an inevitability than they were some thirty-five years ago (CRIC, 2001: 14–15; Mendelsohn, 2003). In the EU, where integration is obviously more extensive and advanced than in North America, survey data on individuals' self-identification reveal complicated patterns of allegiance and evidence of the 'coexistence of different expressions of multiple forms of nationalism, fissiparous and unificationist' (Deflem and Pampel, 1996: 138). For example, there is evidence of mixed multiple identities that are primarily associated with the local, regional and national – there are very few pure cosmopolitans (Deflem and Pampel, 1996; Norris, 2001; Keating, 2001).

On a normative level, cultural postnationalists mistakenly assume that the maintenance or not of a nation's distinctive culture is the basis of its right to self-determination, when it is the right to self-determination itself which is the measure of a nation's right to make choices about culture. We argued this point extensively in chapters 3 and 4, but some of those points bear repeating here. As a start, if a nation chooses and fails to maintain its distinctive culture or if it simply chooses to alter its distinctive culture, the nationalist view is that this has no necessary bearing on the group's retention of the democratic right to self-determination. In other words, from a nationalist standpoint, the democratic right to self-determination is prior to and more fundamental to – rather than derivative of and subordinate to – the right to preserve and promote a distinctive culture. Nationalists will not accept that their right to self-determination necessarily stands or falls on the basis of this cultural argument (Murphy, 2001b). This misunderstanding becomes clear once it is realized that national self-determination is not most fundamentally a cultural right but rather a democratic right. It is the right to choose those with whom we identify, associate and join together in common causes, and to decide how and by whom we will be governed (Philpott, 1995; Murphy, 2001b). It is a democratic right which dominant nations in the international system have long assumed for themselves while denying it to their substate nations, whose demands for a similar degree of self-determination have been called unrealistic, unreasonable or simply unnecessary. Despite the occasional half-hearted initiative seeking its removal, this double standard continues to dominate contemporary state practice (Preece, 1997; Mayall, 1999).

The persistence of this double standard may, in fact, help explain the ease with which cultural postnationalists are willing to discount the significance of national communities and national self-determination. For it is easier to lose sight of the importance of national communities and the various citizenship practices they underpin if one is a member of a dominant nation whose identity and citizenship practices have rarely, if ever, been under threat, given that they are firmly protected and promoted by state institutions. In other words, the relative security enjoyed by dominant national communities may play a large part in the self-confidence with which many postnationalists seek to transcend the confines of nations and nationalism, and which causes them to overlook the fact that substate nationalists are fighting for a right to something which dominant national groups can, and do, take for granted (Ignatieff, 1994: 13–14; Canovan, 2001: 204). Be that as it may, on an empirical level, cultural postnationalists are presented with two political realities which they cannot, or will not, reconcile via the normative stance they have adopted: (1) the incidence of dual identities among citizens (which are interpreted as evidence of the absence of cultural distinctiveness); and (2) increased or persistent demands for political autonomy by these same groups of citizens.

Instrumental and functional postnationalism

Another strand of postnationalist thought is more instrumental in its approach to national self-determination. The core of this instrumental argument is that populations worldwide will soon come to recognize that national citizenship can no longer effectively provide the benefits and security via which it has inspired a sense of common identity, purpose and solidarity. These benefits include the assignment and protection of basic human rights, and the facilitation of meaningful, effective and democratic self-government. From this point of view, citizens will increasingly turn to transnational forms of political community and polity in order to regain the lost dimensions of citizenship that nations and national forms of self-determination can no longer provide (Tambini, 2001: 200). A more functional version of this argument holds that, as social and political mobilization increasingly takes place outside of the bounds of nation-states and national political communities, territory and nationality are coming to play a less important role in the determination of political identities. The end result of all of this transnational mobilization and political participation is said to be effecting a gradual erosion of the sense in which national communities constitute or identify as communities of fate (Soysal, 1998: 210–11; Held, 1999: 99, 102; Dijkstra et al., 2001: 58–60; Tambini, 2001: 198, 212).

The growth of universal human rights norms embodying the recognition and the enforcement of individual rights across state borders is frequently cited as evidence of the reduced importance of nationality in the contemporary global environment. Early examples of the increasing salience of international human rights include the Charters of the Nuremberg and Tokyo War Crimes Tribunals, the Universal Declaration of Human Rights in 1948 and the Covenant on Civil and Political Rights of 1966. These were the precursors of developments at the turn of the twenty-first century, such as the war crimes tribunals associated with the conflicts in Rwanda and the post-Yugoslavian republics and the establishment of an effective International Criminal Court. International practice has also contributed to speculation that long-standing norms of international relations are undergoing a fundamental shift in relation to the challenge of universal human rights. Examples include the challenge to the doctrine of sovereign immunity posed by the attempted prosecution for war crimes of the former Chilean President Augusto Pinochet by the Spanish judiciary. Perhaps more fundamentally, humanitarian interventions in Kosovo and East Timor seemed for many to cast doubt on the doctrine of exclusive state sovereignty and non-interference. Regional developments are also frequently cited in this vein. In Europe, the development of community law such as the European Convention on Human Rights of 1950, in concert with the doctrine of direct effect and the judicial powers of the European Court of Justice, have broken the state's monopoly on granting rights to people living within its borders (Soysal, 1998). Rights related to universal 'personhood' or to European citizenship are transportable across borders, resulting in the penetration of national communities by non-members who have a legal right to state benefits and some citizen participation. These developments in international and Community law have affected three distinct groups of people: refugees or asylum seekers, European Union citizens working in a member state other than their own and third-country nationals who have migrated to the EU for economic reasons. From a citizenship perspective, it is argued that developments in international law limit the ability of states to link benefits exclusively to members (co-nationals). Put differently, states have to give way to the cosmopolitan impulse in certain dimensions of international law, which seems to suggest that states have obligations to non-citizens while these individuals are residing on their territory.

We have a number of objections to the instrumental case for postnational citizenship. The first is that the impact of globalization on the state has been exaggerated. The consensus in the literature on regional and global integration is that, although state sovereignty has been significantly impacted by globalization, the state is far from finished as a key political actor. A more circumspect point of view is that globalization presents state and substate political actors with different constraints but also different opportunities, and thus with a range of choices. Often these are difficult choices, but they are choices just the same (Rosenau, 1995: 39; Coleman and Perl, 1999: 702; Keohane and Nye, 2000: 15–19).[2] Indeed, in many ways states themselves are essential to the success and spread of globalization, for example through the provision of the rule of law and the stability essential to economic production and a flourishing market (Holton, 1998: chaps 4–5; Coleman and Perl, 1999: 702). States themselves frequently reason that economic diversification and open borders may actually reduce their commercial dependence on a particular state or set of states. Moreover, if successful, the increase in wealth and economic capacity resulting from this economic integration may serve to enhance their role and influence in their regional and international areas of interest (Shulman, 2000: 370). The example of the European Union (EU) is illustrative in this context. Although some interpret European integration as a process that is gradually transcending and dissolving the member states, the evidence in fact suggests that the processes of economic and political integration associated with the European Union are more about the rescue rather than the transcendence of the nation-state, and that European states view their membership in the European Union as a means of preserving and enhancing their policy capacities (Millwood, 1992; Mayall, 1999: 502). MacCormick, for example, argues that although the member states of the EU no longer enjoy exclusive sovereignty in the traditional sense of the term, neither has their sovereignty been lost. Instead, it has been combined and distributed internally and in this way enhanced externally with respect to actors outside of the EU (MacCormick, 1999: 132–3). In this sense, the EU is best viewed as a project that is and must remain rooted in the member states, and the nations and regions of which they are comprised (Bellamy and Castiglione, 2000: 68–9; Keating, 2001: 141). Similar evidence exists with regard to the positive relationship between national self-determination and transnational trade and investment integration in other regions of the world, including North America, Asia and the former Soviet Union (Shulman, 2000).

The same logic applies to substate national units such as the province of Québec. For example, the Québec government has avidly pursued trade and investment integration with the United States as a means of increasing provincial economic capacity and diversification, and thereby increasing its economic and political autonomy *vis-à-vis* the federal government (Lisée, 2001; Shulman, 2000: 370). Moreover, Québec nationalist leaders have expressed a positive attitude towards economic globalization and institutions of transnational governance, but argue that provincial leaders, not the Canadian government, should represent Québec's interests on decision-making bodies which govern these global relationships and interactions (CRIC, 2001: 12). As evidence of this interest, Québec and many Canadian provinces maintain permanent offices abroad to facilitate business and trade with their key partners. Scotland and Wales have expressed similar sentiments regarding their integration and participation in the institutions of the European Union (Keating, 1999) and have set up institutions in Brussels accordingly (Scotland House and the Wales European Centre). Indeed regional economic integration and cross-border initiatives have been a critical pillar in the strategy of Europe's small nations to increase their capacity, profile and bargaining power. Some evidence of this includes inter-regional initiatives for collective action to promote regional agendas, such as the Four Motors for Europe (Baden-Württemberg, Catalonia, Lombardy and Rhône-Alpes). Through cooperative agreements, the Four Motors have introduced a series of initiatives – exchanges, conferences, information-sharing – that involve a wide range of regional actors across sectors: government, industry, labour, research and development, youth and women, etc. Each time elected representatives and citizens participate in these initiatives, they do so as members of a region, thereby reinforcing the view and sentiment that there is something distinctive about their regional community. It is not just that they might have a distinctive history, culture, language and identity but also that they have a different way of doing things – a different set of norms, behaviours and forms of action. Other organizations, such as the Association of European Border Regions (AEBR), Assembly of European Regions (AER), Council of European Municipalities and Regions (CEMR), Conference of Peripheral Maritime Regions (CPMR) and Regions of Europe with Legislative Power (REGLEG), accomplish similar ends. Together, these cross-border initiatives affirm the importance of municipalities and regions as places of economic and political activity and as public spaces in which a form of identity and sense of belonging is constructed. As Keating argues (2000: 30–1), the EU 'creates a new symbolic realm, a discursive space in which minority nationality claims can be advanced without necessarily entering into terminal conflict with the host state'. Many of these nations – and regions with legislative powers generally – have made the representation of their own interests a key demand in projects to reform European institutions.[3] Hence, a critical point for substate nations seeking increasing levels of transnational integration is that processes work to support rather than detract from their goal of national self-determination. Moreover, these integrative processes, and the institutions by which they are governed, must proceed only with the consent of their citizens expressed collectively through their own representatives and autonomous representative institutions (Kymlicka, 1999: 122–3; Wendt, 1999: 130–2; Keating, 2001: 56–7).

Picking up the thread of the earlier argument, states also continue to be the most important actors in conferring and guaranteeing rights of citizenship within their borders. Although international and regional human rights codes have had some impact on domestic practices and legal regimes, these codes must still be agreed to, ratified and implemented by states. So in fact it is more accurate to say that these transnational conventions operate alongside domestic human rights and citizenship regimes, and ultimately states retain the prerogative of deciding which of these regimes takes precedence in any conflict, even if this may come at a cost in terms of their standing in international and regional institutions such as the UN or the EU. The state's continuing monopoly on the provision and protection of the rights of citizenship within its borders is well recognized by the disadvantaged populations seeking more secure access to these rights and entitlements. This point is clearly illustrated by an empirical study of the patterns of human rights claims by migrants and ethnic minorities in Germany and Britain (Koopmans and Statham, 1999). Two of the study's findings are particularly telling. First, organizations representing the rights of these groups based themselves almost exclusively in the host state (Germany or Britain) rather than in closer proximity to rights bodies at the European or international level; moreover, their activities were directed overwhelmingly at those host states, again as opposed to institutions or actors at the European or international level, as an instrumental postnationalist argument might lead one to expect. A second key finding was that the claims advanced by these organizations appealed almost exclusively to rights and norms embodied in host state law, and that virtually no appeal was made to the relevant instruments and conventions at either the European or the international level (Koopmans and Statham, 1999: 679–80, 685).

Some critics offer an even more sceptical analysis of the instrumental postnationalist thesis, arguing that the real impetus for conferring citizenship rights on non-nationals does not in fact come from regional or international human rights codes but from the domestic liberal-democratic norms of host countries (Joppke, 1999). There is a lot of evidence to support this view. Following on a point made above – that international law sets limits on states' ability to exclude non-nationals from accessing benefits – states will, for very practical and self-interested reasons, allow non-nationals or temporary residents to have access to social and economic benefits. The cross-border mobility of people – to study, work or visit – is actively promoted by states, a policy which prompts all sorts of bureaucratic necessities: visas, settlement arrangements (including access to state services), taxation agreements and certain civic rights (such as police protection). If non-nationals, such as temporary foreign workers, have access to publicly funded and provided social and educational services, it is most likely because they pay taxes to their host state. The point is that states have always had measures and policies in place to regularize relations with non-nationals on their territory. Even if the importance of international human rights norms might have enhanced these measures, in the case of refugees for example, it did not give rise to them. Moreover, the longer-term response of countries hosting large numbers of non-nationals with limited rights has not been to assign them some form of postnational citizenship –

which would suggest the predominance of international law – but rather to offer them full citizenship as nationals by significantly relaxing naturalization criteria.[4]

A similar argument holds with regard to the recognition and enforcement of rights across borders. For example, much of the help sought and sometimes secured for suffering populations through the international community derives from decisions taken by states, materials provided by states and actions taken by states, either alone or in concert through their participation in international institutions such as the United Nations (Wedgwood, 2002). This assistance often comes too late and in too short supply (a motivating concern for postnationalists), but the reality is that there is no alternative transnational polity, acting independently of any member states, that is capable of filling this gap.[5] It is therefore important to acknowledge the beneficial role played by states, not only with regards to their own citizens, but with regards to the less privileged non-members targeted by cosmopolitan and postnationalist concern, a role that continues to justify their existence. Granted, states are not in the habit of assisting non-nationals or other actors outside of their borders unless such action is in their own interests (or at least not inimical to their own interests), and many a preventable humanitarian disaster has unfolded as a result.[6] Nevertheless, to dismiss the state in the absence of any postnational actor capable of filling its (admittedly rather small) shoes is to deprive needy and suffering populations of even the limited hope held out by the possibility of outside state intervention.

Instrumental postnationalism also raises an important argument about democracy. Specifically, it calls for transnational forms of citizenship and self-determination to close the so-called democratic deficit engendered by increasing levels of regional and global integration. The democratic deficit refers to the perceived mismatch between the normative core of democracy as 'rule by the people' and the limitations of democratic self-government in a world characterized by complex interdependence and the reduction of state autonomy and where, as a consequence, the populations of sovereign states increasingly face decisions made by transnational governmental and non-governmental actors who do not govern with their direct consent (Archibugi et al., 1998; Bellamy and Castiglione, 2000). Redressing this democratic deficit thus requires transnational democratic institutions and corresponding forms of transnational political community and solidarity that are capable of restoring the conditions of effective and democratic citizenship and democratic governance where national communities and institutions are no longer up to the task (Tambini, 2001; Weinstock, 1999). We accept the basic tenor of this argument with some key qualifications. To begin with, as should be clear from the arguments in the preceding paragraphs, we dispute the degree to which globalization has subverted the possibility of effective and democratic self-government. Nevertheless, we do agree that globalization has fundamentally challenged the 'myth' that sovereignty is something to be exercised exclusively by states. Regional and global integration does create both a need and an opportunity for new forms of citizenship and self-rule, but we share with Keating the conclusion that the end of exclusive state sovereignty entails neither the end of states nor the end of nations and national self-determination. Rather, it opens up new opportunities for post-sovereign models of citizenship and self-determination wherein democracy will continue to be organized around national communities of fate, but in a political system that provides for a more equitable distribution of sovereignty among majority and minority nations in multinational states (Keating, 2001: vi–ix; see also MacCormick, 1999: 142). In this system of multilevel governance, there also needs to be room for regional and global level transnational institutions to cope with the democratic deficit. However, these institutions will not replace but rather will operate parallel to self-determining national polities, and in fact will continue to derive their authority and mandate through the direct participation and consent of the representatives of their constituent nations (Marks et al., 1996: 346; Wendt, 1999: 130–2; Kymlicka, 1999: 122–3).

The resilience of national identity

In our view, then, effective and democratic governance will continue, for the foreseeable future, to be organized on the basis of populations characterized by national identities. One of the most persuasive arguments in favour of this position is that the postnationalist claim regarding the dissolution of national identity is simply not borne out by the available evidence. In fact, national identities remain remarkably resilient at both the state and substate levels, and transnational identities show little signs of increased momentum.[7] Moreover, the age-old connection between territory and national identity is as resilient and powerful as it ever was, particularly among stateless nations

(Connor, 1999: 164–7; Keating, 2001: 57–98).[8] For example, Eurobarometer polls from the early 1970s onwards show little evidence of a shift away from local, regional or national identities towards an exclusively or even primarily European identity (Deflem and Pampel, 1996; Norris, 2001: 157). Granted, the data clearly demonstrate that there are multiple and overlapping identities (for example, feeling both Basque and Spanish), but it is significant that these identities are limited to the different territorial levels within the state and rarely extend to include the European level.[9] Evidence gathered from World Values Survey data covering the periods 1990–1 and 1995–7 produces similar patterns, with 47 per cent citing a primary identification with their locality or region of the country and 38 per cent citing a primary identification with their nation. A cosmopolitan identification with one's continent or the world as a whole is not inconsequential at 15 per cent of those surveyed, but it is significantly outweighed by more localized territorial identities. In fact, only 2 per cent of those surveyed considered themselves pure cosmopolitans (Norris, 2000: 161).

Indeed, globalization may even serve as a means of reinforcing rather than dissolving distinctive national identities and loyalties. In one scenario this can take the form of a defensive reaction to protect a particular national community and to preserve its autonomy in the face of external interference or control. This sort of defensive nationalism is often portrayed as irrational or bloody-minded tribalism (Barber, 1992; Held, 1999: 108) but it can also be viewed as a democratic impulse to preserve and promote what is valuable and essential to any national community. In another scenario, regional and global integration may even be actively pursued by nationalists as a conscious strategy of shoring up a distinctive national identity and increasing support for the goal of national self-determination, or even independence. This argument has been made persuasively in the case of the member states of the European Union (Millwood, 1992; Mayall, 1999: 502), and also in the case of their substate nations such as Catalonia, Flanders, Scotland and Wales (MacCormick, 1996; Requejo, 1999: 278). There is also evidence that nationalist leaders in Québec pursued increasing transnational trade and financial integration as a means of enhancing the province's economic viability and versatility and thereby lowering the perceived costs of independence among voters (Meadwell and Martin, 1996; CRIC, 2001: 12; Newman, 2000: 31–2). Moreover, a strong sense of attachment to a regional identity does not require a rejection of global institutions. The Inuit Circumpolar Conference

(ICC), which seeks to promote the rights of the Inuit at the international level, could not have come into being without the help of global forms of communication, technology and travel. Even though it works to ensure the preservation of Inuit customs and traditions at the local level, it uses global technologies, such as the internet and distance education, not only to disseminate information about Inuit culture to non-members – thereby creating an awareness of Inuit culture as a living, thriving culture – but also to provide members of this culture with opportunities to practise and promote it. The message of the Inuit people is clear and is repeated by other substate national or Aboriginal peoples across the globe: there is a recognition that globalization can pose a threat to local cultural norms but this threat can be curtailed if these groups harness the potential of globalization for their own purposes. Another example of this is 'Wales. World Nation' – the particular strategy of devolved Wales for presenting itself to the world and articulating its vision and strategy for the collective future of those residing in Wales.[10] Globalization offers substate national and Aboriginal peoples the opportunity to put themselves on the map like never before.

It is not even clear that the populations that would seem to have the most to gain from a postnational identity (refugees, migrant workers) are making this turn away from their traditional national identifications. Although a Turkish migrant worker in Germany would undoubtedly be glad to receive a full complement of social, economic and civil rights, it is not at all clear that this individual would gladly abandon her national identity in favour of some postnational alternative as part of the bargain. In fact, there is evidence in cases such as these that the opposite is true, in that migrant workers in countries such as Germany maintain a strong identification with their homeland nationality (Koopmans and Statham, 1999: 677–8). Granted, identification with the homeland nationalities tends to fade among second and third generation migrants (the children and grandchildren of the original guest workers), but it is replaced, not by a postnational identity, but instead by a stronger identification with the host, now 'home', country.

National identity as social construct

Postnationalists may retort that arguments such as these have the tendency to reify national identities and cast them as permanent and unchanging features of political life. As such, we may be charged with a failure to recognize national identities as social constructs that are subject to revision, reinvention or even rejection. As Daniel Weinstock argues, national identities are political-historical contingencies, formed by a combination of factors, including deliberate state policy (through its control of the machinery of state such as educational, legal and military institutions), habit formation arising from shared practices and common enterprises (for example, working together in common institutions) and sheer accident or chance (wars, treaties, conquests, etc.). The story involving the particular blend and sequence of these various factors can be told in numerous plausible versions, but the point is that national identity is a construction, and what has been constructed can (and in his view ought to be) purposefully deconstructed (Tambini, 2001: 196–8; Weinstock, 2001: 56–8). In reply, we fully accept that national identities are socio-political constructs, but accepting this point does nothing to blunt the force of the empirical arguments we have cited. For regardless of how national identities are constructed and reproduced, if particular groups of people do in fact manifest a strong sense of national identity, they will organize and mobilize around it. Therefore, in a straightforward practical political sense nationalism will continue to be an important force that politicians and social scientists will have to address in symbolic, institutional and policy terms. It may well be the case that national identities will someday run their course and be superseded by different forms of cosmopolitan or postnational identification, but this is neither the world we face at present nor in the near to medium future. For the foreseeable future nationalism, and substate nationalism, will continue to be key features of the contemporary global scene, features that cannot be sidestepped or dismissed by philosophical argumentation alone.

To be fair, a reasonable rejoinder to this argument may be that there is no reason a priori to conclude that new forms of transnational identity could not be constructed in the same way as national identities have been in the past, through a similar combination of deliberate policy, institution-building, habit formation and sheer accident (Weinstock, 2001: 57). In fact, for theorists like Weinstock, the creation of postnational identities and citizenship practices poses a seemingly uncomplicated challenge. Following the lessons learned from the nation-building practices of the modern state, the architects of the postnational world can simply avail themselves of similar institutional means of overcoming those very same national identities their predecessors helped create (Weinstock, 2001: 66). There are several important objections to this argument. The first is that there is much less of a consensus in the nation-building literature than Weinstock assumes on the question of how, and in terms of which contributing factors, national identities came to be formed and consolidated. Tambini, for example, identifies at least six different approaches to this question, all with different normative, theoretical and political starting points (Tambini, 2001: 196). So the supposed straightforward question of identity construction is already looking much more complicated than Weinstock's account might lead us to believe. How, for example, do we decide which of these six sets of assumptions regarding the relationship between institution-building and national identity is the correct one (assuming there are only six in the first place), when this question is the subject of such intense contestation in the literature? And presuming we could come to some sort of a decision in the case of national identity construction, how can we be confident that the same set of assumptions or conditions will meet with success in the construction of postnational identities? Why should we so confidently assume the same sets of variables are involved in these two cases? Moreover, what if several different sets of variables are relevant to the construction of postnational identities? And if there are several factors involved, which are most important? Are all of these variables equally essential to success, or are some of them more important than others? What balance of each is necessary, and is there a particular temporal ordering in which they must appear? Generally speaking, the postnationalist literature offers little, if any, guidance on these matters.

Another difficulty with Weinstock's account is that he identifies not just deliberate policy and institution-building as contributing factors in the construction of national identities, but also chance or historical accident and the use of coercion and violence by the state. Beginning with the first of these additional contributing factors, even if it were somehow possible to calculate the precise role played by chance in prior processes of identity formation, does not the very idea of chance imply that it is a set of circumstances that cannot be deliberately and successfully recreated? If so, where does this leave our chances for creating postnational identities? Similarly, to what degree did state coercion and violence contribute to the successful consolidation of national identities, and therefore how difficult will it be to construct postnational identities in an era where such measures would appear to be wholly unacceptable? Weinstock accepts that the postnationalist project is made all the more difficult by the inadmissibility of violent and coercive measures to processes of transnational identity construction, but he provides no specific idea as to *how much more difficult* this project becomes, and does not entertain the very real possibility that it may render it impossible, at least in the near to medium term. To summarize the concerns of the last two paragraphs, the claim that the architects of a postnational future can learn from the lessons and techniques of their nationalist predecessors is ultimately lacking in persuasive power because its proponents are unable to say with any confidence or precision which lessons or techniques are relevant, how they are supposed to perform their function and what other factors are likely to contribute to their failure or their success.

The poverty of national partiality?

Postnationalists may be willing to acknowledge the persistence of national identities, but most will nevertheless argue that, from an ethical perspective, there are no convincing reasons why these identities are particularly deserving of our recognition and respect. In effect, they challenge the assumption that nations, as opposed to any other sort of identity community, are deserving of a 'special' right to self-determination and the rights and entitlements of citizenship that entails. This argument is frequently directed at substate nations whose claims to self-determination are dismissed as reactionary, tribalistic, irrational or otherwise unworthy of recognition and respect (Waldron, 1995: 100–2; Barry, 1998). Postnationalists argue that our goal should be to seek the transcendence both of national parochialisms and of the system of states in favour of a truly liberal universal human community and transnational institutions that will provide for individual needs without reference to differences of language, ethnicity, nationality or the like (Preuss, 1998: 149). In this postnationalist framework, the distribution of the rights and benefits of citizenship around the globe should be organized along something like the humanity principle as opposed to the principle of nationality. The ethical motivation of this critique is the observation that the principle of national partiality, and its affiliated doctrines of national self-determination and national citizenship, distracts us from our ethical obligations to those who are not fellow nationals, and inures us to forms of suffering and injustice of those who are not members of our national community. Nations may very well provide for the comfort, security and freedoms of their own members, but in this sense they are also self-serving and therefore difficult to justify in a world where the suffering and even death of non-members can be treated with almost casual disregard. In this view, the principles of national self-determination and national partiality have been a dismal failure in the face of monumental tragedies affecting those who are not part of 'our' nation and, therefore, not entitled to the range of rights, freedoms and protections which the state provides for 'our' citizens.

The power of this argument lies in the intuition that it is morally repugnant to stand by while non-nationals experience grievous injury, suffering, deprivation or even death when we, or our governments, are capable of making a difference to their plight. We share this intuition, but we are not persuaded that postnationalism offers a plausible means towards its resolution. We have already outlined a series of practical reservations regarding postnationalism, and here we would like to enter some normative reservations. The most significant of these is the observation that the simple transcendence of nationality or national identities provides no guarantee that people or governments will be any more attentive to inequalities, suffering and oppression than they are at present in a world where national identities retain their recognition and resilience. For example, is it really the case that national partiality is the *primary* driver of global inequality and the quiescence of more fortunate nations in the face of the suffering of outsiders? Or is it states' interests, their commitment to a particular international order or the political ideology of democratic majorities? And would the transcendence of nations and nationalism therefore necessarily remove these barriers to a more just and equal world? Political ideologies and the preferences they support can exist independently of nations and nationalism. Would transcendence of nations and nationalism necessarily have any positive impact in terms of increasing global justice? The answer to these questions is at best unclear. For example, there is plenty of evidence to suggest that existing global economic inequalities stem at least as much from an ideological commitment to neoliberal internationalism as they do from the principle of national partiality. Indeed, it is distinctly plausible that in a postnational world global inequality might be even more pronounced as a result of strict adherence to a radical neoliberal economic program implemented by institutions of postnational decision-making. The point to be taken here is that global inequality is equally possible in a world with or without nations and national self-determination.

To make a broader point, we have no good reason to believe that a postnational global community would be less separated by divisions, conflicts and inequalities attached to any of a variety of identity-related differences other than those based on nationality. Indeed, human history provides us with an abundance of examples that suggest otherwise. We have already pointed to some potential problems with ideological divisions that are historically rooted in class differences, but there are other examples. Religious identities provided the incentive in the Crusades and the Inquisitions, racial identity fuelled the oppression of apartheid-era South Africa and class identities helped drive the genocidal policies against the peasants or Kulaks of the former Soviet Union (Kuper, 1981: 147–9). What reason do we have to believe that similar events would be impossible or even unlikely in a postnationalist world? Indeed, is it not possible that divisions based on class, religion, political ideology, intelligence or even genetic stock would gain new prominence in the absence of national divisions, and themselves become an increasing source of mistrust, fear, discrimination and conflict? Even if it were possible to imagine a world where such divisions did not exist, individuals will continue to hold particular interests that will influence political decision-making, including issues of redistributive justice, the appropriate role of the state in legislating issues of conscience and the appropriate balance between the public and private spheres. There is more at issue here than simply the question of how to institutionalize a postnational political order – problems we have already flagged in the preceding sections of the chapter; there is also the question of what will motivate people to extend to all human beings the same degree of interest and ethical concern that they currently demonstrate towards co-nationals and various sub-communities within the nation. What is it about postnationalism that will suddenly move people to recognize and respect equally some trait or quality in all other human beings and which will thereby motivate them to extend their sense of ethical responsibility beyond their more local communities of fate? National solidarities have not eliminated violence, inequality and oppression and in many cases have even contributed to their increase. Nevertheless, the bottom line is that postnationalists have failed to demonstrate that a world wherein national differences have been transcended constitutes an adequate, let alone better, normative alternative. Postnationalists have identified a clear normative ideal, but they have not provided an adequate political theory that explains how that normative ideal can be achieved in concrete socio-historical circumstances.

In this sense, postnationalism fails on two distinct levels. First, its assurances that a world without nations or states offers more hope for the plight of stateless peoples or populations suffering at the hands of ruthless or uncaring regimes are fundamentally unconvincing. Indeed, postnationalists cannot even assure such populations that the limited assistance and relief they currently receive from states or international organizations (of states) will be matched in a postnationalist world order. Second, for those populations who continue to assert the right to self-determination as the basis on which citizenship and secure and democratic self-government is to be constructed, postnationalism has equally little to offer. Postnationalism may provide a valuable critique of some of the shortcomings of national partiality, but it fails to demonstrate why or how some alternative form of transnational community of fate is capable of replacing nations as an effective associative basis for citizenship and democratic self-government in the modern world (Smith, 1995a: chap. 6).

For all its imperfections in practice, the principle of national self-determination continues to be the most viable model upon which citizenship and self-government can be organized in the contemporary world. Moreover, unlike postnationalism, its proponents have articulated a rich body of theory that explains the empirical and normative import of nationalist assumptions. To summarize some of the more important theoretical observations, the principle of nationality continues to serve as one of the key means of demarcating the political units within which political participation and democratic self-government are realized (Nodia, 1994; Harty, 1999; Murphy, 2001b, 2003). Nations as communities of fate and solidarity also continue to play a central role in facilitating stable governance, the proper functioning of liberal-democratic institutions, the assignment and protection of citizen rights and responsibilities, the realization of individual autonomy and the conditions for meaningful political deliberation (Tamir, 1993: chap. 6; Kymlicka, 1995: chaps. 5–6; Kymlicka, 2001a: 225–8). Moreover, people continue to be profoundly attached to their national identities, which provide them with a sense of security and belonging and frequently with a sense of pride, accomplishment and self-worth (Margalit and Raz, 1990: 439–61; Taylor, 1994; Connor, 1999: 164–6). It is not necessary to hold, as some critics of nationalism seem to suggest, either that nations are the only type of political community with which people strongly identify or that they are the only type of political community that currently supplies the sorts of goods described above (Weinstock, 2001: 59–62). For example, there is no denying the importance of more localized communities of fate in this regard (Norris, 2001: 161). The point is rather that national identities are one of the most significant and abiding forms of self-identification and association characteristic of the modern period, and that national communities continue to play an essential part in the secure realization of the most basic human rights, benefits and entitlements.

One final point bears consideration. Postnationalists need to consider the likelihood that the denial of claims to national self-determination may lead to the inflammation and radicalization of nationalist claims, the consequences of which in turn include civil unrest and the real possibility of violence and bloodshed (Horowitz, 1991: 224; Connor, 1999: 169–70; Kymlicka and Opalski, 2002: 224). On its face, this appears to be more of a pragmatic than a normative objection to postnationalism, but in fact it is a bit of both. There is a tendency, when facing questions of unity and stability, to conceptualize them as purely a matter of pragmatic political deliberation, considerations which must then be traded off against more purely ethical or normative concerns. This is partially accurate in the sense that the practicality and viability of political arrangements must in a sense be weighed against the imperatives of ideal justice; however, it is important not to lose sight of the fact that these so-called practical considerations themselves have a deeply normative component, which is their implications for the safety and well-being of the communities and the individuals concerned. Hence, it is not as if the choice is simply between what is right and what is feasible; rather, it is about what is both right and feasible under a given set of circumstances.

Conclusion

Our aim in this chapter has not been to celebrate the state's continuing monopoly in terms of defining and implementing citizenship regimes, but rather to demonstrate that the idea of a postnational alternative which seeks the complete transcendence of the state system and the principle of national self-determination is both unrealistic and maybe even counterproductive. Although we find common cause with some of these theorists in the challenge they pose to the doctrine of exclusive and undivided state sovereignty, we are not persuaded by their vision of a world without nations and states. There may indeed come a day when nations and states are thoroughly irrelevant from an empirical and a normative point of view, but that day is neither upon us nor close at hand. In the meantime, national identities provide an imperfect but nevertheless valuable source of solidarity and mutual concern, and a solid foundation for distributing the rights and entitlements of citizenship. In the absence of a more powerful and promising alternative, we should be very wary of calls for their transcendence. For their part, states continue to be the most important institutional means of securing and implementing the basic rights, entitlements and protections associated with citizenship, both within and beyond their own borders. This is not to say that the state system does not have profound practical and ethical shortcomings, for indeed it does. Nevertheless, as we see it, these shortcomings should be taken as incentive for state reform rather than state replacement.

Conclusion

The political world we inhabit at the beginning of the twenty-first century is still very much a world of nations and states. Yet it is not the same world of nations and states that emerged in the aftermath of the previous century's two great wars. Instead, its contours and political trajectories have been challenged, and in places transformed, by immensely powerful forces, both internal and external to the nation-state. These forces have thrown into question both the connection between self-determination and exclusive state sovereignty, and the link between national identity and citizenship: relationships that have provided the very backbone of domestic and international politics in the modern period. Our primary focus in this book has been on a particular set of internal challenges to the idea of the *mononational* state as the sole legitimate site of citizenship and self-determination in the modern world. The challenge comes in the form of substate national and Aboriginal peoples seeking recognition of their equal right to self-determination, and for differentiated forms of citizenship in terms of which these rights can be exercised within the context of a *multinational* state. In this book we set out to defend a model of multinational citizenship, grounded in basic principles of democracy, that recognizes an equal right of self-determination for majority and minority nations, built around an understanding of sovereignty that is shared or distributed among state, substate and possibly suprastate actors.

We have developed this defence of multinational citizenship in relation to a parallel set of external challenges to the nation-state, this time from a cosmopolitan or postnationalist point of view. Postnationalists argue that the forces of regional and global integration have drastically eroded, if not destroyed, the empirical and normative foundations of state sovereignty and the doctrine of national self-determination. Postnationalists conclude that, in order to keep pace with the practical and normative imperatives of an increasingly interdependent world 'without borders', we must look to transnational forms of citizenship, political community and democratic governance that are not constrained by the arbitrary and increasingly irrelevant paradigms of nations and states.

One of the central aims of this book has been to demonstrate that the case for a postnational world order has been overstated. In empirical terms, states have not been replaced as the most important and powerful actors in the global arena. While there is no doubting the fact that regional and global integration has altered the way that states exercise sovereignty at home and abroad, the evidence supports neither predictions of the state's imminent demise nor the anticipated rise of any viable transnational actor capable of taking its place. Similarly, territorially grounded national identities and corresponding forms of political community are not inexorably giving way to transnational forms of identification and community as the postnationalist thesis would lead us to expect. This is especially true at the substate level, where Aboriginal peoples and minority nations continue to press vigorously for the recognition and implementation of their right to self-determination. There may come some time in the distant future when nationality is no longer relevant to citizenship, but for now, and for the foreseeable future, citizenship and self-determination will continue to find their normative locus in territorially grounded national communities. Looking back on the previous chapter, we also remain unconvinced by postnationalism as a normative alternative to national self-determination. To be fair, this stems at least partly from the fact that the primary object of our respective studies differ: while we seek to address the concerns of subordinated substate nations, their focus tends to be directed to the concerns of non-nationals and various stateless populations (for example, refugees, internally displaced populations, migrant workers). Hence the questions of rights of substate nations are often not even raised in the postnationalist framework, at least not explicitly (Archibugi et al., 1998: 198–228). Nevertheless, our normative enterprises come into direct conflict to the extent that postnationalists call for the complete transcendence of the world of national communities and national self-determination, which presumably means at both the state and substate levels. As we have tried to demonstrate, postnationalism first of all fails to deal justly with the democratic claims to self-determination of substate nations, a claim whose legitimacy remains largely unconsidered in their normative framework. Second, as we argued in chapter 6, postnationalism fails on its own terms, since it cannot establish with any reasonable degree of confidence that a postnational world order can deliver and distribute justice with a comparable, let alone superior, degree of efficacy than a world where nations and states continue to thrive.

We draw these conclusions with full knowledge of the many profound ethical shortcomings of the state system in the face of humanitarian disasters, oppressive and murderous domestic regimes, and the plight of stateless peoples whose search for even the most minimal securities and entitlements of citizenship are met with hostility, suspicion or indifference. The true value of postnationalist thought is its capacity to bring these ethical shortcomings to our attention, and to demand that they be addressed. Where we part company with postnationalists is in our conclusion that the most realistic means of addressing these ethical shortcomings lies in the reform or augmentation of the international system of states rather than its wholesale replacement. This is consistent with the ethical realist approach we alluded to in chapter 6. Such an approach directs us to seek ethical ideals to which prevailing institutions and political practices should aspire, but nevertheless ideals which we feel have a reasonable chance of being realized, given existing political circumstances and constraints. As we indicated in chapters 1 and 6, a segment of the postnationalist school of thought has begun to articulate precisely such a middle-ground position, seeking a complementarity among the principles of state sovereignty and national self-determination, on the one hand, and the recognition of rights and obligations beyond the borders of particular nations and states, on the other (Nielsen, 1999; Lu, 2000; Kymlicka, 2001b: 324; Turner, 2002). This is promising work, whose scope and detail needs to be expanded, nowhere more so than in the area of determining how such theoretical models can be translated into political practice.

But this is not the task we set for ourselves in this book. Our own project has proceeded along a parallel track. In our vision of multinational citizenship, the same fundamental challenges to the nation-state identified by postnationalists create both a need and an opportunity for a greater acceptance and recognition of the political demands of stateless nations. We have first of all tried to show that the recognition, and institutionalization, of claims to self-determination at the substate level need not be perceived as a threat to the state, and may in fact play a defining role in its stability, prosperity and survival. Secession, the long-held fear of states harbouring minority nations, is not the only viable means of satisfying claims to self-determination at the substate level, nor is it an option desired by the majority of populations struggling to secure this basic democratic right within a multinational state. Moreover, the more difficult it becomes for states to claim that minority nationalism is necessarily a threat to their survival, the more difficult it becomes for states to perpetuate the normative double standard by means of which their own claims to self-determination are used to trump those articulated by their substate nations. Indeed, as we have demonstrated with examples throughout the book, and particularly in chapter 5, states have already engaged in processes of distributing or sharing their sovereignty with the substate nations and Aboriginal peoples in their midst. Countries like Belgium, Canada and Spain have a relatively longer historical experience with this sort of practice, but even traditionally unitary countries like the United Kingdom and New Zealand have devolved substantial powers and authorities to substate nations or Aboriginal peoples in their midst. We believe this is a trend in political development that will continue in the decades to come, and we have constructed a positive vision of the broad outlines we feel those developments should take. In particular, we have emphasized the need to transform the stubbornly persistent model of the mononational state with forms of citizenship and belonging that speak to the rights, identities and solidarities of the plurality of national communities within contemporary multinational states. We have also emphasized the need for states to relinquish their comprehensive sovereignty over their substate nations, and for parties on both sides of the fence to imagine a greater range of institutional designs that can bridge the gap between state domination and secession.

Finally, throughout the book we have also been at pains to demonstrate that political mobilization in favour of self-determination for substate national and Aboriginal peoples should be conceptualized as part of the broader trend towards democratization that has been sweeping the globe. Our model of multinational citizenship seeks to place democratic decision-making and institutional design more firmly in the hands of the communities whose fates these institutions are intended to serve and protect. It seeks to minimize the capacity of states to interfere with or dominate the internal self-government of their constituent nations; to encourage institutions of shared and cooperative decision-making in areas of common or overlapping interest; and to build intergovernmental relationships anchored in the principles of equality of peoples and mutual consent. In setting this task for ourselves, we are aware of the many obstacles and constraints blocking the road to implementation, but we are persuaded that these are hurdles that can and must be overcome if there is to be a just and stable accommodation among nations that share a state.

Notes

1 Citizenship and Belonging

1 We use the terms 'substate nation' to refer to national groups which are territorially concentrated in one region of the state. We recognize that this terminological use actually contradicts the larger citizenship model we are advocating in that we are essentially arguing for plurinational or multinational states in which there is no hierarchy of nations. We rationalize the use of the term 'substate nation' on the grounds that we are describing current, not desired, reality. A second reason for using this term is that it will be more readily understood by the reader and should therefore not present any conceptual impediments to the comprehension of our analysis.

2 Although there is some controversy over whether it is appropriate to examine the institutions of the EU as constituting a 'superstate'. Andrew Moravcsik (2003) argues that the EU is effective and successful because it practises limited government.

3 We are not taking the view that democratic deficits engendered by the institutionalization of transnational forms of multilevel governance will disappear in our model of multinational citizenship. The challenge of creating multilevel decision-making institutions which are effective, but also accountable and democratic, remains. However, we believe that our model better serves the cause of democratization than competing models of cosmopolitan or postnational citizenship that foresee the transcendence of democratic self-rule at either the state or substate level. We develop this argument in greater detail below and in chapters 4 and 6.

4 We further develop these responses in chapter 3 (for liberal nationalists) and chapter 6 (for postnationalists).

5 Moore (2001) is an exception in that she uses case studies to argue her point and pays particular attention to the politics of nationalist demands.

6 Both Carens's insights and our own bear a certain resemblance to Rawls's (1971) concept of a reflective equilibrium between ideal theory and current political practice.

7 For example, recent survey data from Québec (2001) shows that 68 per cent of respondents said they would vote against outright independence in a referendum. The same survey revealed that the number of people who say that Québec will one day become an independent country continues to decline: only 23 per cent hold this view, while 69 per cent believe Québec will remain a part of Canada. Indeed, 54 per cent of respondents viewed sovereignty as an outdated idea (CRIC, 2002: 27–8). For the Basque Country,

in the July 2003 edition of the 'Sociometro vasco' (a poll conducted by the regional government of the Basque Autonomous Community), respondents were asked whether they were in favour of independence for the Basque Country. Results show that 22 per cent were unconditionally in favour of independence; 33 per cent said it would depend on the circumstances; 32 per cent said they were not in favour; and 13 per cent either did not know or did not have an answer. See 'Un de cada cinc bascos vol la independència i un terç més l'accepta segons les condicions', *Avui* (internet edition), 12 July 2003.

8 We use both primary and secondary sources when presenting the views of political parties or associations.

9 To date, party politics are not a part of the universe of local-level indigenous politics. However, in countries like New Zealand, where Māori make up a relatively larger portion of the population (15 per cent), and where special provision is made for Aboriginal parliamentary representation, Aboriginal peoples have become heavily involved in party politics, taking up party leaderships, forming Aboriginal political parties, and taking up senior ministerial posts when their party wins elections.

10 We are here limiting ourselves to cases where Aboriginals are living together in communities on land that is either recognized as theirs or is the subject of a land claim. For the most part, we do not consider the representation of Aboriginals living in urban centres, although we do look at hybrid cases such as the province-wide system of First Nations government under negotiations in Saskatchewan that will have jurisdiction both on and off-reserve (including urban areas).

11 It is possible that nationalists would abandon the secessionist option if shared sovereignty became a reality. In other words, shared sovereignty might satisfy all or most of secessionist demands and preferences.

2 Citizenship in Multination States: Historical Precedents

1 Cairns is silent on the nature of common citizenship (is it the citizenship of the majority nation?). Moreover, it is not clear whether it is based on nationhood or shared values. Finally, he has nothing to say about how this common citizenship is decided and by whom. For another account of common citizenship see Parekh (1999).

2 The literature tends to use the term 'minority' when referring to substate national groups in the inter-war period and we follow that convention here. However, we agree with Michael Keating's (2001: 20) definition of minority nations, viz., 'groups located territorially within a wider nationality but who do not identify with it, often because they identify with a group elsewhere, including one in another state'. In our view, this is not the

same as a substate nation, which does not usually identify with a group in another state. Minority nations are particular to the circumstances of inter-war East–Central Europe, which was marked by the disintegration of empires.

3 For a discussion of the various arguments deployed to lay claim to territory, see Moore (2001: chap. 7).

4 Wilson's speeches can be found in various collected sources. We refer the reader to the series edited by Princeton University Press, which includes all important letters, speeches, interviews, press conferences and public papers on Woodrow Wilson.

5 The politicization of the cultural revival movement by regional social elites corresponds to phase B in Hroch's model.

6 As we will argue in the next chapter, many contemporary liberal nationalists also base claims to self-determination on cultural arguments. For a critique of this position, see Murphy (2001b).

7 We do not wish to overstate this possibility: obviously Jewish minorities in Europe faced systematic discrimination even when they were ethnically members of the majority nation.

8 Another informative discussion of this problem is found in Seton-Watson (1975).

9 Compare this position with that advocated by contemporary substate nationalist parties, such as the Scottish National Party: 'On all six key economic tests, small European countries do best. We could do just as well. Yet we're lagging behind countries such as Luxembourg, Ireland, and Iceland. And why is this [that small countries perform better economically]? Because all these small countries have the power to compete on their own terms. They are led by politicians whose utmost priority is about creating a better future for their people and their country. They have the advantage of sitting at Europe's top table and arguing for their own interests and industries' (SNP, 2003: 27).

10 We have already noted that there is a tension in the work of liberal nationalists around the integrative function of citizenship: they support it and are concerned that their own work might run counter to it. Our own criticism is that the integrative function of citizenship does not stand or fall on a national culture. We will have more to say about this in chapter 3.

11 For example, the Spanish Constitution (s. 158) states that 'With the aim of redressing interterritorial economic imbalances and implementing the principle of solidarity, a compensation fund shall be set up for investment expenditures'. The Interterritorial Compensation Fund, as it is formally known, is a system of redistribution across the seventeen Autonomous Communities of Spain that is managed through a legal framework set out in the Organic Law on the Financing of the Autonomous Communities (LOFCA). But two of the 'have' regions in Spain – Basque Country and

Catalonia – are also strongly nationalist and object to the fact that their money is supporting members of nations other than their own. For a commentary on the relationship between the fund and the promotion of diversity and equality, see Castells (2000).

12 The Commission came to three main conclusions, each of which spoke to the need for provincial governments to receive 'own-source revenues' (the tax monies collected from residents of a given province) so that they can assume responsibility for programs and policies in their jurisdiction and be held accountable by the taxpayers residing in their jurisdiction. See Québec (2002: 157).

13 An alternative interpretation of the Scottish case is that the more individualistic and *laissez-faire* policies of the Thatcher era were increasingly in conflict with the arguably more collectivist and welfare state oriented predispositions of the Scottish public (Keating, 1996; Brown et al., 1998), the end result of which was more Scottish citizens questioning the historic place of Scotland in the United Kingdom. By placing social policy under the authority of a Scottish Parliament, devolution can then be seen as a means of removing a source of disintegrative tension by reassuring the Scottish citizenry that their distinctive identities and interests can still be achieved within, rather than outside of, the United Kingdom.

3 Liberal Nationalism

1 This literature is too extensive to reference in a comprehensive manner, but we can point to a few classic studies. Materialist accounts include Tilly (1975), Gellner (1983), Downing (1992), Mann (1992). Institutionalist accounts include Levi (1988), North (1990) and Spruyt (1994). Historical accounts include Colley (1992) and Boyd (1997).

2 Difference theorists differ from one another in terms of the emphasis they place on the importance of the individual in group-differentiated theories of justice. Young, for example, is adamantly opposed to group-differentiated theories of justice that are willing to sacrifice the rights of the individual for the greater good or unity of the group. Instead, the liberal commitment to individual freedom and the consequent plurality of definitions of the good must be preserved in any group-differentiated conception of justice (Young, 1990: 36–7). See also Young (1995).

3 See also Waldron (1995), Fierlbeck (1996), Barry (1998) and Tempelman (1999).

4 In her earlier work Young was reluctant to accede to decentralized power vested in autonomous or independent communities (Young, 1990: 249–50). However, in her more recent writings, Young has shown greater support

for claims to self-determination for Aboriginal and substate national groups which are currently subjected to state domination (Young, 2000a, 2000b).

5 The causes for the emergence of late twentieth-century nationalism in East and West Europe are probably quite different but have not been systematically compared in the theoretical or case-study literature on nationalism. In part, this is due to the different time periods for their emergence and the catalyst of the downfall of communism for setting the context for nationalism in East–Central Europe. Yet there are crosswalks between the arguments used for the two different regions, particularly those which focus on markets as organizing principles. So, Claus Offe has argued for East–Central Europe, the absence of a market in the immediate post-communist period meant that societies had to fall back on a pre-capitalist organizing principle: ethnicity. It was not possible to distinguish citizens along class lines but it was possible to do so along ethnic lines. Similarly, arguments for the emergence of substate nationalism in Western Europe draw on levels of economic development. Here again, the market is always assumed: there are economically 'backward' nations which fall back on their national identity and economically backward states which prompt thriving regional national groups to mobilize around their ethnic identity.

6 The idea of a hierarchy of nations and civilizations was a dominant one among thinkers along the entire range of the political spectrum in the nineteenth century. It became one of the primary justifications (often after the fact) of the second wave of European colonialism (Tully 1993; Kymlicka, 1995 52–3, 69–70) and is an idea that continues to command support amongst some twenty-first-century liberal scholars (Flanagan, 2000: 27–47).

7 For similar reconstructions of the liberal nationalist argument see Harty (1999), Moore (1999), Patten (1999), Murphy (2001b).

8 The Parti Québécois was in power in 1976–85 and 1989–2003.

9 The cases in question are, respectively, *R. v. Van der Peet* [1996] 4 CNLR 177, *Delgamuukw v. B. C.* [1998] 1 CNLR 14, and *R. v. Pamajewon* [1996] 4 CNLR 164. See *www.lexum.umontreal.ca*. For additional discussion of these cases see Asch (1999), Barsh and Henderson (1997), Morse (1997) and Murphy (2001a).

10 The case in question is *Members of the Yorta Yorta Aboriginal Community v Victoria* [2002] HCA 58 (12 December 2002), also available on the website of the Australasian Legal Information Institute (AustLII) at *www.austlii.edu.au*.

11 For commentary on additional shortcomings of the consultations, see CAP (2002: 7); AFN (2001b); and Stimson (2001).

12 The 1989 resolution was debated in a parliamentary commission and then passed by the Parliament; in 1998, the resolution was debated and passed in the general session of Parliament. The debates give an indication of the different interpretations of self-determination (Catalunya, 1989, 1998a). The 1998 Resolution was passed, ostensibly, to mark the 50th anniversary

of the UN Declaration of Human Rights and both the Declaration and the Resolution were subsequently published together by the Catalan parliament to drive home the link between them (Catalunya, 1998b). There are civil society groups dedicated to promoting ideas and public debates around self-determination, for example, the Fòrum Català pel Dret a l'Autodeterminació (Catalan Forum for the Right to Self-Determination), at *www.focda.catalunyaonline.com/index.htm*

13 See 'Spain Vows to Block Basque Referendum' (31 July 2001), *Guardian Unlimited, www.guardian.co.uk/international/story/0,3604,529973,00.html.* Chapter 5 will examine the Catalan and Basque cases in greater detail.

14 The Canadian government's position is possibly not sustainable given that a referendum by all Canadians on whether or not Québec has the right to secede would not amount to a collective vote on the self-determination of Canadians. Moreover, Canadians have already 'self-determined', as is evident from the existence of their country, Canada. If the Québécois, or any other nation, wishes to self-determine, it does not make sense to have other nations participate in their process of self-determination. If the Catalans wish to self-determine as a nation, they will obviously not ask the Basques or Galicians or even the rest of Spain to take part in their collective vote. Interestingly, on the question of Aboriginal self-determination in Canada, the federal government has never insisted that all Canadians should vote in self-government referenda, possibly because Aboriginal self-determination does not amount to 'state breaking', although it has certainly 'broken up' the territory of some Canadian provinces.

15 The three questions were: (1) Under the Constitution of Canada, can the National Assembly, legislature or government of Quebec effect the secession of Quebec from Canada unilaterally? (2) Does international law give the National Assembly, legislature or government of Quebec the right to effect the secession of Quebec from Canada unilaterally? In this regard, is there a right to self-determination under international law that would give the National Assembly, legislature or government of Quebec the right to effect the secession of Quebec from Canada unilaterally? (3) In the event of a conflict between domestic and international law on the right of the National Assembly, legislature or government of Quebec to effect the secession of Quebec from Canada unilaterally, which would take precedence in Canada? See Reference re Secession of Quebec [1998] 2 SCR *www.lexum.umontreal.ca*

16 Both the federal government and the provincial government of Québec viewed the Court's pronouncements as a victory: the former applauded the decision that Québec does not have a unilateral right to secession while the latter noted that a strong democratic expression of self-determination on the part of Québec would place an obligation on the federal government to enter into negotiations.

17 The emphasis on clarity is due to two factors: first, in the 1995 Québec referendum on independence, the question that citizens voted on was notoriously ambiguous in its intent. Polls revealed that many Québécois did not in fact understand what they were voting for. Second, there was, and is, a debate over what constitutes a majority in a referendum on independence: the federal government argues that a substantial majority is required whereas the Parti Québécois maintains that 50 per cent + 1 is sufficient.

18 For discussion see McIvor (1992, 1995); Murphy (1996); Nahanee (1993).

19 *Ford v. Quebec* (A.G.) [1988] 2 *SCR* 712–89.

20 For discussion of this and some related Charter cases see Eisenberg (1994).

21 The position of the Welsh Language Board is that the use of the Welsh language has changed considerably in the period 1991–2001 and that the Census results are very mixed. While the population as a whole has 'taken ownership' of the language, primarily though gains in the south-east, there has been a decline of Welsh in the rural areas of the west and north in part due to out-migration. See *www.bwrdd-yr-iaith.org.uk/en/*

22 For an introduction to this material, see Rorty (1986, 1992); Geertz (1986); Kukathas (1992a, 1992b, 1997); Galston (1995); Kymlicka (1995: chap. 8); Fierlbeck (1996).

23 It is also important to note that the exclusion of these non-Aboriginal residents from participating in Sechelt institutions in no way affected their rights as citizens of their provincial and federal governments. Cases such as this are also relatively rare in Canada, where in most cases of territorial Aboriginal self-government, the Aboriginal people comprise the vast majority of the population on the lands in question.

24 For additional discussion of both these cases see Catt and Murphy (2002: chaps 3–7).

25 In this book, we unfortunately do not have the space to consider either the reaction of members of a substate nation to the presence of immigrants on their territory or the effect of these immigrants on the development of national identity in substate nations.

26 Although the issue of who should have a say in the political affairs of different 'nations' in the United Kingdom has been raised in the context of the 'West Lothian question'. Labour MP Tam Dalyell, whose constituency used to be called West Lothian, posed the original question: 'After devolution, why should Scottish MPs at Westminster be allowed to vote on English domestic matters while they would not be allowed to vote on Scottish domestic matters, which would be dealt with by the Scottish Assembly?' But the question is more commonly assumed to challenge the fact that Scottish members at Westminster would continue to vote upon English matters while MPs from England had lost the power to influence Scottish affairs, which had been devolved to Holyrood.

27 This argument echoes our own discussion of external self-determination in chaps 1 and 4.

28 Several English Canadian political leaders declared prior to the 1980 referendum that they would never negotiate economic association (free trade, common currency) with an independent Québec, which is thought to have influenced voters' decisions. The Clarity Act (2000), referred to above, rejects sovereignty-association as a clear option. According to the Act (s. 1.4), 'a clear expression of the will of the population of a province that the province cease to be part of Canada could not result from . . . a referendum question that envisages other possibilities in addition to the secession of the province from Canada, such as economic or political arrangements with Canada, that obscure a direct expression of the will of the population of that province on whether the province should cease to be part of Canada'.

29 These projects will be discussed in greater detail in chap. 5.

4 Multinational Citizenship

1 This chapter draws heavily on Murphy and Harty (2003: 188–93).

2 It should be noted that there are two issues at play with the First Nations Governance Act. The first is related to the process of drafting the Act: we noted in chap. 3 that some groups protest the fact that they were not involved as equal partners. Obviously, there are impediments to doing so: the parliamentary process in Canada does not permit extra-parliamentary representatives' direct involvement. So consultation processes are viewed (by the federal government) as a legitimate alternative. The second issue is related to the content of the bill: there is definitely a division of opinion on the bill itself, but the first issue often eclipses the second. The nature of the controversy surrounding the bill is such that to engage in a debate about its substance is viewed as an endorsement of the federal government's approach to the Act. As the National Aboriginal Women's Association has noted, this is 'too bad because [then] nobody learns what the bills [of the Act] would do'. See 'Native Women Back Overhaul of Indian Act', *Winnipeg Free Press* (6 September 2003), p. B5.

3 Consociationalism has been used in polities where societal cleavages would otherwise impede the attainment of democratic majorities. It is used less frequently where the cleavages are ethnically based for two reasons. First, ethnic groups are normally associated with a territory, thus opening up the door to a devolved or federal solution. Second, in its classic formulation (Lijphart, 1968), consociationalism depended on the commitment of all sub-units to the 'nation'. In cases of ethnic cleavages, this condition cannot easily be fulfilled. However, in practice, it is possible for ethnic groups to commit to the state or to the idea of social cohesion. However, consociationalism has been attempted in some situations of ethnic cleavages, such as Northern Ireland.

[4] This point is made quite forcefully in the international relations literature on the causal factors explaining the end of civil wars. See Walter (2002).

[5] Bhikhu Parekh also makes this argument in the case of multicultural groups in liberal states (1991: 191–2, 196–7).

[6] The types of protest range from criminal action against the property of non-Welsh settlers in Wales to, as in Ceredigion, withholding a portion of the council tax to signal opposition to the council's approval of a plan to build new houses in the area. The protest movement in Ceredigion is known as 'Cant Ceredigion'.

[7] Dafydd Meirion, 'Victory for Welsh language pressure group in the housing market as it turns its sights to English names on Welsh mountains', 28 April 2003, *www.eurominority.org/version/fr/actualite-detail*

[8] This bears a distinct similarity to Kant's discussion of 'cosmopolitan right': the idea that the peoples of the world have been thrown together by the circumstances of history and now need to work out terms on which they can coexist on mutually acceptable terms. For a discussion of this idea in a contemporary context see Waldron (2000).

5 Multinational Citizenship and Demands for Self-Determination

[1] The Cabinet and Senate are consociational. A network of intergovernmental collaborative agreements as well the Court of Arbitration manage interterritorial conflict.

[2] In a survey conducted at the time of the 1995 general elections, respondents were asked to self-identify along a range of options (exclusive Flemish/Walloon through to exclusively Belgian): in Flanders and Wallonia, approximately 40 per cent of respondents reported that they were equally Flemish/Walloon and Belgian.

[3] VU split into two political parties in Fall 2001: N-VA and Spirit. N-VA carries on VU's agenda more clearly than does Spirit, which describes itself as progressive and regionalist. Spirit later merged with the Flemish Socialists.

[4] Although the last province, Newfoundland, was only incorporated in 1949. The original four provinces were: Québec, Ontario, Nova Scotia and New Brunswick. The westward expansion took place between 1870 and 1905. Prince Edward Island, in the east, entered Confederation in 1873.

[5] Major resource co-management and revenue-sharing agreements were concluded between Québec and both the James Bay Cree and the Inuit of Makivik. Copies of the agreements, information bulletins and press releases can be found on the website of the Secrétariat aux affaires autochtones du Québec, *www.mce.gouv.qc.ca/d/html/d0466001.html*. As of 2003, negotiations were also under way among the federal government and Aboriginal

representatives of the territorial and self-governments in Nunavut and the Northwest Territories on the devolution of revenues and responsibilities pertaining to the development of natural resources (Brethour, 2003).

6 Significantly, no Québec government, even that of the Liberal Party, will sign it.

7 There are varying interpretations of voters' motivations for the 1995 referendum. One very plausible one is that they did not understand the question: it was too convoluted. A second one was favoured by the then first minister, Jacques Parizeau, when he conceded defeat following the referenda results: the 'ethnic' and 'money' vote proved to be risk averse and therefore cost the Québécois their independence. Unfortunately, this remark cost Parizeau the leadership of the party; he resigned the day after his speech.

8 The quote in fact accomplishes two things: it acknowledges the requirement of a clear question, as laid out in the Clarity Act, and it makes reference to self-determination by stating that the Québécois will say 'yes to themselves' ('se dire Oui à eux-mêmes')

9 For background on this period see Weaver (1981).

10 Although it is important to acknowledge the positive role played by Canadian courts in securing the recognition of Aboriginal rights by recognizing Aboriginal peoples as original sovereigns. More recently, the courts have decided that Aboriginal rights derive from the distinctiveness of their cultures. See Asch (1999), Murphy (2001a), Borrows (2002).

11 These included the 1983 Penner Report, the 1992 Charlottetown Accord and the 1995 Final Report of the Canadian Royal Commission on Aboriginal Peoples.

12 The province of Newfoundland recently completed a Royal Commission that examined its place in the federation in response to the devastation of its main economic activity, the fishery, and the consequent out-migration of nearly 12 per cent of its population. The outcome of the Commission was to seek a new partnership with Canada, placing pressure on the federal government to respond. See Newfoundland and Labrador (2003).

13 The federal government has responsibility for English and French language minorities living in various provinces (for example, Nova Scotia, New Brunswick, Québec, Ontario, Manitoba and Alberta).

14 See, for example, the Act Relating to Self-Government for the Sechelt Indian Band (Canada, 1986); and the Umbrella Final Agreement between the Government of Canada, the Council for Yukon Indians, and the Government of the Yukon (Canada, 1993). For an informative discussion of the latter agreement, and the specific issue of paramountcy, see Hogg and Turpel (1995).

15 A copy of the press release can be found on the website of the Secrétariat aux affaires autochtones du Québec. See *www.mce.gouv.qc.ca/d/html/d0466001.html*.

16 See also the statements by Rosemarie Kuptana, President of the Inuit Tapirisat of Canada, and Yvon Dumont of the Métis National Council, both quoted in Canada (1992: 6).

17 See in general the Final Report of the Canadian Royal Commission on Aboriginal Peoples (Canada, 1995c), and in particular the section devoted to the residential school system in vol. 1, pp. 333–409.

18 It is worth noting that for groups like the Inuit, whose remoteness from the burgeoning Canadian state meant that its experience of colonialism was relatively less intense, the level of mistrust of the Canadian government is relatively less pronounced. See, for example, Ittinuar (1985).

19 See Hawkes (forthcoming). The Saskatchewan strategy of negotiating an integrated layering of institutions to implement indigenous self-determination is one that is gaining increasing attention in both Australia (Smith, 2002: 25–7) and Canada (IOG, 2000).

20 The section on Spain draws on Harty (2002, 2004).

21 There is the further issue of what Aznar means by the same representation: does he mean the same party representatives who drafted it, the same parliamentary deputies who ratified it, or the same people who voted on it in a referendum?

22 Overall, the all-Spain turnout for the referendum was a disappointment: 33 per cent of eligible voters stayed home; 58 per cent of total eligible voters (or 88 per cent of those who actually voted) supported the constitution while 8 per cent rejected it.

23 When asked to choose among alternative models of the state, the majority of Catalan (51.7 per cent) and Galician (61.9 per cent) respondents selected 'a state of autonomous communities like we have at present'. Basque respondents were fairly evenly divided among three options: 'a state of autonomous communities like we have at present' (33.2 per cent); 'a federal state in which communities have more power' (33.9 per cent); and 'a state which gives nationalities the chance to become independent' (29.8 per cent). See *www.opa151.com*

24 However, at different times, either the Partido Popular (PP) or the Partido Socialista Obrero de España (PSOE) has required the support of Catalan and Basque nationalist deputies in the Spanish Parliament in order to form a majority. During these periods, the nationalists were in a position to bargain some favourable policies or arrangements with the government, but none of these was of the magnitude of a revised Autonomy Statute or a rereading of the constitution.

25 CiU is a coalition of two parties: Convergència democràtica de Catalunya and Unió democràtica de Catalunya.

26 The proposal is available in Catalan, French and English, although the English version is very abbreviated (5 pp compared to 91 pp in the Catalan version). These can be accessed at: *http://195.219.58.179/*

info/cdc/pubDoc.documents. Significantly, the text is not available in Castilian.

27 'Bases per a l'Estatut d'autonomia de Catalunya', available in Catalan and Castilian, at *www.socialistes.org*. Historically, the PSC has a large support base among Spanish migrants who came to Catalonia for economic reasons. As such, the party is very bilingual.

28 ERC is a republican party in a constitutional monarchy, which is one reason why it supports something approximating independence. The ideological conflict it faces is not unlike that which Ireland faced within the United Kingdom at the time of negotiating the Free State Treaty (1921). 'Constitució de L'Estat Lliure De Catalunya', available in Catalan only at *http://www.esquerra.org/arxius/estatut03.pdf*

29 Galician nationalist identity and popular nationalist mobilization is much weaker than in the other two substate nations and at the time this manuscript was completed (September 2003), the Bloque Nacionalista Galego (BNG), which has never ruled in the Galician regional government (Xunta de Galicia), had not produced a draft for a new Autonomy Statute.

6 Postnational Alternatives

1 The classic discussion of the relationship between liberty and authenticity can be found in Berlin (1984). For a reply see Taylor (1979).

2 We recognize that the potential for various actors to benefit from globalization is dependent on their respective goals, capacities and socioeconomic and political contexts (Newman, 2000: 31–4; Shulman, 2000: 373–5; Foreign Policy, 2002).

3 See the 'Declaration of Laeken' (2001) produced by REGLEG (Regions with Legislative Powers) which, among other things, seeks a strong role for regions in the democratization of the institutional system of the EU. See also the Assembly of European Regions (AER) amendments to the European Convention on the Future of Europe, at *www.are-regions-europe.org/*

4 For example, effective January 2000, Germany changed certain requirements in its citizenship laws, which made it easier for foreign workers (*Gasterbeiter*) and their families (including children born in Germany) to become German nationals. The new laws adopted the principle of *jus soli* for non-ethnic Germans born on German soil and facilitated citizenship by naturalization by reducing the length of residency requirement. However, dual citizenship is not allowed, which poses some conflicts for certain foreigners, who might not have any choice about relinquishing their birth nationality.

5 Even international NGOs such as Doctors Without Borders, whose *nom de*

guerre indicates a fundamentally postnationalist orientation, are dependent on the infrastructure of the international system of states which provides for the safe and secure transport of their volunteers and equipment and the stable and peaceful environment to which many of those volunteers will return once their overseas work is completed.

6 Indeed, prevailing state practice suggests that the recognition and implementation of transnational rights norms continues to be subordinated to the self-interest of the states concerned, and will ultimately give way to those interests when push comes to shove. For example, the so-called humanitarian intervention in Kosovo likely had as much to do with the desire to prevent a destabilizing regional war and the resulting economic chaos and massive refugee outflows, both of which had a potentially significant negative impact on the interests of the NATO allies. Moreover, a clear preference for the safety and well-being of their own as opposed to foreign nationals was evident in the decision of the allies not to commit ground troops to prevent more civilian deaths at the hands of the Serbian militias. Universal human rights norms also continue to take a back seat to economic interests and realpolitik, as evidenced in the willingness of the states of Europe and North America to overlook the egregious abuses of their economic and military partners such as Saudi Arabia, Israel, China, Pakistan and Russia.

7 Anecdotally, in the aftermath of 9–11 the ascendance of national identities was brought into the clearest relief. Not only have we been witness to a most intense American patriotic nationalism, we have also been reminded that questions of national self-determination and nation-building remain at the centre of conflicts in Afghanistan, Iraq, Israel–Palestine, Kashmir and Chechnya.

8 See also Smith (1995a: chap. 6); Shaw (1997: s. 4[D]); Holton (1998, 6–7); Joppke (1999: 279–80); Miller (2000: 165–6); Newman (2000: 25); Shulman (2000: 365).

9 See *europea.eu.int/comm./dg10/epo/ eb.html*

10 *www.walesworldnation.com*

References

Abizadeh, A. 2002. 'Does Liberal Democracy Presuppose a Cultural Nation? Four Arguments', *American Political Science Review*, 96, pp. 495–509.

Alfred, G. T. 1995. *Heeding the Voices of Our Ancestors*, Toronto: Oxford University Press.

—— 1999. *Peace, Power, Righteousness: An Indigenous Manifesto*, Toronto: Oxford University Press.

Almirall, V. 1994. *Lo Catalanisme*, Barcelona: Llibreria Verdaguer i Llibreria López, 1886; repr., Les millors obres de la literatura catalana, 22, Barcelona: Edicions 62 i 'la Caixa'.

Anaya, S. J. 1995. 'The Capacity of International Law to Advance Ethnic or Nationality Rights', in W. Kymlicka (ed.), *The Rights of Minority Cultures*, Oxford: Oxford University Press, pp. 321–30.

—— 1996. *Indigenous Peoples in International Law*, New York: Oxford University Press.

Archibugi, D., Held, D., and Köhler, M. (eds). 1998. *Re-imagining Political Community: Studies in Cosmopolitan Democracy*, Cambridge: Polity Press.

Aron, R. 1974. 'Is Multinational Citizenship Possible?', *Social Research*, 41/4, pp. 638–56.

Asch, M. 1999. 'From *Calder* to *Van der Peet*: Aboriginal Rights and Canadian Law, 1973–96', in P. Havemann (ed.), *Indigenous Peoples' Rights in Australia, Canada, and New Zealand*, Auckland: Oxford University Press, pp. 428–46.

Assembly of European Regions (AER). 2003. 'AER Proposals for Amendment of the Draft Constitutional Treaty', 10 April, Brussels, *www.are-regions-europe.org/PDF/CA_Main_Texts/ GB-convention-positionpaper.pdf*

Assembly of First Nations (AFN). 2001a. 'AFN's Key Messages on the Proposed Legislative Initiative on First Nations Governance', *www.afn.ca*.

Assembly of First Nations (AFN). 2001b. 'The AFN's Position on the Federal Legislative Initiative on First Nations Governance', *www.afn.ca/-Programs/Governance/position.html*.

Atkinson, D. 2000. 'Minorisation, Identity and Ethnolinguistic Vitality in Catalonia', *Journal of Multilingual and Multicultural Development*, 21/3, pp. 185–97.

Awashish, P. Forthcoming. 'From Board to Nation Governance: Eeyou Governance and Economic Development in Eeyou Istchee', in M. Murphy (ed.), *Reconfiguring Aboriginal–State Relations: Canada. The State of the Federation, 2003*, Montreal and Kingston: McGill-Queen's University Press.

Azcárate, P. de. 1945. *League of Nations and National Minorities: An Experiment*, trans. E. E. Brooke, Washington, DC: Carnegie Endowment for International Peace.

Barber, B. R. 1992. 'Jihad vs McWorld', *Atlantic Monthly* (March), pp. 1–13.

Barker, E. 1915. 'The Discredited State', *Political Quarterly*, 5, pp. 101–21.

Barry, B. 1998. 'The Limits of Cultural Politics', *Review of International Studies*, 24, pp. 307–19.

Barsh, R. L. 1994. 'Indigenous Peoples in the 1990s: From Subject to Object of International Law?', *Harvard Human Rights Journal*, 7, pp. 33–86.

—— and Henderson, J. Y. 1997. 'The Supreme Court's Van der Peet Trilogy: Naive Imperialism and Ropes of Sand', *McGill Law Journal*, 42, pp. 993–1009.

Beiner, R. 1995. 'Why Citizenship Constitutes a Theoretical Problem in the Last Decade of the Twentieth Century', in R. Beiner (ed.), *Theorizing Citizenship*, Albany, NY: State University of New York Press, pp. 1–28.

Beitz, C. R. 1999. 'Social and Cosmopolitan Liberalism', *International Affairs*, 75, pp. 515–29.

Béland, D., and Lecours, A. Forthcoming. 'The Politics of Territorial Solidarity: Sub-State Nationalism and Social Policy Reform in Canada, the United Kingdom and Belgium', *Comparative Political Studies*.

Bellamy, R., and Castiglione, D. 2000. 'The Uses of Democracy: Reflections on the European Democratic Deficit', in E. O. Eriksen and J. E. Fossum (eds), *Democracy in the European Union: Integration through Deliberation?*, London: Routledge, pp. 65–84.

Bentley, M. 1977. *The Liberal Mind, 1914–1929*, Cambridge: Cambridge University Press.

Berlin, I. 1984. 'Two Concepts of Liberty', in M. Sandel (ed.), *Liberalism and its Critics*, New York: New York University Press, pp. 15–36.

Bhabha, J. 1999. 'Belonging in Europe: Citizenship and Post-National Rights', *International Social Science Journal*, 51, pp. 11–23.

Blanke, R. 1993. *Orphans of Versailles: The Germans in Western Poland, 1919–1938*, Lexington: University Press of Kentucky.

Bonime-Blanc, A. 1987. *Spain's Transition to Democracy: The Politics of Constitution-Making*, Boulder, CO: Westview Press.

Borrows, J. 2000. 'Landed Citizenship: Narratives of Aboriginal Political Participation', in W. Kymlicka and W. Norman (eds), *Citizenship in Diverse Societies*, Oxford: Oxford University Press, pp. 327–42.

—— 2002. *Recovering Canada: The Resurgence of Indigenous Law*, Toronto: University of Toronto Press.

Bourne, A. K. 2002. 'Defending Basque Taxation Devolution in the European Union: The Price of European Integration', *International Journal of Iberian Studies*, 15/2, pp. 103–14.

Boyd, C. P. 1997. *Historia Patria: Politics, History, and National Identity in Spain, 1875–1975*, Princeton: Princeton University Press.

Brethour, P. 2003. 'A Territorial Ultimatum', *Globe and Mail*, web edition, Wednesday, 17 September.

Brown, A., McCrone, D., and Paterson, L. 1998. *Politics and Society in Scotland*, London: Macmillan.

Brubaker, R. 1996. *Nationalism Reframed: Nationhood and the National Question in the New Europe*, Cambridge: Cambridge University Press.

Buchanan, A. 1989. 'Assessing the Communitarian Critique of Liberalism', *Ethics*, 99, pp. 852–82.

—— 1991. *Secession: The Morality of Political Divorce from Fort Sumter to Lithuania and Quebec*, Boulder, CO: Westview Press.

—— 1995. 'The Morality of Secession', in W. Kymlicka (ed.), *The Rights of Minority Cultures*, Oxford: Oxford University Press, pp. 350–74.

—— 1998. 'What's so Special about Nations?', in J. Couture, K. Neilson and M. Seymour (eds), *Rethinking Nationalism*, Calgary: University of Calgary Press, pp. 283–309.

Cairns, A. C. 1993. 'The Fragmentation of Canadian Citizenship', in W. Kaplan (ed.), *Belonging: The Meaning and Future of Canadian Citizenship*, Montreal and Kingston: McGill-Queen's University Press, pp. 181–220.

—— 2000. *Citizens Plus: Aboriginal Peoples and the Canadian State*, Vancouver, University of British Columbia Press.

—— Courtney, J. C., MacKinnon, P., Michelmann, H. J., and Smith, D. E. (eds). 1999. *Citizenship, Diversity and Pluralism: Canadian and Comparative Perspectives*, Montreal and Kingston: McGill-Queen's University Press.

Cameron, David R. 2002. 'Canada', in A. L. Griffiths (ed.), K. Nerenberg (coord.), *Handbook of Federal Countries 2002*, Montreal and Kingston: Forum of Federations and McGill-Queen's University Press.

Campbell v. Attorney General (British Columbia) 2001 BCSC 1400.

Canada. 1986. *An Act Relating to Self-Government for the Sechelt Indian Band*, Ottawa: Statutes of Canada, 33–34–35 Elizabeth II, Chapter 27.

—— 1991. *The Path to Electoral Equality*, Committee for Aboriginal Electoral Reform, Royal Commission on Electoral Reform and Party Financing, Ottawa: Minister of Supply and Services.

—— 1992. Royal Commission on Aboriginal Peoples, *The Right of Aboriginal Self-Government and the Constitution: A Commentary*, Ottawa: Minister of Supply and Services.

—— 1993. *Umbrella Final Agreement between the Government of Canada, the Council for Yukon Indians, and the Government of the Yukon*, Ottawa: Minister of Supply and Services.

—— 1995a. *Aboriginal Self-Government: The Government of Canada's Approach to Implementation of the Inherent Right and the Negotiation of Aboriginal Self-Government*, Ottawa: Public Works and Government Services.

—— 1995b. Royal Commission on Aboriginal Peoples, *Aboriginal Self-Government: Legal and Constitutional Issues*, Ottawa: Minister of Supply and Services.

—— 1995c. Royal Commission on Aboriginal Peoples, *Final Report*, Ottawa: Minister of Supply and Services.

—— 1995d. Royal Commission on Aboriginal Peoples, *Treaty Making in the Spirit of Coexistence: An Alternative to Extinguishment*, Ottawa: Minister of Supply and Services.

—— 1997. *Gathering Strength: Canada's Aboriginal Action Plan*, Ottawa: Public Works and Government Services.

—— 1998. *Nisga's Final Agreement*, Ottawa: Federal Treaty Negotiation Office.

—— 2000. *Clarity Act, laws.justice.gc.ca/en/C-31.8/index.html.*

—— 2002. Commission on the Future of Health Care in Canada, *Building on Values: The Future of Health Care in Canada. Final Report*, Ottawa: The Privy Council Office.

Canovan, M. 2001. 'Sleeping Dogs, Prowling Cats and Soaring Doves: Three Paradoxes in the Political Theory of Nationhood', *Political Studies*, 49, pp. 203–15.

Carens, J. 1995. 'Aliens and Citizens: The Case for Open Borders', in W. Kymlicka (ed.), *The Rights of Minority Cultures*, Oxford: Oxford University Press, pp. 331–49.

—— 2000. *Culture, Citizenship and Community: A Contextual Exploration of Justice as Evenhandedness*, Oxford: Oxford University Press.

Carr, E. H. 1941. *The Future of Nations: Independence or Interdependence?*, London: Kegan Paul.

Castells, A. 2000. 'The Role of Intergovernmental Finance in Achieving Diversity and Cohesion: The Case of Spain', Working Paper 2002/2, Barcelona: Institut d'economia de Barcelona.

Catalunya. 1989, 1998a. *Butlletí Oficial del Parlament de Catalunya*, Barcelona: Generalitat de Catalunya.

—— 1998b. *Declaració Universal dels Drets Humans*, Barcelona: Generalitat de Catalunya.

Catt, H., and Murphy, M. 2002. *Sub-State Nationalism: A Comparative Analysis of Institutional Design*, London: Routledge.

Centre for Research and Information on Canada (CRIC). 2001. 'Trade, Globalization and Canadian Values', *The CRIC Papers*, Montreal: CRIC.

Cheah, P., and Robbins, B. (eds) 1998. *Cosmopolitics: Thinking and Feeling Beyond the Nation*, Minneapolis and London: University of Minnesota Press.

Chevrier, M. 1997. *Laws and Languages in Québec: The Principles and Means of Québec's Language Policy*, Québec: Ministère des Relations Internationales.

Christiansen, T. 1997. 'Second Thoughts on Europe's Third Level: The European Union's Committee of the Regions', *Publius Journal of Federalism*, 26/2, pp. 93–116.

——, Bórras-Alomar, S., and Rodriguez-Pose, A. 1994. 'Towards the "Europe of the Regions"? Evaluation and Reflection from a Critical Perspective', *Regional Politics and Policy*, 3/3, pp. 1–27.

Cobban, A. 1945. *National Self-Determination*, Royal Institute of International Affairs, Oxford: Oxford University Press.

—— 1969. *The Nation State and National Self-Determination*, London: Collins.

Coleman, W. D., and Perl, A. 1999. 'Internationalized Policy Environments and Policy Network Analysis', *Political Studies*, 47, pp. 691–709.

Colley, L. 1992. *Britons: Forging the Nation*, New Haven: Yale University Press.

Commission of the European Communities (CEC). 2001. *European Governance: A White Paper*, CEC Website, *europa.eu.int/comm/governance/index_en.htm*.

Congress of Aboriginal Peoples (CAP). 2002. *Final Report, Phase 1 Consultations. Federal First Nations Governance Initiative*, Ottawa: Congress of Aboriginal Peoples, *www.abo-peoples.org*.

Connolly, W. E. 2000. 'Speed, Concentric Cultures, and Cosmopolitanism', *Political Theory*, 28, pp. 596–618.

Connor, W. 1972. 'Nation-Building or Nation-Destroying?', *World Politics*, 24, pp. 319–55.

—— 1999. 'National Self-Determination and Tomorrow's Political Map', in A. C. Cairns, J. C. Courtney, P. MacKinnon, H. J. Michelmann and D. E. Smith (eds), *Citizenship, Diversity, and Pluralism: Canadian and Comparative Perspectives*, Montreal and Kingston: McGill-Queen's University Press, pp. 163–76.

Convergència i Unió (CiU). 2003. 'Bases per a un nou Estatut nacional de Catalunya', Barcelona, April 2003, *www.convergencia.org/locals/img/general/nouestatut.pdf*

Costa, J. 2003. 'Catalan Linguistic Policy: Liberal or Illiberal?', *Nations and Nationalism*, 9/3, pp. 413–32.

Crawford, J., and Marks, S. 1998. 'The Global Democracy Deficit: An Essay on International Law and its Limits', in D. Archibugi et al. (eds), *Re-imagining Political Community: Studies in Cosmopolitan Democracy*, Cambridge: Polity Press, 72–90.

Cutler, A. C., Haufler, V., and Porter, T. (eds). 1999. *Private Authority and International Affairs*, Albany: State University of New York Press.

Dahl, R. A. 1999. 'Can International Organisations be Democratic? A Skeptic's View', in I. Shapiro and C. Hacker-Cordon (eds), *Democracy's Edges*, Cambridge: Cambridge University Press, pp. 19–36.

Deflem, M., and Pampel, F. C. 1996. 'The Myth of Postnational Identity: Popular Support for the European Unification', *Social Forces*, 75, pp. 119–43.

De-Shalit, A. 1996. 'National Self-Determination: Political, Not Cultural', *Political Studies*, 44, pp. 906–20.

Deutsch, K. 1953. *Nationalism and Social Communication: An Inquiry into the Foundations of Nationalism*, Cambridge, MA: MIT Press.

Dijkstra, S., Geuijen, K., and De Ruijter, A. 2001. 'Multiculturalism and Social Integration in Europe', *International Political Science Review*, 22, pp. 55–84.

Dion, S. 1996. 'Why is Secession Difficult in Well-Established Democracies? Lessons from Québec', *British Journal of Political Science*, 26, pp. 269–83.

Dodds, E. 1920. *Is Liberalism Dead?*, London: George Allen & Unwin.

Dodson, M. 1996. 'Equity and Social Justice: A Dysfunctional Relationship between Government and Indigenous Peoples', in C. Fletcher (ed.), *Equity and Development Across Nations*, St Leonards: Allen & Unwin, pp. 57–64.

Downing, B. 1992. *The Military Revolution and Political Change: Origins of Democracy and Autocracy in Early Modern Europe*, Princeton: Princeton University Press.

Drets de les Minories, Els, Societat de les Nacions. 1924. *Apellació en favor de Catalunya*, Geneva: League of Nations.

Duchesne, S., and Frognier, A.-P. 1995. 'Is there a European Identity?', in O. Niedermayer and R. Sinnott (eds), *Public Opinion and Internationalized Governance*, Oxford: Oxford University Press, pp. 193–226.

Duhamel, M. 1929. *La Question bretonne dans son cadre européen*, Paris: André Delpeuch.

Dunne, T. 1998. *Inventing International Society*, London: Macmillan.

Durie, M. 1998. *Te mana, te kawanatanga: The Politics of Maori Self-determination*, Auckland: Oxford University Press.

Dworkin, R. 1984. 'Liberalism', in M. Sandel (ed.), *Liberalism and its Critics*, New York: New York University Press, pp. 60–79.

Earle, R. L., with Wirth, J. D. (eds). 1995. *Identities in North America: The Search for Community*, Stanford, CA: Stanford University Press.

Eisenberg, A. 1994. 'The Politics of Individual and Group Difference in Canadian Jurisprudence', *Canadian Journal of Political Science*, 27, pp. 3–21.

Elazar, D. J. 1984. *American Federalism: A View from the States*, New York: Harper & Row.

Esquerra Republicana de Catalunya (ERC). 2003. 'Constitució De L'Estat Lliure De Catalunya', Barcelona, April, *www.esquerra.org/arxius/estatut03.pdf*

Estelrich, J. 1929. *La Question des minorités et la Catalogne*, Lausanne: Librairie Payot & Cie.

Falk, R. 1998. 'The United Nations and Cosmopolitan Democracy: Bad Dream, Utopian Fantasy, Political Project', in D. Archibugi et al. (eds), *Re-Imagining Political Community: Studies in Cosmopolitan Democracy.* Cambridge: Polity Press.

Fierlbeck, K. 1996. 'The Ambivalent Potential of Cultural Identity', *Canadian Journal of Political Science*, 29, pp. 3–22.

Feit, H. A. 1989. 'James Bay Cree Self-Governance and Land Management', in E. N. Wilmsen (ed.), *We are Here: Politics of Aboriginal Land Tenure*, Berkeley: University of California Press, pp. 68–98.

Flanagan, T. 2000. *First Nations? Second Thoughts*, Montreal: McGill-Queen's University Press.

Fleras, A. 1985. 'From Social Control towards Political Self-Determination? Maori Seats and the Politics of Separate Maori Representation in New Zealand', *Canadian Journal of Political Science*, 18, pp. 551–76.

Foreign Policy. 2002. 'Globalization's Last Hurrah?' The Second Annual A. T. Kearney/Foreign Policy Magazine Globalization Index, Web version, January/February Issue, *66.113.195.237/issue_janfeb_2002/global_index.html*

Freeman, M. 1999. 'The Right to Self-Determination in International Politics: Six Theories in Search of a Policy', *Review of International Studies*, 25, pp. 355–70.

Fukuyama, F. 1992. *The End of History and the Last Man*, Harmondworth: Penguin.

Galston, W. 1995. 'Two Concepts of Liberalism', *Ethics*, 105, pp. 516–34.

Geertz, C. 1986. 'The Uses of Diversity', *Michigan Quarterly Review*, 25, pp. 105–23.

Gellner, E. 1964. *Thought and Change*, London: Weidenfeld & Nicolson.

—— 1983. *Nations and Nationalism*, Ithaca, NY: Cornell University Press.

Goodin, R. E. 1988. 'What is so Special about our Fellow Countrymen?', *Ethics*, 98, pp. 663–86.

Gosnell, J. 2002. Keynote address to the conference on 'Re-configuring Aboriginal-State Relations in Canada', Institute of Intergovernmental Relations, Queen's University, Kingston, Ontario.

Gourevitch, P. A. 1979. 'The Reemergence of "Peripheral Nationalism": Some Comparative Speculations on the Spatial Distribution of Political Leadership and Economic Growth', *Comparative Studies in Society and History*, 21, pp. 303–22.

Grand Council of the Crees (GCC). 1992. *Status and Rights of the James Bay Crees in the Context of Québec's Secession from Canada*, submitted by the Grand Council of the Crees (of Québec) to the United Nations Commission on Human Rights, Forty-Eighth Session.

—— 1998. *Never without Consent: James Bay Crees' Stand Against Forcible Inclusion into an Independent Québec*, Oakville: ECW Press.

—— 2000. 'The Cree Regional Authority', *www.gcc.ca*.

Guibernau, M. 1999. *Nations without States: Political Communities in a Global Age*, Cambridge: Polity Press.

—— 2002. 'Between Autonomy and Secession: The Accommodation of Catalonia within the New Democratic Spain', ESRC 'One Europe or Several?' Programme, Working Paper 48/02. *www.one-europe.ac.uk/pdf/w48guibernau.pdf*

Gurr, T. 1993. *Minorities at Risk: A Global View of Ethnopolitical Conflict*, Washington, DC: Institute of Peace Press.

—— 2000. *Peoples versus States: Minorities at Risk in the New Century*, Washington, DC: Institute of Peace Press.

Habermas, J. 1992. 'Citizenship and National Identity: Some Reflections on the Future of Europe', *Praxis International*, 12, pp. 1–19.

Hannum, H. 1989. 'The Limits of Sovereignty and Majority Rule: Minorities, Indigenous Peoples, and the Right to Autonomy', in E. L. Lutz, H. Hannum and K. J. Burke (eds), *New Directions in Human Rights*, Philadelphia: University of Pennsylvania Press, pp. 3–24.

—— 1990. *Autonomy, Sovereignty, and Self-Determination: The Adjudication of Conflicting Rights*, Philadelphia: University of Pennsylvania Press.

Hansen, P. 2000. ' "European Citizenship", or Where Neoliberalism Meets Ethnoculturalism: Analysing the European Union's Citizenship Discourse', *European Societies*, 2/2, pp. 139–65.

Harty, S. 1999. 'The Nation as a Communal Good: A Nationalist Response to the Liberal Conception of Community', *Canadian Journal of Political Science*, 32, pp. 665–89.

—— 2001. 'The Institutional Foundations of Substate National Movements', *Comparative Politics*, 33/2, pp. 191–210.

—— 2002. 'Spain', in A. L. Griffiths (ed.), K. Nerenberg (coord.), *Handbook of Federal Countries 2002*, Montreal and Kingston: Forum of Federations and McGill-Queen's University Press, pp. 297–313.

—— 2004. 'The Basques of Spain', in K. Cordell and S. Wolff (eds), *The Ethnopolitical Encyclopaedia of Europe*, London: Palgrave, pp. 139–50.

Hawkes, D. Forthcoming. 'Re-building the Relationship: The Made in Saskatchewan Approach to First Nations Governance', in M. Murphy (ed.) *Re-Configuring Aboriginal State Relations*. Canada: The State of the Federation 2003. Montreal and Kingston: McGill-Queen's University Press.

Heater, D. 1996. *World Citizenship and Government: Cosmopolitan Ideas in the History of Western Political Thought*, New York: St Martin's Press.

Hechter, M. 1975. *Internal Colonialism: The Celtic Fringe in British National Development, 1536–1966*, Berkeley: University of California Press.

Held, D. 1999. 'The Transformation of Political Community: Rethinking Democracy in the Context of Globalisation', in I. Shapiro and C. Hacker-Cordón (eds), *Democracy's Edges*, Cambridge: Cambridge University Press, pp. 84–111.

Henderson, J. Y. 1994. 'Empowering Treaty Federalism', *Saskatchewan Law Review*, 58/2, pp. 241–332.

Heraclides, A. 1997. 'Ethnicity, Secessionist Conflict and the International Society: Towards a Normative Paradigm Shift', *Nations and Nationalism*, 3/4, pp. 493–520.

Herperger, D. 1991. *Distribution of Powers and Functions in Federal Systems*, Ottawa: Minister of Supply and Services.

Hicks, J., and White, G. 2000. 'Nunavut: Inuit Self-Determination through a Land Claim and Public Government?', in J. Dahl, J. Hicks and P. Jull (eds), *Nunavut: Inuit Regain Control of their Lands and their Lives*, Copenhagen: International Work Group for Indigenous Affairs, pp. 30–115.

Hirst, P. and Thompson, G. 1996. *Globalization in Question: The International Political Economy and the Possibilities of Governance*, Cambridge: Polity Press.

Hobhouse, L. T. 1927. *Social Evolution and Political Theory*, New York: Columbia University Press.

—— 1964. *Liberalism*, Oxford: Oxford University Press.

Hobsbawm, E. J. 1992. *Nations and Nationalism since 1780: Programme, Myth, Reality*, 2nd edn, Cambridge: Canto.

Hogg, P., and Turpel, M. E. 1995. 'Implementing Aboriginal Self-Government: Constitutional and Jurisdictional Issues', *Canadian Bar Review*, 74, pp. 187–224.

Holton, R. J. 1998. *Globalization and the Nation State*, Basingstoke: Macmillan.

Hont, I. 1994. 'The Permanent Crisis of a Divided Mankind: "Contemporary Crisis of the Nation State" in Historical Perspective', *Political Studies*, 42, pp. 166–231.

Hooghe, L. 2003. 'Belgium: From Regionalism to Federalism', in J. Coakley (ed.), *The Territorial Management of Ethnic Conflict*, London: Frank Cass, pp. 73–99.

—— 2004. 'Belgium: Hollowing the Center', in U. Amoretti and N. Bermeo (eds), *Federalism and Territorial Cleavages*, Baltimore: Johns Hopkins University Press, pp. 55–92.

—— and Marks, G. 2001. *Multi-Level Governance and European Integration*, Boulder, CO: Rowman & Littlefield.

Horowitz, D. 1985. *Ethnic Groups in Conflict*, Berkeley: University of California Press.

—— 1991. *A Democratic South Africa: Constitutional Engineering in a Divided Society*, Berkeley: University of California Press.

Hroch, M. 1985. *Social Preconditions of National Revival in Europe*, Cambridge: Cambridge University Press.

Ignatieff, M. 1994. *Blood and Belonging: Journeys into the New Nationalism*, New York: Farrar, Straus & Giroux.

Inglehart, R. 1997. *Modernization and Postmodernization: Cultural, Economic, and Political Change in 43 Societies*, Princeton: Princeton University Press.

—— Nevitte, N. and Basañez, M. 1996. *The North American Trajectory: Growing Cultural, Economic and Political Ties between the United States, Canada and Mexico*, New York and Berlin: Aldine de Gruyter.

Institut d'Estudis Autonòmics. 2003. *Informe sobre la reforma de l'estatut*, Barcelona: Generalitat de Catalunya.

Institute on Governance (IOG). 2000. 'Governance Models to Achieve Higher Levels of Aggregation: Literature Review', *www.iog.ca*.

Isin, E. F., and Turner, B. S. (eds). 2002. *Handbook of Citizenship Studies*, London: Sage.

Ittinuar, P. 1985. 'The Inuit Perspective on Aboriginal Rights', in M. Boldt and J. A. Long (eds), *The Quest for Justice: Aboriginal Peoples and Aboriginal Rights*, Toronto: University of Toronto Press, pp. 47–53.

Jones, B., and Keating, M. (eds). 1995. *The European Union and the Regions*, Oxford: Oxford University Press.

Joppke, C. 1999. *Immigration and the Nation-State: The United States, Germany, and Great Britain*, Oxford: Oxford University Press.

—— and Lukes, S. (eds). 1999. *Multicultural Questions*, Oxford: Oxford University Press.

Keating, M. 1988. *State and Regional Nationalism: Territorial Politics and the European State*, London: Wheatsheaf.

—— 1996. *Nations Against State: The New Politics of Nationalism in Quebec, Catalonia and Scotland*, London: Macmillan.

—— 1998. *The New Regionalism in Western Europe: Territorial Restructuring and Political Change*, London: Edward Elgar.

—— 1999. 'The United Kingdom as a Multinational State', in D. MacIver (ed.), *The Politics of Multinational States*, Toronto: Macmillan, pp. 215–36.

—— 2000. 'The Minority Nations of Spain and European Integration: A New Framework for Autonomy?', *Journal of Spanish Cultural Studies*, 1/1, pp. 29–42.

—— 2001. *Plurinational Democracy: Stateless Nations in a Post-Sovereignty Era*, Oxford: Oxford University Press.

Keohane, R., and Nye, J. 2000. 'Introduction', in J. Nye and J. Donahue (eds), *Governance in a Globalizing World*, Washington, DC: Brookings Institution, pp. 1–41.

Keynes, J. M. 1984. *The Economic Consequence of the Peace 1919*, London: Macmillan.

Kohli, M. 2000. 'The Battlegrounds of European Identity', *European Societies*, 2/2, pp. 113–37.

Koopmans, R., and Statham P. 1999. 'Challenging the Liberal Nation-State? Postnationalism, Multiculturalism, and the Collective Claims Making of Migrants and Ethnic Minorities in Britain and Germany', *American Journal of Sociology*, 105, pp. 652–96.

Krasner, S. D. 2001. 'Rethinking the Sovereign State Model', *Review of International Studies*, 44, pp. 17–42.

Kukathas, C. 1992a. 'Are there Any Cultural Rights?', *Political Theory*, 20, pp. 105–39.

—— 1992b. 'Cultural Rights Again: A Rejoinder to Kymlicka', *Political Theory*, 20, pp. 674–80.

—— 1997. 'Liberalism, Multiculturalism and Oppression', in A. Vincent (ed.), *Political Theory: Tradition and Diversity*, Cambridge: Cambridge University Press, pp. 132–53.

Kuper, L. 1981. *Genocide: Its Political Use in the Twentieth Century*, New York: Penguin.

Kymlicka, W. 1989. *Liberalism, Community, and Culture*, Oxford: Oxford University Press.

—— 1995. *Multicultural Citizenship: A Liberal Theory of Minority Rights*, Oxford: Oxford University Press.

—— 1999. 'Citizenship in an Era of Globalization: Commentary on Held', in I. Shapiro and C. Hacker-Cordón (eds), *Democracy's Edges*, Cambridge: Cambridge University Press.

—— 2001a. 'Multiculturalism and Citizenship-Building in Canada', in *Building Citizenship: Governance and Service Provision in Canada*, Ottawa: Canadian Policy Research Networks, pp. 47–70.

—— 2001b. *Politics in the Vernacular: Nationalism, Multiculturalism, and Citizenship*, Oxford: Oxford University Press.

—— and Norman, W. 1994. 'Return of the Citizen: A Survey of Recent Work on Citizenship Theory', *Ethics*, 104, pp. 352–81.

—— and —— (eds). 2000. *Citizenship in Diverse Societies: Theory and Practice*, Oxford: Oxford University Press.

—— and Opalski, M. (eds). 2002. *Can Liberal Pluralism be Exported? Western Political Theory and Ethnic Relations in Eastern Europe*, Oxford: Oxford University Press.

Ladner, K. 2001. 'Negotiated Inferiority: The Royal Commission on Aboriginal People's Vision of a Renewed Relationship', *American Review of Canadian Studies*, 31, pp. 241–64.

Lake, D. A., and Rothchild, D. (eds). 1998. *The International Spread of Ethnic Conflict: Fear, Diffusion, and Escalation*, Princeton: Princeton University Press.

Laski, H. J. 1936. *The Rise of European Liberalism: An Essay in Interpretation*, London: George Allen & Unwin.

Latham, R. 1998. *The Liberal Moment: Modernity, Security and the Making of the Postwar International Order*, New York: Columbia University Press.

Lecours, A. 2001. 'Political Institutions, Elites, and Territorial Identity Formation in Belgium', *National Identities*, 3/1, pp. 51–68.

—— 2002. 'Belgium', in A. L. Griffiths (ed.), K. Nerenberg (coord.), *Handbook of Federal Countries 2002*, Montreal and Kingston: Forum of Federations and McGill-Queen's University Press, pp. 59–73.

Levene, M. 2000. 'The Limits of Tolerance: Nation-State Building and What it Means for Minority Groups', *Patterns of Prejudice*, 34/2, pp. 19–40.

Levi, M. 1988. *Of Rule and Revenue*, Berkeley: University of California Press.

Life in the United Kingdom Advisory Group. 2003. 'The New and the Old', *www.ind.homeoffice.gov.uk/filestore/ old_and_new_text.pdf*

Lijphart, A. 1968. *The Politics of Accommodation: Pluralism and Democracy in the Netherlands*, Berkeley: University of California Press.

Lindsay, A. D. 1914. 'The State in Recent Political Theory', *Political Quarterly*, 1, pp. 128–45.

Lindseth, P. L. 1999. 'Democratic Legitimacy and the Administrative Character of Supranationalism: The Example of the European Community', *Columbia Law Review*, 99, pp. 628–738.

Linklater, A. 1998. 'Cosmopolitan Citizenship', *Citizenship Studies*, 2, pp. 23–41.

Lisée, J.-F. 2001. 'Is Quebec a North American Region-State?', *Policy Options*, 22, pp. 25–32.

Litfin, K. T. (ed.). 1998. *The Greening of Sovereignty in World Politics*, Cambridge, MA: MIT Press.

Lord, C., and Beetham, D. 2001. 'Legitimizing the EU: Is there a "Post-Parliamentary Basis" for its Legitimation?', *Journal of Common Market Studies*, 39, pp. 443–62.

Lu, C. 2000. 'The One and the Many Faces of Cosmopolitanism', *Journal of Political Philosophy*, 8, pp. 244–67.

Lustick, I. 1979. 'Stability in Deeply Divided Societies: Consociationalism versus Control', *World Politics*, 31, pp. 325–44.

Macartney, C. A. 1934. *National States and National Minorities*, Oxford: Oxford University Press.

MacCormick, N. 1996. 'Liberalism, Nationalism and the Post-Sovereign State', *Political Studies*, 44, pp. 553–67.

—— 1999. *Questioning Sovereignty: Law, State, and Nation in the European Commonwealth*, Oxford: Oxford University Press.

McGarry, J. 1999. 'The Nature of the British–Irish Agreement', *New Left Review*, 233, pp. 66–96.

—— and O'Leary, B. 1995. 'Five Fallacies: Northern Ireland and the Liabilities of Liberalism', *Ethnic and Racial Studies*, 18/4, pp. 837–61.

MacIver, D. (ed.). 1999. *The Politics of Multinational States*, Toronto: Macmillan.

McIvor, S. 1992. Submission to the Royal Commission on Aboriginal Peoples, Public Hearings, Round One, Toronto, Ontario (26 June).

—— 1995. 'Aboriginal Women's Rights as Existing Rights', *Canadian Women Studies*, 15, pp. 34–7.

McKim, R. and McMahan, J. 1997. *The Morality of Nationalism*, Oxford: Oxford University Press.

Macklem, P. 1995. 'Normative Dimensions of the Right of Aboriginal Self-Government', in Royal Commission on Aboriginal Peoples, *Aboriginal Self-Government, Legal and Constitutional Issues*, Ottawa: Minister of Supply and Services, pp. 1–54.

McLeay, E. M. 1991. 'Two Steps Forward, Two Steps Back: Maori Devolution, Maori Advisory Committees and Maori Representation', *Political Science*, 43, pp. 30–46.

Maioni, A. 1998. *Parting at the Crossroads: The Emergence of Health Insurance in the United States and Canada*, Princeton: Princeton University Press.

Mann, M. 1992. 'The Emergence of Modern European Nationalism', in J. A. Hall and I. C. Jarvie (eds), *Transitions to Modernity*, Cambridge: Cambridge University Press, pp. 137–66.

—— 1997. 'Has Globalization Ended the Rise and Rise of the Nation-State?', *Review of International Political Economy*, 4/1, pp. 472–96.

Margalit, A. and Raz, J. 1990. 'National Self-Determination', *Journal of Philosophy*, 87, pp. 439–61.

Marks, G., Hooghe, L., and Blank, K. 1996. 'European Integration from the 1980s: State-Centric v. Multilevel Governance', *Journal of Common Market Studies*, 34, pp. 341–79.

Marshall, T. H. 1950. *Citizenship and Social Class*, Cambridge: Cambridge University Press.

Marx, K. 1978. 'On Imperialism in India', in R. C. Tucker (ed.), *The Marx–Engels Reader*, 2nd edn, New York: Norton, pp. 653–64.

Masterman, C. F. G. 1920. *The New Liberalism*, London: Leonard Parsons.

Mayall, J. 1990. *Nationalism and International Society*, Cambridge and New York: Cambridge University Press.

—— 1999. 'Sovereignty, Nationalism, and Self-Determination', *Political Studies*, 47, pp. 474–502.

Meadwell, H., and Martin, P. 1996. 'Economic Integration and the Politics of Independence', *Nations and Nationalism*, 2/1, pp. 67–87.

Mendelsohn, M. 2003. 'Birth of a New Ethnicity', *Globe and Mail*, online edition, Monday, 9 June, *www.globeandmail.com*

Mill, J. S. 1954. *Representative Government*, in Everyman's Library, Philosophy and Theology, 482, London: J. M. Dent & Sons.

Miller, D. 1989. 'In What Sense must Socialism be Communitarian?', *Social Philosophy and Policy*, 6, pp. 51–73.

—— 1995. *On Nationality*, Oxford: Clarendon Press.

—— 2000. *Citizenship and National Identity*, Oxford: Polity Press.

Millwood, A. S. 1992. *The European Rescue of the Nation State*, London: Routledge.

Moore, M. (ed.). 1998. *National Self-Determination and Secession*, Oxford: Oxford University Press.

—— 1999. 'Beyond the Cultural Argument for Liberal Nationalism', *Critical Review of International Social and Political Philosophy*, 2, pp. 26–47.

—— 2001. *The Ethics of Nationalism*, Oxford: Oxford University Press.

Moravcsik, A. 1998. *The Choice for Europe: Social Purpose and State Power from Messina to Maastricht*, London: Routledge/ UCL Press.

—— 1999. 'A New Statecraft? Supranational Entrepreneurs and International Cooperation', *International Organization*, 53, pp. 267–306.

—— 2003. 'Reassessing the Legitimacy of the European Union', in J. H. H. Weiler, I. Begg, and J. Peterson (eds), *Integration in an Expanding European Union*, Oxford: Blackwell, pp. 77–98.

Morse, B. W. 1997. 'Permafrost Rights: Aboriginal Self-Government and the Supreme Court in *R. v. Pamajewon*', *McGill Law Journal*, 42, pp. 1011–42.

Muir, R. 1917. *Nationalism and Internationalism: The Culmination of Modern History*, London: Constable & Co.

Murphy, M. 1996. 'After All, Violence is Not a Traditional Value: First Nations, Self-Government, Gender Equality and the Charter', in M. Jackson and N. K. S. Banks (eds), *Ten Years Later: The Charter and Equality for Women*, Vancouver: Simon Fraser University Press, pp. 39–76.

—— 2001a. 'Culture and the Courts: A New Direction in Canadian Jurisprudence on Aboriginal Rights?', *Canadian Journal of Political Science*, 34, pp. 109–29.

—— 2001b. 'The Limits of Culture in the Politics of Self-Determination', *Ethnicities*, 1, pp. 367–91.

—— 2004a. 'Understanding Indigenous Nationalism', in Michel Seymour (ed.), *The Fate of the Nation State*, Montreal and Kingston: McGill-Queen's University Press, pp. 271–94.

—— 2004b. 'Looking Forward Without Looking Back: Jean Chrétien's Legacy for Aboriginal–State Relations', *Review of Constitutional Studies*, 9, Special Issue: The Chrétien Legacy, pp. 151–69.

—— and Harty, S. 2003. 'Post-Sovereign Citizenship', *Citizenship Studies*, 7, pp. 181–97.

Musgrave, T. D. 1997. *Self Determination and National Minorities*, Oxford: Clarendon.

Nahanee, T. 1993. 'Dancing with a Gorilla: Aboriginal Women, Justice and the Charter', in Canada, Royal Commission on Aboriginal Peoples, *Aboriginal Peoples and the Justice System: Report of the National Round Table on Aboriginal Justice Issues*, Ottawa: Minister of Supply and Services, pp. 359–82.

Nairn, T. 1977. *The Breakup of Britain: Crisis and Neo-Nationalism*, London: New Left Books.

—— 2000. *After Britain: New Labour and the Return of Scotland*, London: Granta.

Nault, R. 2001. 'Speech to Announce the First Nations Governance Initiative', 30 April, Siksika First Nation High School, Saskatchewan. Indian and Northern Affairs website, *www.fng-gpn.gc.ca*

Newfoundland and Labrador, Government of. 2003. *The Royal Commission on Renewing and Strengthening our Place in Canada*, St John's: Office of the Queen's Printer.

Newman, S. 1991. 'Does Modernization Breed Ethnic Political Conflict?', *World Politics*, 43, pp. 451–78.

—— 2000. 'Nationalism in Postindustrial Societies: Why States Still Matter', *Comparative Politics*, 33, pp. 21–41.

Nicolson, H. 1937. *Peacemaking 1919*, London: Constable & Co.

Nielsen, K. 1999. 'Cosmopolitan Nationalism', *Monist*, 82, pp. 446–68.

Nodia, G. 1994. 'Nationalism and Democracy', in L. Diamond and M. F. Plattner (eds), *Nationalism, Ethnic Conflict and Democracy*, Baltimore and London: Johns Hopkins University Press, pp. 3–22.

Norris, P. (ed.). 1999. *Critical Citizens: Global Support for Democratic Governance*, Oxford: Oxford University Press.

—— 2001. 'Global Governance and Cosmopolitan Citizens', in J. S. Nye, jr. and J. Donahue (eds), *Governance in a Globalizing World*, Washington, DC: Brookings Institution, pp. 155–77.

North, D. C. 1990. *Institutions, Institutional Change and Economic Performance*, New York: Cambridge University Press.

Nuñez Seixas, X. M. 1995. 'Nacionalismo y politica exterior: España y la politica de minorias nacionales de la Sociedad de las Naciones (1919–1936)', *Hispania*, 55, pp. 229–65.

Nussbaum, M. 1994. 'Patriotism and Cosmopolitanism', *Boston Review* (October–November), pp. 2–18.

Nye, J. S., and Donahue, J. D. 2000. *Governance in a Globalizing World*, Washington, DC: Brookings Institution.

Offe, C. 1991. 'Capitalism by Democratic Design? Democratic Theory Facing the Triple Transition in East Central Europe', *Social Research*, 58/4, pp. 865–92.

Ohmae, K. 1990. *The Borderless World*, London: Collins.

—— 1995. *The End of the Nation State*, New York: Free Press.

O'Leary, B. 1999. 'The Nature of the British–Irish Agreement', *New Left Review*, 233, pp. 66–96.

O'Neill, S. 2001. 'Mutual Recognition and the Accommodation of National Diversity: Constitutional Justice in Northern Ireland', in A. Gagnon and J. Tully (eds), *Multinational Democracies*, Cambridge: Cambridge University Press, pp. 222–41.

Orsini, M., and Ladner, K. 2004. 'De infériorité négociée à l'inutilité de négocier: la Loi sur la governance des Premières Nations et le maintien de la politique coloniale', *Politique et Sociétés*, 23/1, pp. 59–87.

Osiander, A. 1994. *The States System of Europe, 1640–1990*, Oxford: Oxford University Press.

Parekh, B. 1991. 'British Citizenship and Cultural Difference', in Geoff Andrews (ed.), *Citizenship*, London: Lawrence & Wishart, pp. 183–204.

—— 1999. 'Common Citizenship in a Multicultural Society', *The Round Table*, 351, pp. 449–60.

Partido Nacionalista Vasco (PNV). 2002. 'A New Political Agreement for Co-existence', 27 September, *www.eaj-pnv.com/documentos/documentos/discurso_pol_27092002_i.doc*

Parti Québécois (PQ). 2003. 'Québec: Un pays d'Amérique', *Le Bulletin*, (Winter).

Partit dels Socialistes de Catalunya (PSC-PSOE). 2003. 'Bases per a l'Estatut d'Autonomia de Catalunya, Barcelona', March, *www.aramaragall.com*

Paterson, M. 1999. 'Interpreting Trends in Global Environmental Governance', *International Affairs*, 75, pp. 793–802.

Patten, A. 1999. 'The Autonomy Argument for Liberal Nationalism', *Nations and Nationalism*, 5/1, pp. 1–17.

—— 2002. 'Democratic Secession from a Multinational State', *Ethics*, 112, pp. 558–86.

Paul, T. V., Ikenberry, J., and Hall, J. (eds). 2003. *The Nation-State in Question*, Princeton: Princeton University Press.

Pearson, D. 2002. 'Theorizing Citizenship in British Settler Societies', *Ethnic and Racial Studies*, 25, pp. 989–1012.

Penn, A. 1995. 'The James Bay and Northern Québec Agreement: Natural Resources, Public Lands, and the Implementation of a Native Land Claim Settlement', in Canada, Royal Commission on Aboriginal Peoples, *For Seven Generations: An Information Legacy of the Royal Commission for Aboriginal Peoples*, Ottawa: Libraxus (CD-ROM).

Philpott, D. 1995. 'In Defence of National Self-Determination', *Ethics*, 105, pp. 352–85.

Pogge, T. 1992. 'Cosmopolitanism and Sovereignty', *Ethics*, 103/1, pp. 152–224.

Preece, J. J. 1997. 'National Minority Rights vs. State Sovereignty in Europe: Changing Norms in International Relations?', *Nations and Nationalism*, 3/3, pp. 345–64.

—— 1998. *National Minorities and the European Nation-States System*, Oxford: Oxford University Press.

Preuss, U. K. 1998. 'Citizenship in the European Union: A Paradigm for Transnational Democracy?' in D. Archibugi et al. (eds), *Re-imagining Political Community: Studies in Cosmopolitan Democracy*, Stanford: Stanford University Press, pp. 138–51.

——, Koenig-Archibugi, M., and Lefebvre, E. 2003. 'Traditions of Citizenship in the European Union', *Citizenship Studies*, 7, pp. 3–14.

Putnam, R. D. 2000. *Bowling Alone: The Collapse and Revival of American Community*, New York: Simon & Schuster.

—— with Leonardi, R. and Nanetti, R. Y. 1994. *Making Democracy Work: Civic Traditions in Modern Italy*, Princeton: Princeton University Press.

Québec, Government of, Commission on Fiscal Imbalance. 2002. *A New Division of Canada's Financial Resources*, Québec: Gouvernement du Québec.

Rae, H. 2002. *State Identities and the Homogenisation of Peoples*, Cambridge: Cambridge University Press.

Ramos, H. 2000. 'National Recognition without a State: Cree Nationalism *within* Canada', *Nationalism and Ethnic Politics*, 6, pp. 95–115.

Rawls, J. 1971. *A Theory of Justice*, Cambridge, MA: Belknap Press of Harvard University Press.

—— 1993a. 'The Law of Peoples', *Critical Inquiry*, 20, pp. 36–68.

—— 1993b. *Political Liberalism*, New York: Columbia University Press.

Reiss, H. (ed.). 1978. *Kant's Political Writings*, Cambridge: Cambridge University Press.

Requejo, F. 1999. 'Cultural Pluralism, Nationalism and Federalism: A Revision of Democratic Citizenship in Plurinational States', *European Journal of Political Research*, 35, 255–86.

Resina, J. R. 2002. 'Post-Nation Spain? Post-Spanish Spain?', *Nations and Nationalism*, 8/3, pp. 377–96.

Reynolds, H. 1996. *Aboriginal Sovereignty: Reflections on Race, State and Nation*, St Leonards: Allen & Unwin.

Rico, A. 1997. 'Regional Decentralization and Health Care Reform in Spain (1976–1996)', in M. Rhodes (ed.), *Southern European Welfare States: Between Crisis and Reform*, London: Frank Cass, pp. 115–34.

—— 2000. 'Health Policy under Asymmetric Federalism: Twenty Years of Regional Devolution in Spain', *Eurohealth*, 6/3, pp. 28–9.

Roca i Codina, A. 1918. *Catalunya i la Guerra*, Barcelona: La Artista.

Rorty, R. 1986. 'On Ethnocentrism: A Reply to Geertz', *Michigan Quarterly Review*, 25, pp. 525–34.

—— 1988. *Contingency, Irony, and Solidarity*, Cambridge: Cambridge University Press.

—— 1991. 'Feminism and Pragmatism', *Michigan Quarterly Review*, 30, pp. 231–66.

—— 1992. 'A Pragmatist View of Rationality and Cultural Difference', *Philosophy East and West*, 42, pp. 581–96.

Rosenau, J. 1995. 'Governance in the Twenty-First Century', *Global Governance*, 1, pp. 13–43.

Royle, E. 1998. *Issues in Regional Identity*, Manchester: Manchester University Press.

Ruggie, J. G. 1982. 'International Regimes, Transactions and Change: Embedded Liberalism in the Postwar Economic Order', *International Organization*, 36, pp. 379–415.

Russell, J. 1994. 'Nationalistic Minorities and Liberal Traditions', in P. Bryden, S. Davis and J. Russell (eds), *Protecting Rights and Liberties: Essays on the Charter and Canada's Political, Legal, and Intellectual Life*, Toronto: University of Toronto Press, pp. 205–41.

Russell, P. 2001. 'Indigenous Self-Determination: Is Canada as Good as it Gets?', Keynote Address at the Conference on *Rethinking Indigenous Self-Determination*, University of Queensland, Brisbane, Australia, 25–28 September.

Rynard, P. 1999. ' "Welcome in, But Check your Rights at the Door": The James Bay and Nisga'a Agreements in Canada', *Canadian Journal of Political Science*, 33, pp. 211–43.

Salée, D. 2002. 'Québec's Changing Political Culture and the Future of Federal–Provincial Relations in Canada', in H. Telford and H. Lazar (eds), *Canadian Political Cultures in Transition: Canada: The State of the Federation 2001*, Kingston and Montreal: McGill-Queen's University Press, pp. 163–97.

Sandel, M. 1997. 'The Procedural Republic and the Unencumbered Self', in

R. E. Goodin and P. Pettit (eds), *Contemporary Political Philosophy: An Anthology*, Oxford: Blackwell, pp. 247–55.

Saward, M. (ed.). 2001. *Democratic Innovation*, London: Routledge.

Schnapper, Dominique. 2002. 'The Ernest Gellner Nationalism Lecture: Citizenship and National Identity in Europe', *Nations and Nationalism*, 8/1, pp. 1–14.

Scholte, J. A., with O'Brien, R. and Williams, M. (1999). 'The WTO and Civil Society', *Journal of World Trade*, 33, pp. 107–23.

Schouls, T. 1996. 'Aboriginal Peoples and Electoral Reform in Canada: Differentiated Representation versus Voter Equality', *Canadian Journal of Political Science*, 29, pp. 729–49.

Scottish National Party (SNP). 2003. 'Release our Potential on May 1st', *www.snp.org*

Seton-Watson, H. 1975. *The Sick Heart of Modern Europe: The Problem of the Danubian Lands*, Seattle and London: University of Washington Press.

Shaw, J. 1997. 'Citizenship of the Union: Towards Post-National Membership?', *Harvard Law School Working Papers, www.jeanmonnetprogram.org/papers/97/97-06-.html*

Shulman, S. 2000. 'Nationalist Sources of International Economic Integration', *International Studies Quarterly*, 44, pp. 365–90.

—— 2002. 'Challenging the Civic/Ethnic and West/East Dichotomies in the Study of Nationalism', *Comparative Political Studies*, 35, pp. 554–85.

Smiley, D. V. 1976. *Canada in Question: Federalism in the Seventies*, Toronto: McGraw-Hill Ryerson.

Smith, A. D. 1995a. *Nations and Nationalism in a Global Era*, Cambridge: Polity Press.

—— 1995b. 'Towards a Global Culture?', in M. Featherstone (ed.), *Global Culture*, London: Sage, pp. 171–206.

Smith, D. E. 2002. 'Jurisdictional Devolution: Towards an Effective Model for Indigenous Community Self-Determination', Discussion Paper No. 233, Centre for Aboriginal Economic Policy Research, The Australian National University.

Smith, G. and Wales, C. 2000. 'Citizens' Juries and Deliberative Democracy', *Political Studies*, 48, pp. 51–65.

Soysal, Y. N. 1994. *Limits of Citizenship: Migrants and Post-National Membership in Europe*, Chicago: University of Chicago Press.

—— 1996. 'Changing Citizenship in Europe: Remarks on Post-National Membership and the National State', in D. Cesarini and M. Fulbrook (eds), *Nationality and Migration in Europe*, London: Routledge, pp. 17–29.

—— 1998. 'Toward a Postnational Model of Membership', in G. Shafir (ed.), *The Citizenship Debates: A Reader*, Minneapolis and London: University of Minnesota Press, pp. 189–220.

Spinner-Halev, J. 1994. *The Boundaries of Citizenship: Race, Ethnicity, and*

Nationality in the Liberal State, Baltimore: Johns Hopkins University Press.

Spruyt, H. 1994. *The Sovereign State and its Competitors*, Princeton: Princeton University Press.

Stephens, J. S. 1929. *Danger Zones of Europe: A Study of National Minorities*, London: Hogarth Press.

Stimson, A. 2001. 'Speech by Chief Adrian Stimson of the Siksika First Nation, at the Announcement of the First Nations Governance Initiative', 30 April, Siksika First Nation High School, Saskatchewan, Indian and Northern Affairs website, *www.fng-gpn.gc.ca*.

Strange, S. 1996. *The Retreat of the State: The Diffusion of Power in the World Economy*, Cambridge: Cambridge University Press.

Sullivan, P. 1996. 'All Things to All People: ATSIC and Australia's International Obligation to Uphold Indigenous Self-Determination', in P. Sullivan (ed.), *Shooting the Banker: Essays on ATSIC and Self-Determination*, Darwin: North Australia Research Unit, The Australian National University.

Supreme Court of Canada (SCC). 1996a. *R. v. Pamajewon, www.lexum.umontreal.ca*

—— 1996b. *R. v. Van der Peet, www.lexum.umontreal.ca*

—— 1998. *B.C. v. Delgamuukw, www.lexum.umontreal.ca*

—— 2003. *R. v. Powley, www.lexum.umontreal.ca*

Tambini, D. 2001. 'Post-National Citizenship', *Ethnic and Racial Studies*, 24, pp. 195–217.

Tamir, Y. 1993. *Liberal Nationalism*, Princeton: Princeton University Press.

Taylor, C. 1979. 'What's Wrong with Negative Liberty?', in A. Ryan (ed.), *The Idea of Freedom*, Oxford: Oxford University Press, pp. 175–93.

—— 1985. 'Atomism', in C. Taylor, *Philosophy and the Human Sciences, Philosophical Papers*, vol. 2, New York: Cambridge University Press, pp. 187–210.

—— 1991. 'Shared and Divergent Values', in R. Watts and D. Brown (eds), *Options for a New Canada*, Toronto: University of Toronto Press, pp. 53–76.

—— 1994. *Multiculturalism and the Politics of Recognition*, Princeton: Princeton University Press.

—— 1995. 'Cross-Purposes: The Liberal–Communitarian Debate', in *Philosophical Arguments*, Cambridge, MA: Harvard University Press, pp. 181–203.

Telò, M. (ed.). 2001. *European Union and New Regionalism: Regional Actors and Global Governance in a Posthegemonic Era*, Aldershot and Burlington: Ashgate.

Tempelman, S. 1999. 'Constructions of Cultural Identity: Multiculturalism and Exclusion', *Political Studies*, 47, pp. 17–31.

Temperley, H. W. V. (ed.). 1920–4. *A History of the Peace Conference of Paris*, 6 vols, London: H. Frowde and Hodder & Stoughton.

Tilly, Charles (ed.). 1975. *The Formation of National States in Western Europe*, Princeton: Princeton University Press.

Tiryakian, E., and Rogowski, R. (eds). 1985. *New Nationalisms of the Developed West*, London: Allen & Unwin.

Tully, J. 1993. 'Rediscovering America: The Two Treatises and Aboriginal Rights', in J. Tully (ed.), *An Approach to Political Philosophy: Locke in Contexts*, Cambridge: Cambridge University Press, pp. 137–71.

—— 1994a. 'Diversity's Gambit Declined', in Curtis Cook (ed.), *Constitutional Predicament: Canada After the Referendum of 1992*, Montreal and Kingston: McGill-Queen's University Press, pp. 149–98.

—— 1994b. 'The Crisis of Identification: The Case of Canada', *Political Studies*, 42 Special Issue, 77–96.

—— 1995. *Strange Multiplicity: Constitutionalism in an Age of Diversity*, Cambridge: Cambridge University Press.

—— 2000a. 'A Just Relationship between Aboriginal and Non-Aboriginal Peoples of Canada', in C. Cook and J. Lindau (eds), *Aboriginal Rights and Self-Government: The Canadian and Mexican Experience in North American Perspective*, Montreal: McGill-Queen's Press, pp. 39–71.

—— 2000b. 'The Struggles of Indigenous Peoples for and of Freedom', in P. Patton, D. Ivison and D. Saunders (eds), *Political Theory and Indigenous Rights*, Cambridge: Cambridge University Press, pp. 36–59.

Turner, B. S. 1990. 'Outline of a Theory of Citizenship', *Sociology*, 24, pp. 189–217.

—— 2002. 'Cosmopolitan Virtue, Globalization and Patriotism', *Theory, Culture and Society*, 19, pp. 45–63.

Van den Abbeele, G. 2001. 'No Joking Matter: The "Other" Belgium', *Social Identities*, 7/4, pp. 511–24.

Van den Berghe. P. L. 2002. 'Multicultural Democracy: Can it Work?', *Nations and Nationalism*, 8/4, pp. 433–49.

Vivian, H. 1933. *Kings in Waiting*. London: Hamish Hamilton Publishers.

Waldron, J. 1995. 'Minority Cultures and the Cosmopolitan Alternative', in W. Kymlicka (ed.), *The Rights of Minority Cultures*, Oxford: Oxford University Press, pp. 93–119.

—— 2000. 'What is Cosmopolitan?', *Journal of Political Philosophy*, 8, pp. 227–43.

Wales, National Assembly, Culture Committee and Education and Lifelong Learning Committee. 2002. 'Policy Review of the Welsh Language', Cardiff: National Assembly for Wales.

Walker, B. 1997. 'Plural Cultures, Contested Territories: A Critique of Kymlicka', *Canadian Journal of Political Science*, 30, pp. 211–34.

Walker, N. (ed.). 2003. *Sovereignty in Transition*, London: Hart.

Walter, B. F. 2002. *Committing to Peace: The Successful Settlement of Civil Wars*, Princeton: Princeton University Press.

Weaver, S. 1981. *Making Canadian Indian Policy*, Toronto: University of Toronto Press.

Wedgwood, R. 2002. 'Gallant Delusions', *Foreign Policy* (online version). *www.foreignpolicy.com/issue_septoct_2002/wedgwood.html*

Weiler, J. H. H. 1997. 'To be a European Citizen: Eros and Civilization', *Journal of European Public Policy*, 4/4, pp. 495–519.

Weinstock, D. 1999. 'National Partiality: Confronting the Intuitions', *Monist*, 82, pp. 516–41.

—— 2001. 'Prospects for Transnational Citizenship and Democracy', *Ethics and International Affairs*, 15/2, pp. 53–66.

Weiss, L. 1998. *The Myth of the Powerless State: Governing the Economy in a Global Era*, Cambridge: Polity Press.

—— (ed.). 2003. *States in the Global Economy: Bringing Domestic Institutions Back In*, Cambridge: Cambridge University Press.

Welsh Assembly Government. 2002. 'Bilingual Future: A Policy Statement by the Welsh Assembly Government', Cardiff: Welsh Assembly Government.

—— 2003. 'Iaith Pawb: A National Action Plan for a Bilingual Wales', Cardiff: Welsh Assembly Government.

Wendt, A. 1999. 'A Comment on Held's Cosmopolitanism', in I. Shapiro and C. Hacker-Cordón (eds), *Democracy's Edges*, Cambridge: Cambridge University Press, pp. 127–33.

White, G. 2002. 'Treaty Federalism in Northern Canada: Aboriginal–Government Land Claims Boards', *Publius*, 32, pp. 89–114.

Williams, M. 1998. *Voice, Trust, and Memory: Marginalized Groups and the Failure of Liberal Representation*, Princeton: Princeton University Press.

—— 2003. 'Sharing the River: Aboriginal Representation in Canadian Political Institutions', unpublished paper, on file with the authors.

Wilson, W. 1984. *The Papers of Woodrow Wilson*, vol. 45: *November 11, 1917–January 15, 1918*, and vol. 46: *January 16–March 12, 1918*, ed. A. S. Link, Princeton: Princeton University Press.

Woods, N., and Narlikar, A. 2001. 'Governance and the Limits of Accountability: The WTO, the IMF, and the World Bank', *International Social Science Journal*, 170, pp. 569–83.

'X.7' 1925. *The Return of Kings: Facts about the Conspiracy for the Restoration of the Monarchy in Central Europe*, London: Everleigh, Nash & Grayson.

Young, I. M. 1990. *Justice and the Politics of Difference*, Princeton: Princeton University Press.

—— 1995. 'Together in Difference: Transforming the Logic of Group Political Conflict', in W. Kymlicka (ed.), *The Rights of Minority Cultures*, Oxford: Oxford University Press, pp. 155–76.

—— 2000a. 'Hybrid Democracy: Iroquois Federalism and the Postcolonial Project', in D. Ivison, P. Patton and W. Saunders (eds), *Political Theory and the Rights of Indigenous Peoples*, Cambridge: Cambridge University Press, pp. 237–58.

—— 2000b. *Inclusion and Democracy*, Oxford: Oxford University Press.

Index